The Quest for Therapy in Lower Zaire

Comparative Studies in Health Systems and Medical Care

NUMBER 1

The Quest for Therapy in Lower Zaire

JOHN M. JANZEN

with the collaboration of William Arkinstall, M.D.

Foreword by Charles Leslie

UNIVERSITY OF CALIFORNIA PRESS

Berkeley · Los Angeles · London

University of California Press
Berkeley and Los Angeles, California
University of California Press, Ltd.
London, England
Copyright © 1978 by
The Regents of the University of California
I S B N 0-520-03295-0
Library of Congress Catalog Card Number: 76-19982
Printed in the United States of America

1 2 3 4 5 6 7 8 9 0

Contents

Illustrations

PLATES (*Between pages 106 and 107*)

MAPS

Foreword

The holistic description of a medical system should describe the full range of practices in a society, and it should explain how these practices coexist in a changing structure of customs and social relationships. Few historians, sociologists, or other specialists have yet approximated these goals, and until now no anthropologist has attempted to describe a medical system in this manner. Herein lies the originality of *The Quest for Therapy in Lower Zaire* by John Janzen. In scale, complexity, and analytic cohesiveness it sets new standards for research in medical anthropology.

Books as rich in facts and ideas as this resist labels. It is an anthropological study, with the qualifying adjectives *social, medical, humanistic,* and *applied.* Because it describes a region of Zaire, it could also be classified among African studies books. But it will interest those who are neither anthropologists nor Africanists, for it is written so any reader, layman or specialist, who particularly wants to know how medical systems work, can understand and learn from it. It does this by inviting the reader to compare his own experience and knowledge with the facts reported here. The invitation is implicit in the concepts Janzen uses. His central concept is that of the lay therapy managing group consisting of kinsmen and friends, which is mobilized when illness strikes an individual, and which acts to define the situation and to search for a remedy. The size and composition of the group varies according to circumstances. Though Janzen is describing a region in Zaire, readers will readily see comparisons with therapy management groups that exist in other societies they know about. Because the concept includes an aspect of events that can be observed in any society, and because Janzen uses it well, his description of particular facts in Kongo society reveal general truths about whole systems of action.

Books as rich as this one resist summary. The lay therapy management group is only one of its many concepts, all of which have in common Janzen's effort to describe the historical structure of medical pluralism. With the possible exception of a few small and very isolated societies, all medical systems in the world today are pluralistic. As the degree and organization of this pluralism varies, the central problem for a comparative study of medical systems is to develop theoretical paradigms to describe it.

In our own culture the influence of biomedical science and of doctors is such that it is essential to distinguish health systems from medical systems in order to define Janzen's subject, and to understand that medical systems, defined objectively, include all forms of practice. This book is *not* about the health system in Lower Zaire. If it were, it would analyze the adaptive and dysfunctional relationships between the human population and its parasites, the patterns of nutrition, fertility, mortality, and so on. It would be an epidemiological and ecological study about the interrelationships between species as they affect the normal functions of human beings. It might use social categories, but its fundamental theories and perspective would be drawn from clinical medicine, biology, and the cultural norms of medical practitioners. Quite the contrary—this book has a different perspective and theoretical structure, for it describes a regional medical system.

Medical systems are social and cultural. In contrast to health systems, their boundaries are not those of biological populations, species and ecological networks, but of political organization and cultural exchange. Medical systems are generated by acts of consultation between laymen and specialists, or by concerted acts among laymen to cure, alleviate, or otherwise cope with physical affliction.

Medical systems use the categories of thought and sentiment common to many occasions and interests, which is to say that they are part of the general culture in a society. For example, the concepts of humoral medicine in Hindu, Chinese, and European tradition involve cosmological theories of an equilibrium of forces and elements in nature and of correspondences between the human body and the universe that are used in religious ritual, sorcery, food choices, art, and literature. In the present volume Janzen has written a fascinating chapter on the medical cosmology of Nzoamambu, a master *nganga*. He begins with an assertion, which is really a descriptive hypothesis: "It is characteristic of cosmologies to provide the material by which dominant cultural metaphors are organized." One might think this to be true in the so-called traditional cultures but not in "modern scientific medicine." In the conclusion to the chapter on Nzoamambu, however, Janzen comments on "the cultural embeddedness everywhere of symptom and disease language" by telling us that "only 55 percent of the entries in the World Health Organization's widely used 'International Classification of Diseases' (I.C.D.) are . . . reducible to single, universal, and duplicable, sign-symptom complexes . . . In other words, cultural assumptions rather than laboratory experiment pervade much of the I.C.D."

Medical systems become more defined institutional structures as the division of labor includes more specialist roles. In the past century the professionalization of medicine on a world-wide scale has created secular bureaucracies protected by state regulated limitations on practice, extended courses of socialization and training for different occupational roles within these bureaucracies, and a concerted effort by bureaucrats to reduce the degree of pluralism within medical systems. Janzen uses the term "Western medicine" to describe this system in Zaire. I prefer the term "cosmopolitan medicine" since the system evolved throughout the world—in Japan and Brazil, as well as in the colonial powers of Western Europe and North America.

Cosmopolitan medicine coexists everywhere with other systems of practice, forming more or less pluralistic, more or less integrated, and more or less syncretic regional systems. Janzen describes four coexisting systems among the Kongo people of Lower Zaire, of which the three indigenous systems are, from the perspective of laymen, tolerant, accessible, and experimental in attitude. On the other hand, he writes, "By failing to recognize etiological questions and by denying the validity of alternate therapies, Western medicine's practitioners communicated to their clients the closed, limited nature of Western medicine."

Janzen's strategy for describing medical pluralism in Zaire is to begin with what film-makers would call "an establishing shot." This is a long and comprehensive view, showing the topography of the region, the various settlements and kinds of people in it, their medical traditions, the effects on them of conquest and domination by an alien colonial power, and the on-going changes occurring since Zaire became an independent nation. The details of this description all serve to define the historical context of a rapidly evolving set of medical institutions.

Part II is edited in close-ups that show afflicted individuals, their kinsmen, friends, and the specialists they consult. Each chapter is a story of people caught up in the quest for therapy, describing on the ground level, in intimate detail, how the system works. The point of view in these narratives remains firmly that of Janzen and his collaborator, Dr. William Arkinstall, but they are told with a grasp of "the inside view" that characterizes truly distinguished anthropological field research.

In Part III Janzen shifts perspective, using tracking shots, more close-ups, long shots, and middle-distance views. His purpose requires this variety because he analyzes the patterns that link the historical structures described in Part I to social processes exemplified by the narratives in Part II. Each chapter in this final section of the book analyzes in a different manner "the logic of therapeutic systems" (another concept that will interest readers who may never plan to visit Zaire, but who want to learn how medical systems work).

Janzen's book makes an excellent beginning for a new monograph series, Comparative Studies in Health Systems and Medical Care. The purpose of the series is to build a field of scholarship that will bring together in a complementary fashion the work of medical specialists, historians, sociologists, and anthropologists, and it will publish new research reported in theoretically interesting ways. Scientists or humanists, interested in the nature of health systems and in the ways that medical systems evolve and vary, will find this first volume a source of pleasure and instruction.

CHARLES LESLIE

Preface

Publication of this book comes a decade after Dr. Arkinstall and I realized the necessity for the study on which it is based. Much has changed in health care and medical policy in Zaire during the interim. Emergency medical work by foreign agencies during the immediate postindependence era has given way to a more regulated approach within a national ministry of health firmly in the hands of nationals, many of whom have their M.D. degrees. The ideological isolation of Western medicine has given way to a realization of its prohibitive costs and an awareness of other modes of prevention and treatment.

But one learns to approach evidence of change in Zaire, as anywhere, with caution. Whenever I return to Zaire, duly impressed with apparent transformations since a previous visit, a round of French and KiKongo conversations with old acquaintances usually suffices to persuade me that little has changed at all. To what extent is this true of the medical culture of the country?

Alongside the training of more doctors, nurses, and technicians in national schools, there has been an official rediscovery of traditional medicine. Under the aegis of President Mobutu's nationalistic culture policy, Health Commissioner Nguete Kikhela has launched a survey of traditional health methods across Zaire in order to eventually codify this sector as a health resource for inclusion in a comprehensive national health scheme. This survey is underway as I write these lines, financed in part by the Canadian International Research and Development Corporation. Zaire is not alone in this venture. A recent World Health Organization regional conference in Brazzaville brought together numerous representatives of other African nations to compare strategies for the incorporation of traditional healers and health methods in a coordinated health system with modern medicine.

These endeavors suggest that what has changed is not so much the de facto relationship of Western or modern medicine to techniques and roles derived from traditional medicine, but the manner in which officials see that relationship.

This book presents an "on the ground" ethnographic account of how medical clients of one region of Lower Zaire diagnose illness, select therapies, and evalute treatments, a process we call "therapy management." The book is intended to clarify a phenomenon of which central African clients have long been cognizant, namely that medical systems are used in combination. Our study is aimed primarily at readers interested in the practical issues of medical decision-making in an African country, the cultural content of symptoms, and the dynamics of medical pluralism, that is, the existence in a single society of differently designed and conceived medical systems.

In the course of preparing this book, a number of theoretical issues in social science and medicine emerged, and are developed to some extent. Our key analytical idea pertaining to therapy management came to us in the field as we dealt with kinsmen and other escorts of the afflicted. The idea took firmer shape in seminars at McGill University, as the nature of decision-making, transactions, and resource evaluation was studied in therapy management groups that effectively mediated between sufferer and healing specialist. We are indebted to Professor Don Bates of the Department of History of Medicine at McGill and the students in our seminars for their contribution to the analysis.

Once the nature of the therapy managing group had come into focus, subsidiary themes were worked out. One of these was the idea of a therapeutic or medical system consisting of practices, illness and therapy concepts, and practitioner roles. Related to this was the issue of medical pluralism. Also, given the prominent place of nonprofessional therapy managers in Kongo society, we could develop an understanding of the significance, in therapy itself, of consensus between specialist and sufferer, and amongst the sufferer's advocates. These ideas were important in contextualizing the analysis of classification ideas in use, and the nature of central African colonization and efforts of decolonization within illness and therapy. Many of these issues are pertinent to medical analysis everywhere and will be dealt with more fully in forthcoming work.

Historical circumstances have, in one significant respect, given this book an already-dated cast. Following our research in 1969, names were changed in Zaire for reasons relating to Mobutu's new cultural policy. We have had to use some of the old names, for example those appearing in governmental documents. Wherever possible we have updated names to conform to current usage. A few of these name transformations need to be explained.

"Lower Zaire" refers to the region on both banks of the Zaire River, from about Kinshasa and Brazzaville to the Atlantic Ocean (see Map 1). "Zaire" is an old Portuguese derivation of the local appellation for the grand river, Nzadi, a term which in native thinking denotes both the visible river and the river of the dead. In devising nationalistic names for his country and its landmarks, Mobutu selected the old and widespread term "Zaire" in lieu of the local term "Nzadi," one of many up and down the Zaire River. Lower Zaire used to be called Lower Congo, or Bas-Congo. This term "Congo" was derived from the name used by the Kongo people who, about two to three million strong, inhabit parts of northwestern Angola, western Zaire, Cabinda, and the western area of the Republic of Congo, the site of the ancient Kongo Kingdom. These people, the BaKongo (to use the Bantu plural; singular, MuKongo) speak the KiKongo language. In scholarly and administrative circles, a linguistic convention has arisen to distinguish the Kongo people from the Congo region (as in Belgian Congo, now Zaire, or the Republic of Congo). Today, the term "Congo" is used only by the People's

Republic of Congo Brazzaville (formerly a part of French Equatorial Africa). This book thus deals with the Kongo people in a part of Lower Zaire in the Republic of Zaire.

When President Mobutu ordered name changes of landmarks, he requested his fellow citizens to drop their non-African personal names. We have followed this usage in recording our cases and in identifying other persons. In medical publications, however, another issue enters, that of confidentiality. Following what we believe to be correct in both Kongo society and medical anthropological analysis, most clients' names and those of their advocates have been disguised through pseudonyms. Healers, on the other hand, who in Kongo society and in Zaire are public figures, have been referred to with their true names. We offer special acknowledgment to all with whom we had extensive dealings: Bayindula, Masamba, Kitembo, Bilumbu, Mama Marie Kukunda, the late Kunata and his uncle Madeko, Luamba, Makunzu, Mama Mankomba, Nguma, Yambula, Tambwe, and Nzoamambu.

This book would have been impossible without the consent of individuals who appear in its pages. We deeply appreciate their cooperation; they answered most of our questions willingly, and gracefully declined to answer a few. We hope we have accurately conveyed the many Kongo therapy managers' and therapists' insights into the human condition.

A few individuals should be given special acknowledgment. Kusikila kwa Kilombo, chief of Kivunda Sector during our study, was an ever-available guide, as interested in the subject of our study as we were. His knowledge of clan politics permitted a better comprehension of the therapy management phenomenon. He once told us: "When you hear me speak in French, I am just a secondary school graduate. But when I speak in KiKongo you might think I have a Ph.D." We are grateful that he shared his KiKongo-level wisdom with us.

Fukiau and Dianzenza gave fully of themselves, both of their hospitality and their knowledge of Kongo culture. The guest house they had built for Arkinstall and me permitted us to work with freedom and still touch base with good friends nightly to share discoveries and problems.

Nzoamambu, his wives and his son Tezulwa, graciously hosted us for a week during which time we learned his medical world view and observed his practice as master *nganga*. Without his lessons we would not have been able to include Chapter 10 on the ideas behind Kongo customary medicine, ideas which made much of our other data intelligible.

We must also acknowledge the contributions by Drs. Nsonde and Bazinga who took time to share their views on the role of modern medicine in Zairian society, and in relation to the work of traditionalists named above. Along with these members of the new generation of medical doctors we mention Sister Emily of Mangembo Hospital; the medical staff at Sundi-Lutete, Karen, Kayuma, and Batumunitu; the staff at Kibunzi, Barbro and Tata Nsinga. All were helpful and understanding.

Governmental officials in Zaire assisted our project, granting the necessary permits so we could conduct our work peaceably. For this we are grateful to them. The Social Science Research Council of New York provided the original grant, recognizing the importance of a joint team of a medical doctor and an anthropologist. Without their funds, the project could not have happened. Supplemental small grants were made by McGill University and the University of Kansas.

Once our work was in manuscript form, it benefitted from the criticism of most capable readers. Dr. Glen Tuttle encouraged us after reading a rough early draft. The late Dr. Kurt Kauenhoven, Dr. Don Bates, and Professors Allan Young, Wyatt MacGaffey, Brooke Schoepf, and several anonymous readers are acknowledged for their varied and helpful comments. Professor Charles Leslie was our most thorough critic. He wanted this book to reach completion as much as we did.

The book's coverage of matters medical would not have been possible without the collaboration of Dr. William Arkinstall, cofieldworker, participant in the McGill siminars, and colleague in several later work sessions. Bill and his wife Karen shared in the whole experience of this project; their presence is acknowledged in the content of the book as well as matters of style and logic. Their friendship has been inestimable.

Reinhild, my wife, alone knows the true cost of this book. Her poignant criticism of all aspects of the work has been excelled only by her encouragement when needed. Bernd, Gesine, and Marike have generously given of their father so that this might happen.

A cup (*mbungu*) to all who were involved!

Heubuden   JOHN M. JANZEN
July 22, 1976

PART I

THE AREA OF STUDY

CHAPTER ONE

The Human Setting of Healing in Lower Zaire

The Management of Illness and Therapy

This study of therapy among the BaKongo in Lower Zaire includes both Western medicine and practices derived from pre-colonial traditions. Beginning about 1890 the work of Western doctors and nurses has taken place alongside the work of *banganga*, who are native doctors, and *bangunza*, who are inspirational diviners and prophets. The people of Zaire recognize the advantages of Western medicine and seek its drugs, surgery, and hospital care, but contrary to what might have been expected, native doctors, prophets, and traditional consultations among kinsmen do not disappear with the adoption of Western medicine. Rather, a modus vivendi has developed in which different forms of therapy play complementary rather than competitive roles in the thoughts and lives of the people.

Hospital workers in the Lower Zaire often observe that patients interrupt treatment to return to their homes, or, upon arrival at the hospital, patients bear telltale scratches of an *nganga*'s treatment. Many people believe that some illnesses evade treatment by the doctor in a hospital and must be taken to a diviner-seer or before a council of fellow kinsmen. The professionals and laymen involved in this process act in a pragmatic manner to deal with immediate problems and do not take a comprehensive view of the whole system in which diverse procedures are interrelated. This book provides such a broad view of therapy in Zaire.

It is difficult to get an overall view of the interrelatedness of therapy practices in Kongo society by looking at the specialists who perform them. The interrelatedness of alternate therapies is most accessible by observing how they are evaluated and used by their clientele. An observer notes very quickly the ubiquitous "family" around the sufferer: now they are feeding the patient; later they are chatting or just sitting with him; at another time they are washing his clothes. If his condition deteriorates they may begin to mourn for him. But they are never absent, often to the consternation of the Western-trained hospital staff who feel the patient should be left alone "to rest and recover." The selection of therapy is largely a responsibility of kinsmen, and it is they who must be studied to discover the interrelations of alternative therapies in Kongo society.

The management of illness and therapy by a set of close kin is a central aspect of the medical scene in central Africa. Such kinsmen or their advocates constitute what we shall call the "therapy managing group." Its persistence gives continuity to modern Kongo medical institutions. A therapy managing group comes into being whenever an individual or set of individuals becomes ill or is confronted with overwhelming problems. Various maternal and paternal kinsmen, and occasionally their friends and associates, rally for the purpose of sifting information, lending moral support, making decisions, and arranging details of therapeutic consultation. The therapy managing group thus exercises a brokerage function between the sufferer and the specialist, whether this be for a hernia operation by a Western doctor or a plant cure known to a traditional practitioner for the treatment of sterility.

The therapy managing group has been neglected in the literature on African societies. Only a few writers have explicitly referred to the phenomenon or systematically analyzed it: Margaret Read has recognized the importance of the family in therapy management in her work in Ghana[1]; D. M. Boswell has identified the place of the "escort" in therapy-seeking behavior in urban Zambia and has analyzed the kin and extra-kin settings of problem-solving.[2] We will return later in this book to their ideas. In the majority of works on African societies, the therapy managing group is entirely ignored or described sketchily without proper recognition of its central role in shaping the fabric of health care.

Michael Gelfand, who has long experience as a physician and teacher among the Shona of southern Africa, identifies the process in a few illustrative passages in his prolific writings. During late pregnancy and childbirth the Shona woman goes to live with her mother. When three months are left in the pregnancy, her kin engage a midwife who medicates and dilates the maternal passages to facilitate birth. Mother, grandmother, and mother-in-law are on hand at these visits by the midwife. In "Consultations and Fees," Gelfand makes reference to the patients' relatives, their families, and family delegations, particularly in consultations with diviners where patients are often not even present. Gelfand's work gives random accounts of kin managers and their interaction with specialists.[3]

Paul Parin, in a psychoanalytic study of the Agni of the Ivory Coast—a people with a social structure akin to that of the BaKongo—describes the therapy managing process but only to explain psychological phenomena. One middle-aged woman described in his study developed a dual strategy for coping with her problems. She provoked a crisis so that her mother, her headman, a friend, and a judge would enter her case to help her out. Alternatively she indulged in witchcraft fantasies and consulted magicians, but only, says Parin, in her "weaker" moments. By involving other individuals in her case, she put her problem "outside

1. Margaret Read, *Culture, Health and Disease* (London, 1966), Chapter 2.
2. D. M. Boswell, "Personal Crises and the Mobilization of the Social Network," in *Social Networks in Urban Situations*, ed. J. Clyde Mitchell (Manchester, 1969), pp. 245-96.
3. Michael Gelfand, *The Sick African* (Capetown, 1955); *Medicine and Custom in Africa* (London, 1964), p. 115; *Witch Doctor* (New York, 1965), p. 102.

herself" and could return to normal life again for a time.[4] Parin describes the therapy managing group as the social fabric that maintains normalcy for a sufferer.

Similarly, in an account of *akombo* therapy among the Tiv of Nigeria we find a description of the therapy managing group, to explain religious phenomena. After a sufferer has consulted a diviner to learn which kinsmen are involved in his troubles, he calls on them—brothers, mother's brothers, father, or other combinations of kinsmen—to placate the *akombo* forces active in their relationship.[5] Here, in a fashion typical for studies in Africa, social and mystical causes are shown to be present in notions of illness. But we are not told how an individual comes to consult a diviner (all alone?), what he does if he is too sick to make the journey, and so on.

A few references to the therapy managing concept are to be found in studies pertaining not to medicine at all, but to politics and society. In a book on Kinshasa, Jean LaFontaine provides an excellent, but again isolated, account of the phenomenon. In residential compounds of the kind most Kinois inhabit, neighbors are frequently not kinsmen. The owner of the compound may have some kinsmen living with him, but strangers from other ethnic groups and home regions rent additional small quarters in the compound. LaFontaine notes that in this setting, quasi-kinship functions emerge, including the management of therapy. She witnessed the case of an elderly man who fell ill while living alone in one of these compounds. He was cared for entirely by another tenant and his wife who were not kinsmen. They took him to the hospital, brought him food daily, and acted as caretakers for his room during his absence.[6] Here, then, the therapy managing group acted as a go-between for the sufferer and the Western institution, fulfilling the dictum derived from tradition that "neighbors should help one another."

4. Paul Parin, Fritz Morgenthaler, and Goldy Parin-Matthèy, *Fürchte deinen Nächsten wie dich Selbst* (Frankfurt am Main. 1971), pp. 303-04.
5. D. R. Price-Williams, "A Case Study of Ideas Concerning Disease Among the Tiv," *Africa* 32 (1962): pp. 123-31.
6. Jean S. LaFontaine, *City Politics* (Cambridge, 1970), p. 131.

Therapy management as it exists in Kongo society is thus not an isolated phenomenon, although it has received little systematic treatment in the literature. Most studies of traditional African medicine focus on the specialists, who are spectacular enough to distract attention from ordinary routines of treatment. The descriptions leave an impression that lone individuals consult specialists, whether herbalists, diviners, or magicians. This impression is belied by occasional evidence to the contrary. Medical writers on African medical practices such as Gelfand, Harley,[7] and most recently Jansen,[8] have transported their Western conception of the physician normatively confronting an individual sufferer to African settings, where native therapy is reported as if the same thing occurs there. This perspective creates an illusion that traditional specialists have superficial functions within the society. It leads one of these writers, for example, to suggest that once witch doctors have been suppressed by "civilization," the deleterious fear of witchcraft will disappear.[9] However, if, as we propose in this study, norms and beliefs concerning illness and therapy are profoundly coded into the lives and minds of sufferers and their kinsmen, friends, and neighbors, the theoretical and practical issues of medical usages come into quite another perspective. The therapy managing group phenomenon becomes a generic concept with probably universal representation in all societies. The "sick role" can be analyzed as a way of defining and mobilizing rights and duties within a community of persons who take responsibility from the sufferer and enter into brokerage relationships with specialists.[10] The doctor-patient relationship

7. George W. Harley, *Native African Medicine* (Cambridge, 1944). This work, although lacking systematic treatment of therapy management, is a model of the naturalistic study of traditional medicine, plants, and techniques used.

8. G. Jansen, *The Doctor-Patient Relationship in an African Tribal Society* (Assen, 1973).

9. Gelfand states, specifically, that "the *nganga* is the hub round which the spiritual world revolves, and so long as he functions as a dispenser of antidotes to witchcraft, so long will the African's bondage to fear continue." *Witch Doctor*, p. 120.

10. The writing of Talcott Parsons is central in this discussion of the "sick role:" See, for example, his "Definition of Health and Illness in the Light of American Values and Social Structure," in *Patients, Physicians, and Illness*, ed.

has complex meaning when the therapy managing group has a prominent place in mediating that relationship.[11] In this situation, Western practitioners who are trained to confer directly with the patient must learn to be sensitive to the family members who piece together the picture of therapeutic progress and decide the next step of action. Health educators may take note that the therapy managing group and not the sufferer alone is the appropriate focus of public health instruction.

Broad cultural premises about illness and health must be seen in the context of therapy managing groups. BaKongo make a fundamental distinction between an illness that is natural in cause, which they call an illness of God (*kimbevo kia Nzambi*), and one that entails human causes, which is an illness of man (*kimbevo kia muntu*). Generally, mild conditions which respond readily to therapy when no particular disturbance exists in the immediate social relationships of the sufferer are thought to be diseases or misfortunes of God. Illness or death amongst the elderly or neonate are often considered to be natural. The notion "of God" does not imply divine intervention or retribution but simply that the case is an affliction in the order of things, unrelated to human intentions.[12] Long before a case ever comes before a specialist, the relegation of a sickness to one or the other of these categories is an essential task of the therapy managing group. Western medicine is considered efficacious in the treat-

E. G. Jaco (Glencoe, 1958), pp. 165-87. More recently, Eliot Freidson has reviewed the literature on the sick role in his *Profession of Medicine* (New York, 1971).

11. Several leading works we have found helpful in working through this important subject are: L. J. Henderson, "The Patient and Physician as a Social System," *New England Journal of Medicine*, 212 (1935): 819-23; M. Balint, *The Doctor, His Patient, and the Illness* (New York, 1957); Samuel W. Bloom, *The Doctor and His Patient* (New York, 1963); Jean Pouillon, "Malade et médecin: le même et/ou l'autre? Rémarques ethnologiques," *Incidences de la Psychanalyse: Nouvelle Révue de Psychanalyse* 1 (1970).

12. The classic work on African disease and misfortune causality is of course E. E. Evans-Pritchard's *Witchcraft, Oracles, and Magic Among the Azande* (Oxford, 1937). Kongo categories introduced here are similar in general lines, although differences will become evident later in our book. Robin Horton has provided a good framework with which to analyze the tenacity of metaexplanation and premise in African thought in his "African Traditional Thought and Western Science," *Africa* 37: (1967): 50-72, 155-87.

ment of natural illnesses, as are some of the therapies of the herbalist *nganga*. But a variety of signs, from the slow healing of a wound or sore to overt conflict in the social group of the sufferer, may shift the perceived etiology to the category of illness caused by man. Once this etiology is entertained by the therapy managing group, an alternative set of therapeutic endeavors is undertaken, involving reasoned efforts at conflict resolution, counterspells to ward off hostility and suspicion, and purification rituals to "heal" discord.

A feature of therapy management in Kongo society is the collective orientation of medicine. The whole diagnostic apparatus is sensitive to the social causes of physiological affliction. African traditional medicine has been criticized by Western missionaries and colonials as superstition that victimizes individuals ostensibly to benefit the social group. But it could be equally well argued that Western medicine focuses on the individual patient and leaves the social context of his illness in pathological chaos. Kongo therapeutic attitudes, like those in many other African societies, are composed to discern the social and psychosomatic causes of illness. Tension is known by BaKongo to cause illness, anger is "dangerous," and anxiety is thought to be prevalent. These assessments of the social situation are accurate; for African society, like Western society, is anxiety-evoking, and illness can be caused or exacerbated by social stress. Disputes over land, property, marriage, and death, and the role conflicts inherent in customary social structure, are sources of anxiety; the growing influence of the mass media which lauds prosperity and new life styles is another source of anxiety that particularly affects the elite. A neurotic concern about heart trouble, impotence, weak legs, and abdominal pain were common symptoms of anxiety in the cases we analyzed. They were taken very seriously by the therapy managing groups who attributed them to anxiety-producing situations.

The logic of decision-making within ad hoc and more formalized managing groups was analyzed by recording decision after decision as they were made in a number of cases. By analyzing alternative options and choices in these cases we have formed

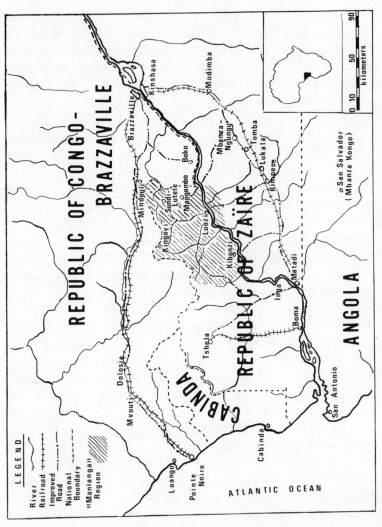

MAP 1. Lower Zaïre, extended region of study

LEGEND

River
Railroad
Improved Road
National Boundary
"Manianga" Region

REPUBLIC OF CONGO-BRAZZAVILLE

REPUBLIC OF ZAÏRE

CABINDA

ANGOLA

ATLANTIC OCEAN

Kinshasa
Mudimba
Brazzaville
Mbanza-Ngungu
Tumba
Lukala
Boko
Mindouli
Sundi-Lutete
Kingoyi
Mangembo
Kimpese
San Salvador (Mbanza Kongo)
Luozi
Kibunzi
Matadi
Inga
Tshela
Boma
Dolosie
Mvouti
San Antonio
Loango
Pointe Noire
Cabinda

kilometers
0   10   50   90

a conception of the popular images of therapeutic alternatives. The first, Western medicine, is perceived to be independent of local culture, with its practitioners working in isolation of other therapeutic activity in the society. Laymen recognize that Western medicine defines problems as primarily physical, and does so in ways that are not understood very well by laymen, in many cases specifying diseases unknown to the laymen. In fact, it may use specialized diagnostic facilities to uncover specific conditions, such as malaria and hepatitis, or employ unique therapy techniques such as surgery and injections of antibiotics. A second system in Kongo therapy weighed by the therapy managing groups is the art of the *banganga*. Perhaps a slight overlap exists between the methods used by the *banganga* and the practice of the Western system. Each prescribes medication and each deals predominantly with individual physical complaints. An additional choice generates kinship therapy in which the kin become involved actively in diagnosis and therapeutic maneuvers. And finally, there is a set of alternative choices we identify as purification and initiation. Some overlap occurs between the art of the *banganga* and the therapy actions which involve kinsmen. The *banganga* often recommend that the kin independently research possible areas of social conflict, but they do not generally take an active role in the dynamics of kinship therapy. On the other hand, kinship therapy and therapy processes involving purification and initiation rites significantly overlap. In these areas, culturally determined illness concepts are definitely in operation.

The Society and Its History

This study took place among the BaKongo, the KiKongo-speaking people of Lower Zaire (formerly the Lower Congo). The immediate region in which fieldwork was conducted in 1965–1966 and again in 1969, was the Manianga, a term used also to identify the local people. Manianga is a distinct area covering both banks of the Zaire (Congo) River (see Map 1) bordering on the Republic of Congo (Brazzaville) to the north and the Ngombe region to the south. It is approximately midway between Matadi, the ocean port of Zaire, and Kinshasa, the capital. Historically,

the name Manianga was given to a market on the north bank of
the Zaire River and to one of the narrower and easier crossings on
the river, which has rapids, treacherous undercurrents, and
whirlpools along its course from Kinshasa to the ocean.
Manianga was a busy market in the precolonial era.[13] It lay midway between the coastal regions north of the river and the market
at Mpumbu near today's Kinshasa site, the hub of slave trade.
The populations we describe are identified by Murdock as of the
Kongo cluster of the central Bantu, and by Baumann and Westermann as being in the matrilineal Bantu belt of west African
civilization.[14]

The Manianga region has a climate and landscape characteristic of the Lower Zaire. The broad river dominates the landscape,
requiring inhabitants to adapt to it. It is largely responsible for the
isolation of the regions north from the main roads, railroads, and
towns of Lower Zaire. As one leaves Luozi (see Map 1) for the
north Manianga interior, one drives up a steep escarpment that in
good weather is difficult and on rainy days becomes impassable.
The terrain of alternating forest valley and savannah hilltop
shows severe erosion from driving rains that last from September
or October through May. West of Luozi, the fertile Luala River
valley supports good farming for about 75 kilometers upstream,
where a government farm (*paysannat*) has been created. Westward and northward, beyond the escarpment, into the hills,
forests appear more frequently, remnants of a time when much of
the region was forested. In western Manianga, toward Mayombe,
enough forest remains for commercial lumber companies to operate. North and eastward toward Mindouli, in Congo Brazzaville,
one enters a high plateau where the soil is sandy and fertile.

13. Edouard Dupont, *Lettres sur le Congo* (Paris, 1889), and Henry M. Stanley, *Through the Dark Continent* (New York, 1879), report finding Manianga
market in the seventies and eighties a large bustling trade center dealing in goods
necessary for the porters' trek from the coast to Stanley Pool.
14. The populations on the north bank of the Zaire River that are the focus of
this study are classified by Murdock as Sundi, Bembe, Bwende, Dondo, and
Kamba, Group 3 of the Kongo cluster of central Bantu, in George P. Murdock,
Africa, Its Peoples and Their Culture History (New York, 1959). These names
refer to nonterritorial clans recurring throughout the area, not territorial
"peoples" as Murdock's scheme suggests. Also cited, H. Baumann and D. Westermann, *Les peuples et les civilisations de l'Afrique* (Paris, 1967).

This uneven terrain of varying soil composition and seasonal rain results in some highly fertile areas and in others that are quite barren. The western lowlands, less densely inhabited, possess a laterite-clay soil unsuitable for savannah cultivation. Here food-crop gardening is limited to the scarce alluvial soils along a few streams such as the Luala. In the northern highlands, sandier soil prevails, permitting both savannah and forest gardening and a higher population density.[15] Despite this uneven terrain and varied population density, the same food crops are grown throughout the area, representing "African" cultigens in the oil palm tree (*Elaeis guineensis*), assorted fruit trees, and several curcurbits; "Malaysian" cultigens of bananas and yams; and "American" cultigens such as corn, beans (*Phaseolus vulgaris*), squash and groundnuts, sweet potatoes, and manioc. The traditional division of labor continues in respect to these crops, with the women tending shifting savannah fields of manioc, beans, squash, and groundnuts fallowed for at least ten years. Where forests remain or have been planted, men tend orchards of palm and fruit trees, as well as truck crops. Both types of cultivation have been affected by colonial demands for direct food taxation (in the Free State era) and later head tax, fines, and obligatory cash cropping. European merchants began in the twenties to purchase palm oil and nuts, as taxes were levied. In the forties, the Belgian colonial government imposed urena fibers as a cash crop. Sizeable forest tracts were cleared to permit optimal soil for urena, but the collapse of the world fiber market in 1951 made this crop unprofitable and left the soil barren savannah. Despite the erratic history of cash cropping and the continuing problem of marketing, Manianga food sources have been adequate in most areas. Although hunting is practiced by many men and has a strong ritual lore, its nutritional significance is slight. Pigs, goats, sheep, chickens, tse-tse-resistant cattle, and fish provide some animal protein.

The Territory of Luozi—the Manianga—has a population density overall of 13.8 persons per square kilometer, the average for

15. Henri Nicolai, *Luozi: Géographie régionale d'un pays du Bas-Congo* (Bruxelles, 1961), and field notes.

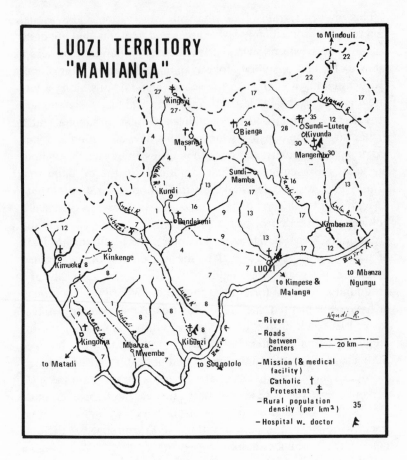

MAP 2. Territory of Luozi, Manianga, major roads, centers, medical facilities, population density (after Nicolai 1961; authors' field notes)

the Lower Zaire. The region is distinctive, however, in the variation from sizeable areas that are totally uninhabited to those inhabited as heavily as 35–40 persons per square kilometer (see Map 2).[16] Several hypotheses for the low population density in the Manianga lowlands have been put forward. One is that the slave trade directly or indirectly removed more than half of the popula-

16. *Ibid.*, appendices; Kivunda Communal Records, Tableaux de recensement de population (1956, 1959, 1962, 1964, 1965).

tion, but historical documentation is lacking. The low population is perhaps more a result of the eary colonial intrusion. Agents of the Congo Free State "recruited" up to 8000 porters annually from the lower Zaire River region beginning in the 1880s, and later many more workers were needed for construction of the railroad. In response, whole settlements fled north across the river into the hilly border area between the two Congos, today densely populated.[17] Many who did not flee died on the projects. Endemic tropical diseases of the area—sleeping sickness, malaria, dysentery—ravaged the local population as colonial expansion upset its ecological adaptation. Kongo villages had been built on hilltops, as forested cemeteries (*makulu*) at the sites of old villages testify. Atop the hills, the insects carrying disease—mosquitoes and flies—were less numerous. With the colonial intrusion, many communities moved down into the sheltered valley forests to escape labor recruiters and agents of the new state. The epidemic of sleeping sickness that hit the Lower Zaire in the first decade of this century and decimated many lowland villages may have been a direct consequence of this shift in settlement form.[18] Later, with the encouragement of the administration, which sought to consolidate several villages into one for its own convenience, villages moved back to the open hilltops, and back into an overall healthier relationship with their surroundings, although the social consequences of forced consolidation were as traumatic and far-reaching on the people as the epidemics had been. Gilles Sautter estimates that the population of the Atlantic coast of central Africa had by the first decade of this century dropped to half the level of the fifteenth century and that it did not begin to grow until the 1930s.[19]

In those areas of the Manianga highland that combine cultivable savannah worked by the women with streamside forest cultivated by the men, the population density reaches 35 persons per square kilometer. In these regions, approximately 80 percent of the adult males remain in the villages to gain their livelihood. In

17. Dupont, *op. cit.*
18. A. Beck, *Changing Lifestyles and Sleeping Sickness* (Cambridge, 1970).
19. Gilles Sautter, *De l'Atlantique au fleuve Congo* (The Hague, 1966).

areas where forest is scarce, population density tapers off and the exodus of men from the villages to urban centers approaches 50 percent, a higher proportion than the average for the Lower Zaire. Over the entire Territory of Luozi, the disproportion of women to men aged 20–45 reaches 250 women for 100 men, though for other age groups there is nearly equal representation of the sexes.[20]

The village settlements are the residences of less than half of the people born in the Manianga. These villages may be small hamlets (*belo*) of a dozen or so inhabitants, either members of a single line of descent with their spouses, or various associates of someone who has withdrawn from a larger community. Villages may also consist of a larger settlement (*vata*) of several hundred individuals and several descent communities. In precolonial times, much shifting and moving of settlements occurred due to a variety of social and ecological reasons. During the colonial era, pressure was put on Africans to consolidate hamlets dispersed alongside a road. Now, older settlements are hidden from view by mature fruit trees, and when a settlement is moved, the old site often becomes the clan cemetery. The trees, left to grow, become the communal property of the descendants.

Another type of settlement in the Manianga is the mission, present since the late nineteenth century. The Swedish Covenant Mission (Svenska Missionsforbundet) (SMF) entered the region north of the river as early as 1887 at Kibunzi and at Mukimbungu, where a large hospital was created, shortly after the turn of the century. The SMF also established mission posts in the Manianga highlands, at Kingoyi, Kinkenge, and Sundi-Lutete with schools and medical dispensaries. The Belgian Catholics of the Redemptorist Order opened missions at Luozi, Mangembo, and elsewhere. The missions hired and trained houseboys, general servants, and craftsmen, and in due course attracted other people to them who became evangelists, pastors, priests, teachers, nurses, and clerks. African quarters sprang up around the European missions, with a somewhat autonomous prestige

20. Nicolai, *op. cit.*, pp. 31-37; Kivunda Communal Records, *op. cit.*

system and an economy related to the mission. From these mission communities the modern Zairian social system based on class and wage differentials, educational levels, and related professions emerged. The missions continue to play an important role in regional and national life. They are frequently the site of the best schools and medical institutions. Since independence, their direction has been assumed by Africans.

Another type of nontraditional settlement sprang up around the colonial administrative post, frequently situated near the mission. Here, too, lived the families of house servants, street sweepers, janitors, and gardeners of the Europeans. The most important role played by Africans in the administration from the first colonial outposts of the Free State in 1885 until present times was that of the gendarme, or policeman. The local contingent of police enforced tax collection; arrested, beat, and jailed, and fined troublemakers; supervised prisoners and surveyed their work projects; and assured that markets were held peaceably. In due course, African clerks began to work in these administrative centers, and when independence was achieved, the administrative apparatus, now fully African, constituted a complex community of salaried officers, agents, guards, party counsellors, and secretaries, each with a private local residence. Luozi, the territorial capital of the Manianga, is a large administrative community, and *secteur* headquarters are smaller replicas of it.

Around the missions and the administrative centers, commercial centers emerged, usually headed by a Belgian or Portuguese merchant. These merchants bought local produce such as palm nuts or oil, manioc, peanuts, vegetables, and fruits for transport to the urban markets. Their most important function was to supply Africans with a variety of manufactured goods such as cloth, sugar, knives, bicycles, gunpowder, hoes, soap, and shoes. As long as the mercantile role was limited to European outsiders, the "staff" did not constitute much of an independent community. But in the postwar era, and especially after independence in 1960, the role of the merchant came increasingly into African hands. In 1974, the government expropriated the remaining foreign merchants of their stores and stocks, and the importing-exporting function moved totally into Zairian hands. In Manianga, a powerful Portuguese family that had operated retail stores and a palm oil extracting plant was replaced by a variety of Zairian merchants who have acquired trucks and other significant capital investments. Several important commercial centers have emerged near the missions and the sector administrative centers. The merchants often live in or near their stores. Clerks, chauffeurs, and mechanics also find residences nearby. To meet their needs, secondary commercial enterprises such as bars, cafes, and hotels are opened and a town nucleus comes into being.

In other areas the "company town" has been created, forming another type of nonvillage settlement. It is in many ways like the commercial post, with a different history. The Congo Free State was largely financed by concessioning areas of the Congo Basin to international companies who were able, with African labor, to extract rubber, ivory, wood, and agricultural products from the region. Wherever this exploitation of resources was localized, as in palm plantations or, later, copper and diamond areas, settlements sprang up inhabited by laborers and their kinfolk, along with attendant personnel such as medics, clerks, mechanics, and teachers. In the Manianga and the Lower Zaire, such company towns appeared near the palm oil industry north of Luozi, the logging operation at the Mayombe border, and the governmental farm in the Luala Valley. None of these centers has prospered in postcolonial times. On the other hand, the cement industry at Lukala on the Matadi-Kinshasa highway, and the Inga hydroelectric project near Matadi, have provided abundant job opportunities for Manianga folk.

Clearly, the Manianga is no longer a "traditional" society. Economic, educational, and other social institutions have been drastically and permanently altered by the massive populational relocation in the colonial setting of the past seventy years. Changes are centered in missions with their hospitals and schools, in the commercial settlements with shops and factories, and in administrative headquarters where police, clerks, and politicians converge. Luozi, with a state hospital, territorial administration, schools, Catholic and Protestant missions, and merchants of various kinds, has become an urban community. In the northern highlands, the government post of Kivunda, with an adjacent commercial post, nearby Protestant and Catholic missions with large medical centers and schools, and the Kimbanguist mission, constitutes an urbanized outpost. And in the western Luala Valley, the state farm, along with schools, medical posts, missions, and a related commercial center, constitutes another such cluster that may become a town if the agricultural industry survives.

These towns and centers have some of the character of the larger cities, from Matadi to Kinshasa and Brazzaville, where Manianga emigrés are to be found. Jean LaFontaine, in her study of Kinshasa, described the Zairian capital as a bustling, sprawling city in which the traditions of tribesmen are rapidly lost. Kinship ties are attenuated in the face of personal incomes spent for ever-rising prices of basic subsistence items and the lure of friendship. Also, social outlooks change as people try to get along with persons of other tribal backgrounds using the lingua franca, Lingala, or the colonizer's language, French. The dividing line between teachers and workers, successful entrepreneurs and barely surviving pushcart drivers, educated governmental officials and newspaper hawkers, is very apparent and displaces the sodality of kinship.[21] Despite these centrifugal forces at work on kin relationships, economic exigency, and the threat of personal crisis make kinship ties a prominent form of urban social organization.

In sharp contrast to the modern city is a final nontraditional settlement, the "holy village." In this category are the headquarters of independent religious movements common in the Lower Zaire, and centers of individual healers in secluded quarters of villages and towns. Some are monastic settlements whose inhabitants are veterans of colonial imprisonment and exile. The prophetic movement from which all others derive began in 1921 around the prophet Simon Kimbangu. Kimbangu began to heal the sick, preach, and "raise the dead." Given the public mood of the time, the gradual erosion of chiefly leadership, and the op-

21. LaFontaine, *op. cit.*

pression of the people, Kimbangu was perceived as a liberator. Since his following was enormous, he and his apostles were arrested and imprisoned for life. Subsequent underground religious movements that derived from this beginning survived throughout the time of colonial persecution, surfacing here and there as local cells of independent Christianity with strong Kongo cultural overtones. When the colonial era ended, dozens of prophetic centers emerged. Most notable is the Church of Jesus Christ on Earth by the Prophet Simon Kimbangu (EJCSK), whose headquarters are in the prophet's natal village just across the river from the Manianga. This church has achieved public recognition and legitimacy in the hands of the prophet's three sons, and vies with the Protestants and the Catholics for public subsidies for its schools and dispensaries. Thousands of followers make annual pilgrimages to the prophet's mausoleum at N'Kamba, and EJCSK missions dot the Zairian and central African region. Less prominent are various cells and orders calling themselves the Church of the Holy Spirit. These groups rarely have schools or dispensaries and are occupied with healing and purification rites. Some of our cases indicate the role they and the individualized prophet-seers play in the Kongo therapeutic process nowadays.

Although various nontraditional settlements provide residence for more than half of the people in the Manianga, the customary social structure continues to influence life decisions and to shape primary groups. We can thus describe its major lines in some detail, for it pertains to all persons, since most BaKongo keep in touch with their natal village homes. The minimal social unit of kinship in Maniangan society is the lineage (*mwelo-nzo*, "door-of-the-house"). It comprises matrilineally traced descendants of a common ancestress, whose adult male descendants live together in a hamlet (*belo*) or urban compound. The lineage is involved in crucial decisions and has a family head who takes charge of distributing the fields annually to dependents: wives, brothers' wives, widowed and divorced sisters. This unit is the minimal unit of westernmost African matrilineal society. We find it involved as the managing group of most of the medical cases. A great deal of sharing and expectation of mutual support occur within it. This is true of both the rural lineage and its counterpart in urban settings, localized in a compound of a large house. The lineage is the setting of competition and suspicion over scarce resources, and it is here that witchcraft is most often believed to be present.

A more inclusive unit of matrilineal kinship is the *nzo*, ("house") or *vumu dikanda* ("clan womb"). If numerically small, it is not distinguished from the lineage. If large, it becomes an extended village (*vata*) with several residential quarters (*bibelo*), each possessing its own men's house for eating, drinking, and palavering. The clan section possesses its own cemetery, usually situated at the heart of the landed estate in a sacred grove of trees marking the site of a former village. This estate is defended against all encroachment before government courts and in traditional open palavers. Although the *belo* residential unit is seldom reconstituted in the urban setting, the *nzo* section is so extended. An urban subchief oversees the needs of urban clansmen, and funds flow back to the village through him for ceremonial obligations. This relationship also serves as an axis of referral in medical cases.

A still more inclusive level of matrilineal clan organization is the extended clan, *dikanda*, comprised of two or three *nzo*. This is the largest effective exogamic unit and the descent group of widest political support. Formerly, in feuds, common *dikanda* membership entailed a mutual ban on fighting.

The broadest level of matrilineal descent reckoning is the *luvila*, a category of putative common descent, not a real social group. In formal legend, all BaKongo descend from twelve female ancestors who accompanied Nimi a Lukeni, founder of the capital of Kongo, Mbanza Kongo, in the thirteenth or fourteenth century when he set up court and sent allies out to govern the provinces. This legend is used to open genealogical exercises in the defense of clan land. It also bestows nominal exogamy upon the clan category, although no effort is made to trace intervening generations or to enforce clanwide exogamy; a ritual sacrifice absolves those who suspect that intraclan "incest" has made them ill.

In addition to the MuKongo's identity in this series of progressively more inclusive matrilineal groups and categories, he is also identified with his father's group. The mother's lineage and house are situated in the principle of *kingudi* ("mother's side") from *ngudi* ("mother" or "center," "first principle"). Father's matrilineage and house are known as *kise*, from *se* ("father"). The *kise* principle of patrifiliation places a person in a category of "children" corporately known as the *bana bambuta* ("children born of the father's clan"). In practice, this patrifilial relationship is as significant as matrilineality, as residence patterns suggest.

The residential unit clusters around a dynamic lineage head who does what he can to keep his sisters' sons and their wives together, to gather his female kin upon their husbands' deaths or their divorce, and, as father and (formerly) possessor of slaves, to retain a following of sons and patrifilial kinsmen through wealth and generosity to dependents. A woman leaves her parental home at marriage to take up residence with her husband. A man is able to choose his residence with father or mother's brother on growing up, depending on which is the more inviting situation for him. Life in Kongo society contains numerous points of individual option, as well as ambiguity and strain.

Although children usually move away from their paternal home when they grow up, the patrifilial children periodically return as a collectivity to celebrate paternal clan affairs. They are reputed for their skill in arbitrating conflicts within their fathers' group of which they are common offspring, not members, and it is they who preside over their fathers' funerals and act as priestly mediators between the living and the dead in their fathers' clan. A patrifilial child is also expected to "marry back" into his father's matrilineage, taking as wife his "father's sister's daughter." This is a classificatory preference that extends to any girl of a young man's generation within his father's matrilineage. "Returning blood" is believed to maintain a balance in descent group identity. Although statistically few marriages fulfill this expectation, those that do are the politically strategic marriages between neighboring landowning clans. Today, most marriages occur on a variety of kinship bases between persons residing in or originating from restricted regions such as north Manianga, or the Ngombe Circle. Clan heads strongly advise against distant marriage with strange families. Several of our medical cases show the difficulties accompanying marriage with strangers, as well as the problem of incest in too close a marriage.

Incest, priesthood of the dead, and witchcraft in social life are vital issues in Kongo religion and cosmology even though most BaKongo are nominal Christians. The Kongo cosmos is divided between the visible world of the living above the earth and the invisible world of the ancestors below. The two are mediated by symbols of water, wine, white clay, and red bark in the hands of patrifilial children and other priestly experts. The other world of ancestors and spirits is frequently symbolized by river chalk or clay (*luvemba*), and dying, that is passing beyond the *nzadi* river of death, is spoken of as "going to the white" (*ku mpemba*). Whiteness conveys a sense of legitimacy, a justification for being, a source of social order and truth. Clan spokesmen defend the estate of the living by rooting it in the prior existence of genealogical forbears.[22]

The mystical source of chiefly power was also symbolized by "whiteness," as well as signs such as the leopard skin and the sword. Grand traditional chiefship ended early in the colonial experience in Kongo, but the clan headman's office (*mfumu dikanda*) retains trappings of mystical power rooted in the other world of lineal ancestors. This source of power is called on to protect the interests of the living, to mitigate against the chaos resulting from unequal distribution of resources (e.g., land), the inappropriate marriage of women, and the mishandling of envy or insubordination. Governance in the clan is expressed in the term *sika*, to rule, order, be vigilant; *sikila dikanda* expresses the headman's duty to guard the clan and maintain its *minsiku*, the prohibitions, sacred emblems, and secrets.

---

22. This principle has been central in traditional etiology of illness and continues to be important in clarifying an afflicted person's social setting. The general phenomenon of legitimation in Kongo tradition is discussed and illustrated in John M. Janzen and Wyatt MacGaffey, *An Anthology of Kongo Religion* (Lawrence, 1974).

The antithesis of ideal governance is witchcraft, *kindoki*; the contrast between competent authority and the disastrous consequences of unbridled envy, anger, and injustice is a recurring theme in the exploration of causality of illness. The chief partakes of the same power as the witch, with the difference that the witch uses it for selfish ends and the destruction of the collectivity, or even to benefit a witchcraft coven, while the chief exercises mystical power and even capital punishment upon individual subjects for the collective good. Witchcraft substance, *kundu*, is present in every local clan section, as is chiefship. Where the *kundu*-holder is someone other than the chief, a troublesome time is thought to ensue. Where the *kundu*-holder is the chief, order will prevail, although fear is expressed of any *kundu*-holder. The theory of witchcraft, as outlined here, does have explanatory significance in Kongo society; rights to property and ascribed social position are matrilineally conveyed, and witchcraft expresses the tensions and contradictions endemic to the society. Increasingly, it is used to explain tensions and contradictions in any social setting.

Some ritual experts work beyond the bounds of lineal descent and share power in the public arena; these are the magicians, diviners, and prophets. The *mpu* holder, for example, was a "chief priest" who maintained an ancestral shrine for prominent clans. Secret societies like Lemba, Kinkimba, and Kimpasi played an important role in maintaining a social elite and inculcating traditional values. They recruited prominent chiefs, judges, and healers who in local polities exercised significant authority. But the secret societies and the public priests were destroyed with the advent of the colonial government and mission work. Only individualized and idiosyncratic *nganga* orders survived.

The erosion of authority of traditional chiefs, priests, and magicians in the early decades of this century resulted in a perceived increase of witchcraft. The colonial government forbade the poison ordeal for witchcraft and usurped chief's rights to execute criminals, thereby eliminating the two ultimate traditional mechanisms to combat social disorganization. The populace resorted progressively to individualized devices of witchcraft protection acquired from remaining individualized and idiosyncratic *banganga*. These "defenses" proved inadequate, seen from within Kongo culture, for neither did they stop the decay of traditional chiefly power in the face of the colonial government, nor did they eliminate the epidemics that ravaged the countryside. Furthermore, they were vulnerable to the criticism leveled by the missions that Kongo magic was weaker than the combined forces of Christianity, colonial might, and modern medicine.

This systematic discrediting of Kongo culture resembled the local effects of colonialism elsewhere in the world. As in Melanesia the cargo cult movement, and in the Plains of the United States the Ghost Dance movement, so in Kongo a prophet movement appeared to cope with the encroachments of colonialism. In 1921, the prophet Simon Kimbangu and his associates advocated literacy, Bible reading, mission education, and cooperation with the colonial government. Addressing Kongo culture itself Kimbangu decreed that *minkisi* medicines, now discredited, should be abandoned, as well as drinking and dancing and other aspects of custom in disfavor with the whites. At the same time he taught that public authority was to be revitalized through renewed attention to the ancestors and worship of the true God Nzambi in lieu of reliance on *minkisi*. Kimbangu's messianism and that of other prophets constituted a desperate attempt to regain integrity in Kongo cultural terms. Despite massive repression, exile and constant surveillance, the prophetic revival persisted and reshaped Kongo society—in inverse proportion to the degree chiefship, healership, and other legitimate public institutions had been destroyed.

Disease, Modern Medicine, and Health

After the tumultous years of early colonialism a new equilibrium was established between the conditions of life in the Lower Zaire, the tropical diseases of central Africa, and available medical care. The endemic killers such as sleeping sickness, malaria, intestinal parasites, tuberculosis, and bilharzia were brought under greater control although none was entirely eliminated. Endemic diseases such as respiratory infections, chronic diarrhea, sickle-cell anemia, poliomyelitis, and postmeasles respiratory infections still take the lives of many children. Malnutrition, nutritional anemia, specific vitamin deficiencies such as beriberi and pellagra still occur. Many of these diseases can be directly related to inadequate knowledge and insufficient supply of proper food.

Recent birth and death statistics for the Lower Zaire—1959, the most recent available—indicate that life expectancy from birth for males is 37.64 years, and for females 40 years. The infant mortality rate (in the first year of life) is 180/1000, half of what it was twenty years earlier, but still very high. The overall mortality rate for all ages declined by 1960 from the 16/1000 figure of 1933, while the birth rate remained constant at about 40/1000.[23] Comparable statistics are available for the years 1965–1970 for the Republic of Congo which borders the Manianga to the north; there, life expectancy from birth is 41 years, and infant mortality 180/1000.[24] These general demographic developments of a declining death rate and a steady birth rate have resulted in a growing rural population in the Manianga which, despite emigration to cities, rose from 70,000 in 1933 to 90,000 by 1961.

Modern medicine has done much to improve the state of general health in Lower Zaire since 1900. The history of this achievement begins with medical missions, in particular the Swedish Covenant Mission. Their first doctor arrived at Mukimbungu in 1891, but died in 1893. Several nurses carried on the work until Dr. Hammar arrived in 1900 to open a hospital at Nganda, near Luozi. When his successor, Dr. Palmaer, arrived in 1911 and moved the hospital to Kibunzi, fully 5 percent of the regional population was infected with sleeping sickness. He attacked this problem directly and opened a nursing school. His successor, Dr. Wiklund, collaborated closely with the colonial government to bring sleeping sickness under control.[25] Medical

23. A. Vilen, *Rapport annuel 1937 de l'oeuvre médical SMF* (Kibunzi, 1938); G. Trolli and Dupuy, *Contribution à l'étude de la démographie des BaKongo au Congo belge 1933* (Bruxelles, 1934); *Statistical Yearbook, 1959* (New York, 1959).

24. *Statistical Yearbook 1971* (New York, 1972); *World Health Statistics Annual 1969* (Geneva, 1970).

25. Vilen, *op. cit.*

stations were established at Kinkenge and later Sundi-Lutete. For years the Swedish Hospital at Kibunzi constituted the center of medical activity in the region, situated as it was near the trade route and river. With the building of the railroad and later the Matadi–Kinshasa highway, the travel and trade routes shifted to the south shore of the Zaire River. Construction of hospitals in Matadi, Kinshasa, and towns in between, and the opening in 1950 of the large Institut Médicale Evangelique (IME) at Kimpese on the main rail and highway routes, meant the gradual isolation of Kibunzi as a regional medical center. The nursing school was closed just before independence, and in 1961 the last Swedish doctor served there.

With the decline of Kibunzi, the dispensaries at the other Swedish stations in more heavily populated areas undertook building and modernization programs, each having about sixty treatment beds and a thirty- to forty-bed maternity ward. The Swedish church has continued to support these dispensary centers with staff where needed, although each has, with local support and growing governmental subsidy, been able to hire an African nurse trained in the government-approved course at IME-Kimpese. These dispensaries continue to do their best with major support and supplies from various international relief funds (e.g., Church World Service, Protestant Relief Agency) and the Zairian government.

The Catholic Church established one major hospital-dispensary at Mangembo in the northeast Manianga region, often without the services of a doctor, and two smaller dispensaries, each run by a mission sister or African nurse. There are some government dispensaries in the area, generally with a few medicines and little equipment, staffed by an African nurse who is also the local health officer. There is a sixty-bed government hospital at Luozi which has had an African doctor in attendance since 1964. This hospital is supplied with medicines from the government, but in 1969 was less well equipped than the mission hospitals. Some private dispensaries operate with various supplies and varying degrees of effectiveness.

These facilities, by themselves inadequate, are hampered by

the bad roads in Manianga and cumbersome travel across the Zaire River. An emergency air ambulance service recently established at IME-Kimpese provides quick access between the dispensaries of Manianga and the medical staff at IME hospital. But there are villages 50 kilometers from a hospital or dispensary without other access than by foot, an infrequent passing merchant's truck, or a mission or government ambulance that must be called by messenger. By comparative standards, Manianga health care facilities are not very rosy. There are only two hospital beds per thousand individuals under the direct care of a physician, less even than the Zairian national average of four beds per thousand, and far below the North American standard of eight beds per thousand population. And the figure of doctors per thousand population also is not very cheerful. During the sixties there were at times three doctors, at other times none, for 90,000 inhabitants. In the early seventies there was again a doctor at Kibunzi and one at Luozi, which gave the region one doctor per 45,000 inhabitants, below the national average in Zaire of one physician for every 30,000 inhabitants (see Figure 1). The remaining formal crtieria of health care in Manianga can be compared with the Zairian average in regard to types of specialists, hospitals or dispensaries, and beds (see Figure 2).

Formal criteria of health care such as physicians and hospital beds per thousand inhabitants require careful interpretation if an indication of health is to be gained. Although Manianga has fewer hospital beds than the Zairian average, the present populace is probably healthier than the Zairian average. Many of the physicians and hospital beds are concentrated in cities, thus skewing the general national averages. Also, the Manianga populace is probably healthier than formal criteria of care indicate because of a favorable diet, climate, and overall adaptation.

The villages of Manianga north of Luozi are constructed on hilltops at an altitude of 300 meters or more above sea level and 150 meters above the Zaire River. These villages, swept clean and kept free of grass, are exposed to wind and consequently are free of insects. Most settlements have a clean artesian spring for cooking and drinking water. In the valleys around the villages the

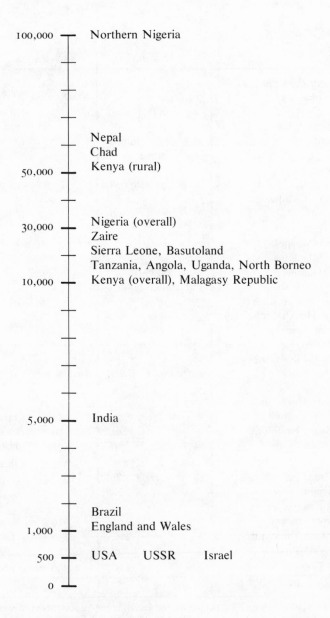

FIGURE 1. Inhabitants per medical doctor in several countries. Based on World Health Organization Records, from M. King, ed., *Medical Care in Developing Countries* (Nairobi, 1969).

	Manianga	Zaire
I *Medical Personnel per Inhabitants:*	90,000	17,000,000
Physicians	2 (1:45,000)	614 (1:28,000)
Medical Assistants	0	106 (1:170,000)
Dentists	1 partially trained nurse	21
Pharmacists	0	103
Midwives	10± (1:9,000)	68+ (1:250,000)
Assistant Midwives	8	205
Nurses	18± (1:4,500)	1,167+ (1:14,000)
Assistant Nurses	7	1,532+
Physiotherapists	0	19
X-Ray technicians	0	68
Veterinarians	several partially trained agronomists	50
Veterinary Assistants	0	50
Other Health Technicians, e.g., lab helpers	8+	73+

II *Medical Facilities per Inhabitants:*	Institutions	Beds	Institutions	Beds
General Hospitals				
Governmental	1	75	157	24,108
Private Nonprofit	2	250	86	12,515
Private Profit	0	0	72	11,658
	3	325	315	48,281
Beds per inhabitants:		(1:280)		(1:355)
Medical Centers and Maternities				
Governmental	3	0	519	3,912
Private Nonprofit	5	235	156	3,022
Private Profit	3	0	155	868
	11	235	830	7,802
Beds per inhabitants:		(1:385)		(1:2,000)

FIGURE 2. Western medical personnel and facilities per inhabitants in Manianga (Luozi Territory) and Zaire, 1969. Based on *World Health Statistics Annual* 1969, vol. 3, and field notes. Figures on facilities do not include specialized hospitals (188), tuberculosis sanatoria (17), leprosaria (32), and psychiatric centers (4).

land is fertile and suitable for gardening. Bathing and washing are done in the pools of small running streams. While many larger streams are infested with bilharzia, the people generally know which waters are so infested, and it is only the occasional village which lacks a clean stream in which to wash clothes and bathe. The nutrition of this area is good. Fresh fruit is available throughout the year. Tree-ripened oranges with ample vitamins A and C, pineapples, mangos, avocados and bananas are eaten in abundance in season, and their juices prepared into liqueurs and wines. The staple food, manioc, heavy in carbohydrate, is mixed with palm oil which contains a variety of fatty acids, and with peanuts, which when eaten with the skin are high in protein, iron, and vitamin B. Leaves from the manioc stalks are prepared as *saka-saka* and provide additional sources of iron and vitamin B (common in dark green, leafy plants). Dried fish is often used as an additional source of protein. Chickens, goats, and pigs are abundant and are eaten principally at festive occasions. Eggs, though available, are eaten sparingly. While there is some regional nutritional variation, there is little disease directly caused by malnutrition.

Despite the factors of positive adaptation and good nutrition, infectious diseases remain endemic, especially among the children, accounting for the high infant mortality rate of 180/1000. Poliomyelitis is a common infliction in the young, and one or more crippled children is seen in every village. Malaria, which is common, is less of a problem in the highlands than in the lowlands, but for children under three it is serious anywhere and may weaken a child with other afflictions. Intestinal parasites are frequent in children and may occasionally be the source of serious anemia complications. Respiratory infections either as primary pneumonia or as a complication of a viral exanthem such as measles or chicken pox is often lethal, killing from 25 to 75 percent of those infected. The complex group of childhood diarrheas has a 10–50 percent mortality rate. Whooping cough, a disease now rare in developed countries due to childhood vaccination, still claims lives in unvaccinated African children. Sickle-cell disease is aggravated by any other condition which may precipitate a crisis in the homozygous patient. And although bilharzia is only a problem in those regions lacking a clean water stream, in those instances virtually 100 percent of the local population is infected. The potential for epidemic outbreaks of the old killer diseases is present, but significant medical progress has been made in the past sixty years, both in public health and in clinical care, so that today the medical staff in Manianga may spend much of their time on routine surgical conditions, injuries, hernias, fractures, and maternity cases rather than on sleeping sickness, smallpox, or yellow fever epidemics.

Methodology of Study

When we went to Zaire in 1969 to investigate the interaction of modern Western and traditional Zairian therapy, illness concepts, and alternate criteria of therapy choice, we had only a vague idea of the specific outcome of the study. But we were not strangers to the region. Arkinstall had been a surgeon at the large IME-Kimpese in 1964/65, and later in 1966, was hospital director at Kibunzi. From late 1964 to 1966, Janzen had worked as field anthropologist on social organization in the north Manianga. During this period the study was conceived and a short preliminary survey undertaken which resulted in Chapter 4 of this book. The study had evoked local interest in the planning stage and received support of both governmental and medical authorities. When the Social Science Research Council granted financial support in 1969, we were free to return to Manianga and pursue whatever methodological course we desired.

We entertained various methodological tactics. With an interest in concepts of illness and therapy, we studied componential analysis following Conklin, Frake, Romney and D'Andrade, and Metzger and Williams.[26] With an interest in case histories we

---

26. Harold Conklin, "Haunuoo Color Categories," *Southwestern Journal of Anthropology* 11 (1955): 339-44; Charles Frake, "The Diagnosis of Disease Among the Subanun of Mindanao," *American Anthropologist* 63 (1961), 1: 113-32; Kimball A. Romney and Roy G. D'Andrade, eds., *Transcultural Studies in Cognition*, American Anthropologist Special Publication, *American Anthropologist* 66 (1964), 3, Part 2; Duane Metzger and Gerald Williams, "Tenejapa Medicine I: The Curer," *Southwestern Journal of Anthropology* 19 (1963): 216-34.

looked closely at the work of Victor Turner.[27] As we entered the field our methodological options were clear and our strategies selected.

Componential analysis promised great things, largely because the techniques of eliciting information appeared simple to administer and productive in the data one could gather. However, original efforts to administer interviews in KiKongo resulted in some bafflement on the part of our otherwise willing interlocuters, having to do with a type of "it-all-depends" perplexity, and a great deal of variety in the results. Responses to such questions as "What kinds of illnesses are there?" or "How is such-and-such an illness treated?" resulted in totally disparate types of answers, with some individuals telling us they only go to Western hospitals, and others telling us about the olden days when diviners, magicians, and paganism ruled, but that this was all bygone now. We were confronted with a type of cultural pluralism we could not control methodologically within the format of formal question-and-answer interviews. Furthermore, we noted that respondents would *say* one thing (e.g., "In bygone days we used to have poison ordeals but now we use the hospital.") but then in the throes of decision-making *do* another (e.g., walk out of the hospital and to the village for a divination session). We then abandoned our primary concern with "what the people think" for a concern with "what they do," and how that is rationalized.

The same reservations expressed with regard to formal elicitation of consciously held opinions of the world of illness and therapy came into play with regard to the possibility of a social epidemiological survey. We felt we did not really know which questions to ask about certain dimensions of therapeutic action, and we were dubious of the accuracy of responses we might receive. We needed answers to questions such as "Why would kinsmen withdraw the sufferer from his hospital bed to hold a clan meeting, and he comply?" or "Why would a well-educated teacher or nurse resort to African therapies lacking any clear chemotherapeutic component, defined only by the symbolic?" We ultimately abandoned the survey approach because we sus-

27. Victor W. Turner, *Drums of Affliction* (Oxford, 1968).

pected there were dimensions and combinations of therapeutic choice we did not yet understand and that our question format would thus be irrelevant. It is now clear that this was an appropriate decision, for in the early days of our field research our thinking was oriented very much to individualistic responses. If we would have set up a survey questionnaire about illness occurrence and therapeutic response, we would have totally "programed out" what we eventually came to perceive as an entire type of therapy, namely collective "kinship therapy."

To find answers to the types of queries that concerned us, we determined early in our fieldwork that we needed to document complex, multiepisodic medical cases that would demonstrate the modes of interconnection between available therapeutic options. These would also demonstrate the dynamics of decision-making in actual cases better than cerebralized and individualized reconstructions of native theory. To identify such cases we established our bases in two well-defined social universes already familiar to us: the village in which Janzen had resided as fieldworker for 18 months in 1965/66, and the nearest large medical mission complex some six and a half kilometers away where Arkinstall was familiar with the personnel and again offered his professional services for the duration of our stay. We resided at yet a third place, in a nearby rural setting. In short order we had identified a dozen or so medical cases which met our criteria.

Our field research strategy from here on was inspired in part by advice from Victor Turner, to whom we are grateful. The salient feature of this strategy, as he had applied it in his work on Ndembu cults of affliction, and explained it to us, amounted to keeping careful records of the course of events surrounding a case: following an event, he would go over his notes and transcriptions with the actors themselves to establish rationales and draw interpretations. Of course, fuller contextual material, genealogies, structural relationships, and life histories would be needed too. With this approach, culture (symbols, concepts, verbal categories) could be convincingly related to society (roles, social groups, and situations) in our methodology. To this social anthropological dimension we added the medical one of monitoring the physical condition of the sufferer. Whatever tensions of change there might be within each of these domains, as well as in the dialectic between them, would become evident in the course of time.

Once we had decided upon the several cases we would study intensively, our time was taken up keeping in touch with them, learning from the patient and his next of kin, and observing the specialists consulted. Thus, we needed to assemble biographical material on individuals, to document the social context of events, to establish treatments received before observations began, and to keep track of ongoing deliberations leading to other therapies. We tried to witness as many of the therapeutic episodes as we could. This sometimes meant second-guessing the kinsmen's intentions as to when and where they might be going, sometimes soliciting an invitation to accompany them on the walk or journey to the therapist.

Once into the research, we discovered that BaKongo in quest of healing are far more peripatetic than we had realized. Not only did they walk vast distances to consult therapeutic specialists, but they had access to motor vehicles. Thus, the cases which are presented in Chapters 3-8 were traced over much of the Lower Zaire: from the rural north Manianga to Mindouli in Congo Brazzaville, westward to Kingoyi and beyond to Ngouedi and Pointe Noire at the coast; southward to Luozi, Kimpese, and Matadi; eastward to Kinshasa. As we added more cases, we found ourselves trying to cope with this phenomenon. We were roused out of bed to walk 15 miles with a clan to a diviner. We drove over nearly nonexistent roads with our old Volkswagen and talked to a healer who had been consulted to add to the record in one of the cases. The method we selected was rewarding and appropriate in that we were put on the track of therapies we would not otherwise have imagined present; we discovered a case-relevant pattern of therapeutic consultation; we became acquainted with a wide variety of representative specialists; most important, we discovered the logic of therapeutic decision-making.

The disadvantages of this method were mostly of a logistical nature. It became impossible to keep up with more than about eight or ten cases simultaneously. We have several fragments of cases which we abandoned for lack of time; several others we began but could not complete for the same reason. We would have preferred to document up to 50 and more cases to better establish the threshhold between complex-episode and -issue cases and single-issue cases, thereby facilitating a statistical grasp of these various therapies in Kongo society. A further disadvantage of our method was the eventual toll it exacted on us, physically, and on our car, mechanically.

While the case studies presented below constitute an important type of evidence, they are not the only evidence. Our extended observations of the several kinds of therapists, the social situation of illness, and the archival research into the historical dimension of all these areas are as important as the cases. We devoted considerable time discussing disease concepts and therapy techniques with healers and laymen, the status of Western medicine in their society, and in collecting medicinal plants. We worked in the mission archives, state post records, and the libraries in Kinshasa and the university.

Still, our case-study approach shaped the final outcome of this book. The cases provide the behavioral sequences that document the variables that our later analysis of decision-making and our charts present in a systematic fashion. These variables include: symptoms and signs generated by the sufferer, his kinsmen, and the diagnosis of the therapist; the therapy techniques deemed appropriate for the affliction and followed in the therapeutic session; the roles of therapists and the social set-roles of those acting out the therapy, especially in kinship therapy where no specialist is involved; and the types and relationships of kinsmen and other people involved in decision-making. This information, based on the cases and constituting a skeleton of the analysis, is available at a glance in Appendix A and figures 9–16.

Plants named in the text may be identified by referring to Appendix B, ''Herbarium of Medicinal Plants,'' and are referred to by Appendix plant number, for example, *wayeya* (106).

CHAPTER TWO

A History of Medical Pluralism in Lower Zaire

Kisi-Nsi *and* Kimundele *in a Single Society*

The quest for therapy in Kongo society leads to consulting practitioners of both indigenous and Western medicine. These respective courses of action are part of more inclusive categories called *kisi-nsi*, native culture (*literally*, "culture of the land"), and *kimundele*, foreign culture (*literally*, "culture of the white man"). The dichotomy pervades education, social relations, and attitudes toward property. Although it is derived from the colonial situation, it is becoming less isomorphic with differences between Africans and Europeans as black elites replace Europeans in role and attitude.

Indigenous therapeutic traditions and imported Western medical practices are intertwined and coexist at every level of society. The therapy managers in individual cases move back and forth between specialists and activities of both systems. Yet the beliefs and practices constituting these systems rest upon different premises. For most people translation from one to the other is difficult, and individuals usually manipulate them separately rather than synthesize them.

A system of knowledge is a way of describing the world and a related, congruent manner of acting.[1] A common descriptive language must exist for intelligible action to occur at all. Since this language indicates the premises of attitudes and the motives of action, it is necessary in the study of a system of knowledge like Kongo therapy to pay careful attention to action and explanation of action, therapeutic moves, and labels such as "illness of God," "clan affairs," and "playing with magic." It is possible to study change within such a system by observing the shifting qualities of action and the verbal efforts to account for or to deny these shifts. Changes may occur in the identification of diseases, the naming of symptoms, and the efforts to restore health. Such changes are not likely to alter the basic premises of the system of knowledge because when changes are explained in the rational terms of language, new premises appear absurd, thus invalid. In this sense Kongo and Western therapy systems are closed systems. Thus, members of African society learn Western culture with ease, but cannot with equal ease reduce African culture to Western categories, or vice versa.

Rationality is not synonymous with modern experimental science. In science, the "common stock of description" may be corrected and replaced by another stock.[2] The aim of science is its self-corrective and renewable nature as a deliberately changing system of knowledge. Although Western medicine claims to be "scientific," it is no more nor less rational than the Kongo healing tradition which reasons that plants should be combined according to their origin from the village and the forest, or that an illness which does not respond to medications or manipulative therapy is likely to be caused by conflict, tension, or hostility in human interaction. Advocates of each system may be dogmatically attached to their system, each convinced his is "rational," or "true." Criticism of the one that uses the other's description of the world is futile, as evidenced in the amusing exchange between David Livingstone (M.D.) and an Mbundu rainmaker long ago.

1. Alsadair MacIntyre, "A Mistake About Causality in Social Science," in *Philosophy, Politics, and Society*, ed. Peter Laslett and W. G. Runciman (Oxford, 1962).
2. Thomas Kuhn, *The Structure of Scientific Revolutions*, 2nd ed. (Chicago, 1970).

Medical Doctor: Hail, friend! How very many medicines you have about you this morning! Why, you have every medicine in the country here.

Rain Doctor: Very true, my friend; and I ought; for the whole country needs the rain which I am making.

M.D.: So you really believe that you can command the clouds? I think that can be done by God alone.

R.D.: We both believe the very same thing. It is God that makes the rain, but I pray to him by means of these medicines, and the rain coming, of course it is then mine. It was I who made it for the Bakwains for many years, when they were at Shokuane; through my wisdom, too, their women became fat and shining. Ask them; they will tell you the same as I do.

M.D.: But we are distinctly told in the parting words of our Savior that we can pray to God acceptably in his name alone, and not by means of medicines.

R.D.: Truly! but God told us differently. He made black men first and did not love us as he did the white man. He made you beautiful, and gave you clothing, and guns, and gunpowder, and horses, and wagons, and many other things about which we know nothing. But toward us he had no heart. He gave us nothing except the assegai, and cattle, and rainmaking; and he did not give us hearts like yours. We never love each other. Other tribes place medicines about our country to prevent the rain, so that we may be dispersed by hunger, and flee to them, and augment their power. We must dissolve their charms by our medicines. God has given us one little thing, which you know nothing of. He has given us the knowledge of certain medicines by which we can make rain. *We* do not despise those things which you possess, though we are ignorant of them. We don't understand your book, yet we don't despise it. You ought not to despise our little knowledge, though you are ignorant of it.

M.D.: I don't despise what I am ignorant of; I only think you are mistaken in saying that you have medicines which can influence the rain at all.

R.D.: That's just the way people speak when they talk on a subject of which they have no knowledge. When we first opened our eyes, we found our forefathers making rain, and we follow in their footsteps. You, who send to Kuruman for corn, and irrigate your garden, may do without rain; we cannot manage in that way. If we had no rain, the cattle would have no pasture, the cows give no milk, our children become lean and die, our wives run away to other tribes who did make rain and have corn, and the whole tribe become dispersed and lost; our fire would go out.

M.D.: I quite agree with you as to the value of the rain; but you can not charm the clouds by medicines. You wait till you see the clouds come, then you use your medicines, and take the credit which belongs to God only.

R.D.: I use my medicines, and you employ yours; we are both doctors, and doctors are not deceivers. You give a patient medicine. Sometimes God is pleased to heal him by means of your medicine; sometimes not—he dies. When he is cured, you take the credit of what God does. I do the same. Sometimes God grants us rain, sometimes not. When he does, we take the credit of the charm. When a patient dies, you don't give up trust in your medicine, neither do I when rain fails. If you wish me to leave off my medicine, why continue your own?

M.D.: I give medicines to living creatures within my reach, and can see the effects, though no cure follows; you pretend to charm the clouds, which are so far above us that your medicines never reach them. The clouds usually lie in one direction, and your smoke goes in another. God alone can command the clouds. Only try and wait patiently; God will give us rain without your medicines.

R.D.: Mahala-ma-kapa-a-a!! Well, I always thought white men were wise till this morning. Who ever thought of making a trial of starvation? Is death pleasant, then?

M.D.: Could you make it rain on one spot and not on another?

R.D.: I wouldn't think of trying. I like to see the whole country green, and all the people glad; the women clapping their hands, and giving me their ornaments for thankfulness, and lullilooing for joy.

M.D.: I think you deceive both them and yourself.

R.D.: Well, then, there is a pair of us.[3]

This ironic dialog described a relationship similar to the one between alternative therapy systems in contemporary Zaire. The great difference is that individuals now entertain separate and unique rational systems of knowledge, and sequentially (occasionally simultaneously) act upon them. The situation resembles that of medicine and psychoanalysis, or the coexistence of different religious traditions in a modern city. Within Kongo history the immediate analog is the diversity and specialization of the traditional cults of affliction around the *minkisi* ("sacred medicines"), each of which tended to develop a distinctive mythology.

The case studies to follow in later chapters show a picture of

3. Henry M. Stanley, *Through the Dark Continent*, 2 vols. (New York, 1879).

specializations of European and African origin in a complex whole which therapy managers manipulate. The fundamental premises of *kisi-nsi* and *kimundele* have changed little, yet practices have evolved, been criticized, adjusted, and amended, much in the same way sufferers and their advocates today make decisions regarding therapy. To describe the historical development of this process let us first consider the colonial period in which traditional therapy was assaulted and a policy imposed to promote Western medicine.

Colonial Medical Policy and Action

Belgian policy can be considered in the framework set forth by the colonial apologist, J. de Hemptinne, Apostolic prefect of Katanga, who in 1928 identified two quite divergent cultural policies. Either the indigenous and European societies could live side by side with little communication between them, or the indigenous order could be subordinated to the European order in the hope of a progressive transformation of it.

In the first hypothesis, the indigenous society would remain true to its traditions, its ethos (*mentalité*), its customs. It would remain itself and perpetuate itself along the lines of its secular institutions. The role of the colonizing people would be limited to purifying the indigenous custom of elements contrary to universal order, without however attempting to bring together the two civilizations living in each others' presence. Each would remain in its traditional sphere, concluding a sort of pact or treaty of association in the aim of satisfying the desires (*cupidité*) of the invader without nullifying the security of the autochthonous race.

According to the second hypothesis, the civilizing nation would try to raise prudently and slowly and surely the black race to a higher level of human existence; the civilizing nation believes in the perfectibility of the indigenous and calls him to take part in the civilizing enterprise, its works and efforts, and the general civilization and general progress of humanity. As a consequence, in policy affairs, the programme will not be that of establishing side by side two administrations in parallel manner, but to have one unique government within which the indigenous people would play their role following their capacity. Transitionally, so as not to destroy the steps of normal evolution, the framework of the traditional (*indigène*) order will be maintained, but this will be done only with the clear idea of causing these traditional powers to evolve towards our pattern and to suppress them where they do not comply with the civilizing advance.[4]

De Hemptinne was committed to an evolutionistic policy that would attempt to create a homogeneous colonial structure. The appearance of autonomous local institutions within the Belgian colonial system had followed a trend that the British carried out in "indirect rule." De Hemptinne warned that if the trend continued, the indigenous people would ask for their independence within fifty years.[5] Massive administrative reforms in 1934 advanced policies that de Hemptinne feared. But in spite of the creation of local government institutions, the "evolutionist," civilizing model was strong in the colonials' attitude to the very end.

The two colonial models were evident in the Belgian public health program. Reorganization of indigenous society, for example, relocation of villages, was enforced in the name of the public good. This was done with little regard for the existing social structures. The rationale was suggested in a report of 1932 entitled "Hygiène des villages."[6] It recommended a stricter control of hamlet dispersement and advocated that large villages be forced to remain intact to facilitate health and administration. "Large villages should be strictly forbidden to segment because that makes the work of our sanitary agents and doctors physically impossible." Small villages were disliked by the territorial agents for the same reason. The report went on to chastise the native authorities (*chefs coutumiers*), warning that "if the overall authority of the customary chief cannot control divisiveness between the clans, it is desirable then that the tutelary authority of the colony substitutes itself for the traditional so as to put to an end these problems." After giving details of numerous improvements in cleaning out the villages, digging toilets, and so on, there

4. J. de Hemptinne, "La politique indigène du gouvernement belge," *Congo* 2 (1928): 1–16.

5. *Ibid.*, p. 10; Michael Crowder, "Indirect Rule, French and British Style," *Africa* 34 (1964), 3: 197-205.

6. Fonds Reine Elisabeth pour l'Assistance médicale aux indigènes du Congo Belge (FOREAMI), *Rapport annuel sur l'exercise 1931* (Bruxelles, 1932).

was a special survey of those regions in which the population was resistant, or had a noticeable disrespect for the spirit of enforced public health. "By their passive resistance, and habitual spirit of malice, the natives hope to test to the limit the physician's motivation to improve their living standard. They will dig a trash pit on order, but not use it; it will then fill with water and become a mosquito breeding hole."

The punishment for not carrying out orders was usually a fine. But the report suggested another threat: "Huge projects of cutting down grass, of destruction of unused buildings, or drainage of marshes and so forth were quickly realized as soon as it was announced that a village relocation would otherwise be enforced." Since "civilization" was a threat with hygiene as its punishment during colonial rule, it is hardly surprising that with independence people often did not fulfill demands that they were earlier forced to meet.

The evolutionary model of colonial medicine was followed in the Lower Congo public health programs, but other areas of medical policy were dominated by the cultural autonomy model. In these areas a different African civilization was acknowledged, but it was considered to be inferior to Western civilization. For example, colonial literature abounds with discussions of the "mentality" of the Congolese, which justify relegating some medical problems to indigenous resources. One report in 1929 commented on "maladies mentales et nerveuses" by observing that there was little hope for any progress in this area "since so little is known about the normal 'mentalité' of the people."[7] The colonial myth of the "native mind" eventually led to the use of psychological tests whose results were published with titles such as "Considerations of the Intelligence of the African Blacks" (1955),[8] "Essay in the Psychology of the Primitive" (1956),[9] "Psychoses and Neuroses in Central Africa" (1957),[10] "Psychotechnic Study

7. G. Trolli, *Rapport sur l'hygiène publique pendant l'année 1929* (Bruxelles, 1931).
8. G. Wintringer, *Considerations sur l'intelligence du noir d'Afrique* (Anvers, 1955).
9. Jean-François Iyeky, *Essai de psychologie du primitif* (Léopoldville, 1956).
10. J. Vyncke, *Psychoses et nevroses en Afrique centrale* (Bruxelles, 1957).

of the Baluba: Experimental Intelligence Test to 485 Baluba Blacks" (1957).[11] While some of these studies meet standards of scientific objectivity in their methodologies, others are little more than a parrotting of ideas announced by Lévy-Bruhl in 1927 to the effect that primitive people have "mythopoetic" or "prelogical" minds, and their thought has peculiar "jumps" in it, accompanied by "flitting eyes."[12] These studies justified colonial attitudes that one should move very slowly in attempting to transform this "mentality," or that since Africans were incapable of abstract thought they were essentially unchangeable and any effort of this kind was futile. According to these views, Africans could master technical skills, but were liable to suddenly revert to their inherent primitive character. In 1969, one still encountered the colonial tradition in individuals like a European priest in charge of a secondary school in Kinshasa who claimed that his students did poorly in mathematics because "since independence the native mentality has not changed one bit!"

The idea that a poorly understood "African mentality" existed at least acknowledged another system of thinking and institutions. To this extent the relativist model prevailed; yet the prescriptive model of Belgian colonial policy remained an evolutionist one. Indigenous therapeutic practices were mentioned within colonial manuals or laws, which sought only to establish in the "backward" colony the more advanced institutions of European society. The only link between the relativist and evolutionist models was that the persistence of indigenous therapeutic practices confirmed the colonial theory of the "*mentalité indigène*." In fact, colonials argued that the native mind could not be understood by Europeans at all, since native culture was "primitive"; therefore it should be replaced by civilized behavior.

The Evolution of Kisi-Nsi

Although colonial medical policy did not take indigenous therapy into account it certainly did have an effect upon it, espe-

11. A. Ombredane, *Etude psychotechnique des Baluba, T. I.* (Bruxelles, 1957).

12. Lucien Lévy-Bruhl, *L'âme primitive* (Paris, 1927).

cially through the Christian missions, moral vanguards of the colonial system. To describe this effect we will first sketch the traditional institutions as they were at the beginning of this century. The traditional system comprised a series of *nganga* roles, linked to one or more *nkisi*, forms of sacred knowledge (*plural, minkisi*). *Nganga* derives from the verb *vanga* ("doer" or "maker"), and *nkisi*, derived from the same root as *kisi* ("custom," "manner," or "language"), is a particular expression of the *nganga*'s art. Thus, *nganga bakulu* is the elder who keeps the ancestor basket and administers the cult of the ancestors (*bakulu*). The *nganga mbwa* is the owner of a dog (*mbwa*) taken to the cemetery and shown to the ancestors before the hunt; *nganga lufu* (also *ngangula*) is the blacksmith, literally, "operator of the forge" (*lufu*), a role that entails many subsidiary *minkisi* and prohibitions. The *nganga buka* (or *mbuki*) is any person who knows herbal remedies and treats sufferers without the intervention of consecrated medicines. A quarrelsome individual was called an *nganga mpaka* ("propagater of quarrels"), and Catholic priests came to be called *banganga Nzambi*, priests of God.[13]

Some indigenous schemas order these and other roles by grouping specialties around the role of the *nganga ngombo*, the diviner, who acts as a "gate opener" or point of reference to the other specialties. The diviner is consulted to direct the sufferer and his kin to an appropriate specialist or cult. In some regions of the Manianga, a schema is devised recognizing twelve *nkisi* cults, each corresponding to one of the twelve original clans around Ne Kongo, founder of the Kingdom of Kongo.

Mpu		Lemba
Mabola		Mbola
Muniangi		Mpansu
Mazinga	Ngombo	Masekula
Kilauki		Mpodi
Mukoko		Mbwanga

13. Jan Van Wing, *Etudes BaKongo* (Bruxelles, 1949), pp. 418-19.

Ngombo recommends appropriate cures from among the other specialities:

> *mpu*, consecrates and inaugurates a chief;
> *mabola*, cures illnesses amongst young women;
> *muniangi*, cures excessive menstrual bleeding;
> *mazinga*, assists in the healthy birth of a child;
> *kilauki*, cures skin diseases and eruptions;
> *mukoko*, cures women's sterility;
> *lemba*, calms the land and the villages;
> *mbola*, treats mouth diseases;
> *mpansu*, cures insanity;
> *masekula*, terminates a pregnancy;
> *mpodi*, uses the cupping horn to remove impurities from the body;
> *mbwanga*, cures headaches.[14]

This set of cures is local to the Kivunda region of the north Manianga, but similar classifications exist throughout Lower Zaire.[15] Another way of organizing the *minkisi* is to make them a cosmological order. In one such classification from 1910 seven *nkisi* were listed as "water" medicines and ten as "land" medicines. Other medicines, especially those used for divination, mediated between these categories and that of "air." Three additional land medicines were under some circumstances transferable to water and three other *nkisi* belonged simultaneously to the water and land categories. *Mukwanga,* for example, was a sky medicine that could cross over into earth. In this cosmological order the three natural categories of water, land, and air were extended into more "human" categories. *Nkiduku* was a war medicine used by men of advanced age, and *bikandu* was a child's medicine. *Funza* was said to be the most important of all medicines, for it belonged to the twin cult and was the source of all the other medicines.[16] These various social and cosmological criteria of organization of *minkisi* are more permanent than the individual *nkisi* which

14. Fukiau-kia-Bunseki, Personal communications, 1969.

15. A review of the *nkisi* names in Karl Laman's *The Kongo II* (Uppsala, 1957), provides documentation on the numerous *minkisi*, large and small, private and public, which have existed and exist.

16. Nsemi Isaki, manuscript, Laman Collection, Svenska Missionsforbundet Archives (Lidingö, ca. 1910).

come into being with a particular creator, then segment, or fuse, and get replaced by a successor. Thus, while only two specific *nkisi* cures appear in the case studies in the following chapters—*mpodi* the cupping horn, *mpu* the chief priest role in the clan—many of the traditional classificatory niches that used to be articulated by an *nkisi* are strongly in evidence. For example, *nkisi ngombo* disappeared earlier this century, but divination as a function remains strong.

Another essential aspect of this tradition is the distinction between natural etiology expressed by "illness of God" and unnatural etiology expressed by a variety of other terms, including the role of the *nkisi* and of witchcraft in illness causation. The German ethnographer-geographer Pechuel-Loesche provides a rare insight into early Kongo thinking on this point. In a report from the Loango coast based on a five-year visit beginning in 1875, he noted that the local BaFiote considered death to be a natural process in the life cycle.[17] They spoke of it without inhibitions, answering questions about an elderly person who had died by saying that "God has called him" (*N sambi a n (nu) tumisi nandi*). But the BaFiote did distinguish such a natural death from one occasioned by evil spirits, murder, poison, or magic. The suspicion of witchcraft was raised only when an otherwise happy (*lebens froher*) person suffered illness, an accident, or death. These afflictions were best warded off through a more careful observance of prohibitions, avoidance of sacrilegious acts and utterances, and examination of possible sins against the *Tschina* clan symbols. Magical defenses were useless against these natural causes. A magician was consulted only after the doctor was at his wit's end in a treatment. In this case, the costs became considerably higher because the risks were greater. Pechuel-Loesche concluded that even in Loango, curers neither healed nor killed (on behalf of their clients) without first collecting a fee.[18]

The etiological category "of God" included sickness caused by a wide variety of abuses, from eating poorly or excessively, to

17. E. Pechuel-Loesche, *Volkskunde von Loango* (Stuttgart, 1907), pp. 332-33.
18. *Ibid.*, pp. 444-45.

violating clan prohibitions and social laws. Unnatural death and illness was limited to the intervention of hostile human and nonhuman forces, which in Pechuel-Loesche's reconstruction appeared to be a residual category.

During the first decades of this century, observers reported the same illness etiologies, with witchcraft gaining prominence. Thus, in Laman's Kongo ethnography, based on village teachers' observations, we find the following, from about 1915:

> To determine the cause of an illness is not difficult . . .; it has been caused by *bandoki* (witches) or by *minkisi* (magic). The sick man himself may be a *ndoki*, and thereby cause both the illness and his own death. This may, for example, be because he has not performed his duty to his fellow *bandoki*. But even if he himself is not a *ndoki*, the sick man may from several causes, e.g., envy or jealousy, be eaten by some *ndoki*, and die.
>
> A *nkisi* causes illness if the sick person has incurred guilt through, for instance, theft, adultery, or perjury, for which the *nkisi* has avenged itself in response to the adjurations of his *nganga,* or again through his defiling himself by the infringement of some prohibition or other. He may also be shot with *nkisi* guns and so forth. If a sick man has his *ndoki*-power proved upon him he may be executed.

Despite the initial mention of *bandoki* and *nkisi* as some illness causes, the text goes on to suggest an additional possibility.

> If, despite all the measures adopted a person cannot be cured, it is often said that Nzambi [God] has eaten him, i.e., it has been his will. Very old and esteemed persons are considered to die a natural death, a Nzambi-death.[19]

In another text from the early decades of this century on the etiology of disease and misfortune, Babutidi, a catechist, wrote that the *nganga* went into ecstasy to perceive the *ndoki* causing an illness or the *nkisi* that was to blame. Treatments for the former included counterattack with an *ndoki*-gun, and a counter-curse or spell so that the *ndoki* would "release" the sufferer. This therapy was always performed in the presence of the sufferer's kinsmen and other people; it is highly plausible that it was intended as much for their benefit as for the sufferer. The attribu-

19. Laman, *op. cit.*, p. 78.

tion of illness to *nkisi* was quite a different matter, according to Babutidi. When an *nkisi* struck a person with illness, its anger was induced by the craft of a spiteful person, or it could be malice within the *nkisi* itself. In either case, the revenge or malice (*mfunyia*) of the attacking *nkisi* had to be neutralized by the *nganga* for a cure to be effected.

Babutidi distinguished, as most BaKongo still do, between "illegitimate" affliction such as an *ndoki* attack in which a weak and unprotected victim is destroyed by forces around him, and "legitimate" affliction in which the victim is the deserving object of an *ndoki*'s, and *nkisi*'s, or a fellowman's revenge for having violated some social precept or his own good judgment. Witchcraft could be treated by counterattacking the witch and seeking protection from him, while other cures required the sufferer himself to reform, and he was himself often accused of "playing with magic." The physical symptoms, for instance, bloody stool or side pain, stated Babutidi, deserved independent medical treatment.[20]

These observations made at the turn of the century suggest that divination ordered human situations into the categories of illness by God, by *nkisi*, and by *ndoki*. Initially, a case would have been handled by private diagnosis or within a restricted social group. If this did not suffice, and accusations arose and became heated to the point that unity was endangered, an outside ritual expert such as the *nganga ngombo* would be called. Possibly also another kinship meeting would be convened. The sufferer would then be recommended for treatment by a particular *nkisi,* or initiation to it. The very fact of his suffering might be considered evidence of displeasure by *nkisi* spirits or cult advocates. Initiation to a cult would constitute the cure. Recruitment of the sufferer reinforced prevailing values of the society and the concepts of that particular cure.

When the Christian missions and the colonial government at the turn of the century launched a concerted attack upon concepts of the *nkisi* and the authority of the *nganga*, they were

20. Babutidi, Notebook 8, Laman Collection, Svenska Missionsforbundet Archives (Lidingö).

successful in ridding the countryside of all kinds of therapy paraphernalia. From 1890 to 1930, region after region in the Lower Zaire responded to the call by abandoning or burning most of their *minkisi*. This crusade was joined by African prophets like Simon Kimbangu.

But none of these movements destroyed the premises regarding the etiology of illness and misfortune, nor the expectation that a divinatory operator must disclose to people the origin of their concerns. Etiological categories in the period from 1910 to 1970 underwent a certain evolution in the way illness was discussed, revealing a tendency to discuss causes of illness in terms of euphemisms such as "relations," "mysteries," "whispers" (gossip), envy, malice, playing with magic, "stepping on fetishes," embezzlement, kidnapping, and so on. Since the sufferer himself or his enemies or kinsmen may be to blame, or the illness may be due to a situation for which a group takes collective responsibility, the mystical cause of witchcraft is often subordinated in diagnosis to an intense analysis of social relations. This is brought out in the comment of one *nganga* to us. "Whenever people introduce ancestors as the cause of illness, I see real living persons hiding behind those ancestors." Perhaps because euphemisms are used, many cases blur or collapse the distinction between *ndoki* and *nkisi* into the category illness of man (*kimbevo kia muntu*). This general etiological category does not appear in the early literature.

These changes do not depart from the traditional premises of *kisi-nsi*, but are rhetorical changes akin to a shift of emphasis from *nganga* to *ngunza* during the colonial period. While an *nganga* (magical operator) may be anyone who has technical skill and ritual paraphernalia, an *ngunza* (prophet) is an iconoclast who has visionary insight and access to spiritual and sometimes to political power. Individuals can be identified as holding one position or the other, according to the rhetoric of the speaker. These roles changed as colonial rule divested chiefs of their authority to judge and sentence wrongdoers to death. The *banganga* were similarly refused the right to engage in ritual inquiry and accusation, and to conduct trial by ordeal. The cults were criticized, misunderstood, and attacked, and wherever they held a political function, they were forcibly put down. Innovative *ngunza* prophets responded directly to this weakening of the chiefship and the *nganga*. The prophet Kimbangu won immediate and widespread recognition in 1921 by adopting Christian forms and Biblical concepts of salvation. The conflicts of value and authority caused by colonial domination set the stage for Kimbangu to forge new rituals of healing, raising the dead, and antiwitchcraft techniques. Other prophets followed his lead.

The colonial reaction to indigenous therapy was sometimes very direct. As late as 1956, village healers in the Kibunzi and Mbanza Mwembe region were rounded up and reprimanded by colonial authorities after a patient had been removed by his relatives from a mission hospital and taken to one of them. On another occasion, a village herbalist was threatened with imprisonment and exile for removing the head of a fetus from a woman who had attended a mission maternity ward where only the body had been born in a breach delivery. Zablon, a well-known orthopedist of Kinganga, claimed to have had little trouble from the colonial government, but the missionaries considered him a dangerous charlatan. He said that at one time the Catholic priests wanted to have him exiled to the Upper Congo, but government officials had disagreed with them, and when the dispute ended he was allowed to continue bone setting and giving massages. An herbalist, Kitembo of Muyeni, told us that he changed his treatment from "leaf-cone" and asperge preparation to "cooking pot" preparation to evade the attention of Europeans. He also planted his *lemba-lemba* herbs deep in the forest instead of in the village where they belonged.

The colonial authorities were inconsistent; healers were harassed by some officials for a period and yet permitted to practice at other times. Colonial officials even protected the work of the *banganga* on rare occasions, and in a few instances Europeans are said to have consulted the *banganga* in a clandestine manner. The prevailing view of the officials was that *banganga* were no great harm, and perhaps even useful in maintaining order. When Catholic and Protestant missionaries complained, however, they would investigate and harass or imprison individual practitioners. This approach to the *banganga* contrasted to the treatment of *bangunza*, whom Belgian colonialists sought out with a paranoia unequalled in other colonial systems. Virtually all individuals who drew attention as *ngunza* were imprisoned, exiled, or kept under surveillance until 1958. The Belgians feared massive insubordination and saw these religious leaders as a real political threat. In 1921, Kimbangu, the most celebrated prophet, was sentenced to death and then imprisoned for life in Katanga, where he died in 1951. Other prophets were exiled to work camps in the Upper Congo.

Nganga and *ngunza* roles were redefined after the Second World War, and particularly after independence from colonial rule. The German defeat of Belgium convinced many Africans that the colonialists were no longer invincible. At the same time, colonial policy became less arbitrary and cruel. Low-level government courts began to function in native hands. The governmental reform of 1935, reenacted after wartime emergency measures were suspended, strengthened the role of African chiefs in local affairs. Sector councils, made up of African elites, began to function, and, as the political emasculation of prewar colonialism was alleviated, religious movements appeared within the established Christian congregations under mission leadership. These African leaders, whom many quietly called *bangunza*, emphasized ecstatic power in the laying on of hands and other spectacular feats and began to practice counselling in a manner similar to the traditional *ngombo* diviner. This counselling was an analysis of social conflicts, or divination by investigation. Thus, divination, previously a task of the *Nganga* role, gravitated to the *Ngunza* role and reappeared as an innovation within the legitimate new structures of the church.[21] The *nganga* role was in dispute within these movements, but it did not disappear. *Banganga*, from the urban herbalists to their country counterparts, received new legitimacy as they were increasingly drawn into the service of politicians and administrators after independence. In-

21. John M. Janzen, "Kongo Religious Renewal: Iconoclastic and Iconorthostic," *Canadian Journal of African Studies* 5 (1971): 135-43.

deed, their relationship to these new patrons is reminiscent of the earlier relationship of *banganga* to chiefs.

Definition and Control of the Art of Healing
Since the Second World War

The concerted effort of the colonial government and the missions to change, even to eliminate indigenous therapy, was far reaching. The only therapist allowed to continue in publicly acknowledged practice was the *nganga mbuki* with his herbs, plus a few specialists in manipulative therapy. Their practice was inhibited by their liability to prosecution as criminals if an accident occurred. But even these practitioners operated outside the pale of governmentally recognized healing institutions. A basic law in this regard had been promulgated in 1952, limiting the "art of healing" to those who held a nurse's diploma. The independent government continued to use this basic legal instrument although auxiliary decrees of 1957 and 1966 sought the elimination of clinics that were "incommodes" and "insalubres."[22] When independence arrived in 1960, the "art of healing" law applied to the many African nurses, medical assistants, and other lower grades of personnel that had been trained in Western medicine; there were as yet no African doctors or public health officials.

With the help of the World Health Organization, a crash program was launched to train several hundred medical assistants as physicians, and by 1964 these African doctors began to fill key positions in hospitals and public health programs.[23] But during the interim period after independence, the colonial medical services collapsed. Europeans, including physicians, fled Zaire when violence erupted shortly after independence was achieved. Private dispensaries appeared overnight to fill the need for medical care. These dispensaries were highly profitable and utilized the readily available pharmaceutical supplies from Brazzaville. In

22. Luozi Territorial Archives. The basic law of the "art of healing" was that of March 19, 1952, put into Ordinance No. 71/81 by the Governor General, February 19, 1958. Ordinance No. 41/81 of February 12, 1953, modified part of the original decree.

23. Willy de Craemer and Renée C. Fox, *The Emerging Physician* (Stanford, 1968).

1961 a regional medical officer (*chef de cercle medical*) wrote that the nurse (*infirmier*) of the state dispensary was not working because too many "private doctors" existed and people preferred them. He called these practitioners "bandes de médecins privés" or "bandes de voleurs" (robber gangs), and said that they peddled their medicines as itinerant merchants.[24]

The illegal market could be advantageous when legitimate centers lacked medicines. In one instance of this sort, smallpox was discovered in a village near a primary school, but none of the nearby medical posts, including a large Catholic hospital, had any vaccine. The school authorities therefore had an "*aide-infirmier*," who brought vaccine from Brazzaville, vaccinate the children. Officials who heard about this illegal vaccination requested local authorities to investigate and report to them. Local authorities, appalled at this insensitivity to human need, let the matter drop.

In a number of instances, illegal practitioners began manufacturing their own medicines. A number of cases came to the attention of officials in which practitioners made pills of plant substances or injected their own formulas intravenously. When one man injected powdered milk in the guise of penicillin, the abuse was brought to the attention of the governor, who urged the district commissioner to curb such practices. The commissioner's edict of September 1961 defined the situation as follows:

> Considering the illegal and illicit installation of dispensaries, "para-dispensaries," and profit-making enterprises spread throughout several localities of the district; considering also that the goal pursued by these dispensaries and persons is more toward lucrative, clandestine profit and harmful to the public health rather than in the public good or humanitarian work; considering the numerous cases of intoxication and death from abuses perpetrated by persons wishing to exploit the present situation and the naiveté of the population; considering the intention of certain religious sects tending toward separatism from the rest of the population by the installation of purely sectarian dispensaries, in spite of the neutrality of the art of healing toward all religious ideologies; considering the necessity of avoiding and combatting at all

24. Luozi Territorial Archives. Dossier P-21, "The Art of Healing" (October 23, 1961).

cost the commercialization of the art of healing by any person, it is decided: Article 1: The installation or creation of an illegal or illicit dispensary of medicines is forbidden; Article 2: Private dispensaries that do not conform to the law shall be closed immediately, and their pharmaceutical supplies seized immediately; Article 3: Infractions will be punished with one month prison and 1000 francs fine; Article 4: The territorial functionaries and law-agents will be responsible for the execution of this decision.[25]

The local officials did not respond with enthusiasm to this edict since it threatened the framework of existing medical care. Perhaps the greatest effect of the edict was to alert private practitioners and set off a confused flood of bureaucratic activity. Some of the two dozen or so persons known to be operating illegal dispensaries in the Luozi Territory in 1962 tried to apply for permits since they did have "diplomas." They found it was difficult to discover how one should apply, let alone to follow through with it. One assistant nurse with 32 years of service in a mission hospital wanted to practice privately with a diploma delivered by the provincial *commissaire* of the colonial region of Leopoldville. The local *secteur* chief wrote to the territorial *commissaire* on his behalf and was told he must apply to the Provincial Ministry of Health. Another elderly nurse with a 1931 aide-*infirmier* diploma and a certificate indicating seniority on the staff of a large Catholic hospital, asked a European doctor to renew his certification, but the territorial administrator ordered him to close his dispensary until his permit had in fact been authorized by the doctor. A third *infirmier* applied for permission to practice by having local officials testify to the need for a dispensary: the place "is twenty-five kilometers from the nearest other medical center, and the qualities of the interested party are noteworthy." The territorial administrator forwarded the letter to the doctor who was the director of the hospital at the territorial headquarters. He refused permission, but he did not answer the point of the request nor indicate how to obtain legal permission to practice. The administrator, seeing the plight of the local com-

25. *Ibid.*, Decision No. 130/P-21, September 6, 1961, by the District Commissioner of Thysville.

munity, wrote the applicant that his request had been rejected, but that he should get an attestation from *any* doctor who could visit and verify his work, with the hope that in the future he might be authorized. The hospital director who had denied authorization to the applicant then wrote to the ministry of public health that the *commissaire* of the police was doing nothing about unauthorized medical establishments in the territory. A copy of this letter was sent to the *commissaire*, who was infuriated and promptly defended his corps. All in all, the application of the "diploma-carrying *infirmier*" to practice legally resulted in 23 letters, 15 of which were mailed after the request was turned down.

A communal councilor at the lowest grade of government described the lack of medical facilities in his area in a letter to the Provincial Ministry of Health.

> I take the privilege of bringing to your attention the difficulties regarding public health in our region. We are thirteen villages and a primary school, with a population of about 4,000 persons, but without even a small dispensary.
>
> No one in the entire population knows where to turn in cases of illness so as to receive adequate treatment, since all other dispensaries are too far removed from here. We got together to resolve the problem and here is our solution: the matter had been presented to the commune (secteur) government but since the commune considered itself incapable of dealing with the issue it asked us to communicate the matter to you, the ministry. So now it's up to you. The whole populace is ready to build a little dispensary if you will send us medicines and an infirmier to aid us in our difficulty and our suffering with various sorts of illnesses (14/8/66).[26]

Later in 1966, officials in the Territory of Luozi claimed that all private African-run dispensaries had been shut down, but this is doubtful. Government zeal to eliminate these dispensaries has been outstripped by the even greater zeal of practitioners to open them and the populace to use them. The tension between government policy and popular practices has been resolved most

26. *Ibid.*, Dossier P-21.

fully only in large urban centers like Kinshasa, where privately owned dispensaries are often run by qualified personnel.

The state legitimatizes Western medicine in Zaire by setting standards for practice, yet the effort to protect laymen from illegal practices that the shortage of qualified physicians and the demand for Western medicine encourage, is not entirely successful. At the same time, cultural norms and the patronage of officials legitimatizes indigenous therapy. Thus, the whole question of legitimacy shifts with the perspective of the actors in different situations, and various medical practices coexist in unstable, evolving relationships.

Postcolonial Legitimization of Kisi-Nsi

It is not easy to define contemporary patterns of governmental policy with regard to *banganga* and *bangunza*, since no official codes describe their status. Yet their activities are not sub rosa. Appointment of traditional practitioners to political roles after independence and the more recent exaltation of traditional medicine in the campaign of "authenticity" indicates they are being publicly legitimized, at least as therapists. Our information is a large file of cases in which direct or mediated relationships exist between government office holders and herbal and ritual practitioners. The cases we came across in archives of official correspondence and in field research must be a sample of the larger situation, but the extent to which we can infer a general social pattern from them is problematic.

A good point of entry to the status of indigenous medicine is the case of an *nganga* who in 1966 convinced the local bourgmestre (chief) to introduce his name to the territorial government for a special legalizing attestation. He had been working six years without any encumbrances, as the efforts to shut down illegal practitioners were not applied to the *banganga*. But he wanted official recognition. The bourgmestre addressed his superior in these words:

> This man has worked for six years now; he knows the plants which remove the infection of empoisonment and other illnesses. It has been

established that for the duration of six years he has never caused an accident with his patients. To this end, I ask you to kindly issue a special attestation for his service (2/8/66).[27]

The superior requested a list of persons the *nganga* had success-fully treated, with the illnesses they had suffered. A list of 184 persons was compiled and submitted. Poisoning cases topped the list with 63; next were 27 cases of sterility; epilepsy, madness, convulsion, indigestion, heart pain, and so forth followed. The territorial administrator then wrote the bourgmestre that he could not write a certificate for someone who did not have a diploma. But he did not suggest that the healer stop practice. What drew his attention was the enormity of the fact that over sixty persons in his jurisdiction had needed treatment for poisoning. He instructed the bourgmestre to make a discreet inquiry to identify the perpetrator of all these poisonings. In this case the *nganga* had been naive about Zairian bureaucracy. Just as the way around the requirement of having permission to run a dispensary for Western medicine from the health ministry was to find a physician to attest to your good work, so to obtain governmental sanction for his work the indigenous curer should have sought direct personal approval from an official.

To illustrate this point we may take the case of an *nganga* who obtained attestations, permits, and other legitimating titles. He carried the following documents in his wallet:

1. République Démocratique du Congo, Kongo Central Province, Office of the Governor: Pass. Mr. X, healer, is authorized to travel throughout the entire province of Kongo Central. Civil and military authorities are requested to permit him free passage. Mpumbu-lez-Léo, 6/2/65, signed, The Governor.
2. République Démocratique du Congo, National Security Administration, Post of Thysville (Ngungu); Permanent passage permit. I the undersigned, X, head commissaire of national security offices, attest by this document that Mr. Y, resident of Z region in the Territory of Luozi and acknowledged healer by the government document of Kongo Central Province, is authorized to travel freely in the entire province of Kongo Central in the interest of his work. I

27. *Ibid.*

request all military and civilian authorities to aid and abet him in every need. 9/3/66, Commissaire of national security at Thysville, signed.

3. République Démocratique du Congo, Luozi Territory, Secteur of X. The named Y, originator of Z village, secteur of Mbanza Mwembe, Territory of Luozi, clan Nsundi, is an acknowledged healer, known throughout the Republic of Congo-Kinshasa, province of Kongo Central, particularly in Luozi Territory. Military and civilian authorities are requested to aid him in his duty. 9/5/67. Signed, the president-judge of the territorial court.

4. Bureau of Judicial Affairs of Master Jean-Marie X, Matadi: Subscription Card. Name, Surname. Profession, Healer. Nationality, Congolese. Bi-annual price, 7 Zaires ($14.00). Takes effect 2/10/68. Signature of defendant. N.B., This is to defend your interest before the courts.

His relationship to lower level officials reflected the importance of his position. For example, on one occasion the victims of a theft appealed to him for help and he wrote their village headman that if the thief did not return the money he "would see to it that the thief is taken care of." The next day the thief confessed and the *nganga* told the headman to turn him over to the police. In much the same way he resolved a case of suspected incest which was believed to be causing illness within a clan by writing a letter to the *ngunza* in charge, telling him to see that the clansmen sacrificed a pig or goat to "cut the remaining blood ties" between the spouses.

On another occasion the judge of a Matadi commune begged this *nganga* to come and simply demonstrate his presence in the communal headquarters. Our field notes record the event in the following manner:

We arrived at Nzanza, and an elderly woman with difficulty seeing came to the *nganga*. She had been operated on for cataracts twice, but without any effect. He treated her and she went away. Also present was the judge of Nzanza, his host. The judge had a job for him which the communal judicial authorities have difficulty handling. They have many cases of assault, theft, and sorcery accusation; "there is work for an *nganga* whenever he can come to Nzanza," said the judge. The commune has a population of 39,000 and over 8000 are Angolan refugees. Many villages have moved up alongside the paved road that runs through the communal territory. All in all the area reflects the breakdown of conventional order and the judge wants the *nganga* to visit several times a month to exert pressure upon the *bandoki*, witches, and the *bankwa mbi* ("people of ill will") to relent in their nefarious activities. He says in effect that just the *nganga*'s presence will be helpful. Other seers, diviners (*bangunza*) and magicians (*banganga*) have worked on the matter, but the judge is unhappy with them. He had called this *nganga* to Nzanza several days earlier because several cases of illness had been caused by fetishes buried around the center. Tonight he and the *nganga* are going to do something about it, but they politely inform us they don't need our presence.

Clearly, the *nganga* has a publicly acknowledged role in helping local officials maintain order.

Where power lies unsurely, one expects struggles to legitimatize or discredit conflicting roles and interests. Our field notes illustrate the ways *banganga* are involved in these processes. The first of the following cases occurred in the Manianga and the second in the capital of Kinshasa.

The great energy and intelligence of Kitembo, *nganga,* may explain the tension between him and the other villagers, especially the *duki*, headman. The young hard-working carpenter of the Kinkwinga quarter told us that Kitembo charges exorbitant rates for his work, higher than the dispensaries. He also accused him of telling people that they wouldn't get better if they went to the dispensary. Furthermore, said the carpenter, Kitembo has some worthless cures like the "grimaces" (facial contortions) which he uses as he sucks out the foreign object in a person's body. (Kitembo told us he had long ago abandoned this treatment, the *mpoka,* which usually requires the cupping horn.) The charge which the *duki* was said to have brought against Kitembo was that he tried to destroy the rest of the village. In particular, he was accused of planting an Mpungu *nkisi* in the cemetery to destroy other clans. (Mpungu works slowly and calmly, driving its victims mad.) There is some confusion about who made the charges. They were formally introduced to the communal court by the *duki*, but according to the communal chief, who followed the affair closely, the neighboring clan section was responsible for the charges. An undersecretary of the commune, while on a tour of the area, ordered the arrest of Kitembo at the request of the *duki*. To handle this affair the communal chief ordered a thorough investigation of the village to check for harmful *minkisi* (relating it to us with a "tongue in cheek" attitude to indicate that this was a tactic). When no horrible fetishes turned up, the plaintiffs withdrew their charges. The communal chief, who likes Kitembo, got him off the hook.

Still, he has stopped treating patients for the time being, although the communal chief authorized him to continue.

The second case, involving an *nganga* called Tambwe, came to our attention when he was stranded in Kinshasa, the victim of a fraud by an unidentified individual who had used forged credentials and the image of a large Lower Zaire hospital to get him to send medicinal plants. Tambwe was lured to the capital with promises of appointment to a favored position in this hospital with a house and car and servants.

With his family and two trunks of medicines (bark, bottles, vials, plants, skins, and so on), Tambwe found temporary refuge in the garage behind one of the communes. The mayor, a university graduate who had studied in Europe, did not consider Tambwe to be a typical welfare case. Although he had no money and few clothes, he had his equipment and could earn money quickly. The mayor gave him the necessary identity papers to live in Kinshasa, and to install his family in the local headquarters of the youth section of the party. We found Tambwe at work several weeks later amidst the wall posters of the president and the party cadres. Dozens of bottles had been set up on counters around the room, and he lived in the back. A sign outside announced "Dr. Herborist." During the hour and a half that we were there a dozen people came by for treatment. Several were ordinary and indistinguishable folk, but one was a judge from Thysville who was treated for blindness, and rode away in a taxi. Another patient, wearing a grey suit and tie, received an injection of Tambwe's homemade plant medication, and bought a bottle of elixer, then left in a chauffeured car.

We have other examples of the ways officials consult *banganga*, give them patronage, and use them as agents of social control. Political figures, of whatever level in government, feel pressures and hostilities against them, and seek protection or clarification of their situation from ritual experts. The cases brought out here suggest that ritual power is an important option used by officials. They tell us something about the *nganga*'s role and the confidence political figures have in ritual power. When a particular *nganga* has established himself as a charismatic authority, he becomes an available tool and vehicle of governmental process. The legitimation is personalized in that an individual *nganga* gives ritual support to a political figure who then gives him protection. A Kongo proverb describes the relationship: "Chiefs are chiefs; magicians are magicians" (*mfumu na mfumu, nganga na nganga*), meaning that they work together, each in his own way. In the words of the commissioner of national security in Thysville on the pass permit, "I request all military and civilian authorities to aid and abet him in every need."

The legitimation of native roles and arts in the postcolonial period extends beyond the personalized relations of politicians and ritual experts, however. It occurs in a climate of faith in certain aspects of *kisi-nsi*, particularly the medicinal plants. African elites laud the ancient medical secrets, stating that soon all will be forgotten unless qualified experts study them. They claim that the medicinal plants are a treasure trove of secrets which, if they were reestablished upon a truly scientific basis, would prove to be of high quality. This common opinion has a mythlike quality among the elite who know little about the older cures but substantiate them with accounts of miraculous cures after Western medicine failed. The plants are always distinguished from magical devices when these claims are put forward. A small collection of herbs was exhibited at the 1968 Kinshasa Trade Fair, indicating that the government considers them to be a resource to develop. Medicinal plants were the only element of indigenous healing that was not denigrated by colonialists or missionaries. Scientific interest was shown in them, and the Catholic priest colloquially known as Tata Paul published a handbook on their uses in KiKongo. He wrote that people could utilize the book rather than suffer the *banganga*'s exploitation and deceit.[28] Ironically, most literate *banganga* have copies of Tata Paul's recipe book today and use it as guide. The legitimation of *kisi-nsi* illustrates the symbolic significance of indigenuous medicine in modern society.

28. "Tata Paul" (Verstig), *Makaya ma Nsi masadisa Nitu*, 9th ed. (Matadi, 1966).

PART II

STUDIES IN KONGO ILLNESS AND THERAPY

An Introductory Note

In the preparation of these studies we have often asked ourselves where, in the wide range of human experience, they belong. Canons of medical anthropology require the systematic reconstruction and analysis of illness. But the urgency of lives hanging in the balance deserves an artful telling. The studies have a tragic dimension that will be evident from the first case, which ends in the death of a youthful mother. The comic dimension is represented as well, although less frequently. Who does not smile at the thought of a therapeutic expert enhancing his allure by nicknaming himself "Mosquito"; or a fertility specialist requiring his clients to name their progeny, the evidence of his skill, after him.

Art and science share an uneasy union in these studies, whose dramatic structure is conveyed by relating a sequence of episodes. Within each episode the impact of colonial medical policy and the new symbolic value of indigenous culture are scrutinized in the decisions made by the therapy managing groups. The episodes are divided into: (1) the recognition of the problem, (2) the diagnosis of its nature and cause, and (3) the application of a particular solution. Alternate diagnoses often generate successive episodes in which different therapies are utilized. A lack of definition and agreement as to what is wrong, or what should be done, along with dissatisfaction over the solutions attempted, propel the quest for therapy from episode to episode. A digest of all episodes is offered in Appendix A.

These studies are complex and typical of serious problems in Manianga and other central African societies. Yet, most illnesses are not so complicated. Zairians, like all people, are afflicted with minor ailments which they treat symptomatically at home or at a medical facility. Such episodes do not require lengthy discussion with other family members.

Because we have concentrated on cases that have escalated into the complex and problematic, most major categories of illness and etiology, modes of treatment, and therapist's roles are illustrated at least once. Some of the afflictions carry biomedical causes such as chronic heart failure, urinary infection, a narrow pelvis; other cases carry primarily psychological and social causes such as fright, role conflict, factional animosity. A good many episodes reveal cultural definers of illness, and we emphasize these to highlight that which is unique about Kongo illness and therapy.

A word is in order with regard to names. Naming and the name changes that frequently occur in Kongo in connection with status changes make this an important and sensitive issue. Few persons wish to have their identity tampered with in publication. But some would rather not have private worries and embarrassments made public. Since anthropological knowledge belongs in the public domain, we have had to decide where to draw the line between naming and disguising our actors. Pseudonyms are used in those cases in which individuals requested it, and where an opinion was not obtained, to protect the privacy individuals expect and deserve. Public figures such as healers and medical institutions have been identified by their true names. Quite often we have generalized our descriptions, using terms such as ''a nearby dispensary,'' ''a distant hospital,'' to spare the reader the task of remembering a multitude of strange names. Similarly, we have considerably pared down rosters of kinsmen and friends in these studies.

Note: Chapters 4 and 6 are adapted from previous publications. The first, "Strife in the Family as Cause of Child's Illness," appeared in the article "Vers une phénoménologie de la guérison en Afrique centrale," in *Etudes Congolaises* XII (1969): 2, 97-115; the second, "The Professional as Kinsman," appeared as the case of Nsimba in "The Dynamics of Kongo Therapy," in *Psychological Anthropology*, ed. T. .R. Williams,. Papers of the Ninth Congress of Anthropological and Ethnological Sciences (Mouton, 1975).

CHAPTER THREE

Disease of God, Disease of Man

This first case illustrates the context in which the major diagnostic differentiation is made in Kongo therapy management between "of God" illness and "of man" illness. Luzayadio, the focus of this case, played a very minor, passive part as a decision-maker in her own therapy, and thereby fulfilled an important criterion of the sick role in Kongo society. Her kinsmen made the crucial decisions as advocates of her therapy. The composition of this managing group varied from stage to stage in the therapy. As her condition deteriorated, her ambiguous marital status provoked anxiety within the very circle of kinsmen who arranged to help her, raising the suspicion that hers was a special human-caused affliction.

Luzayadio was born in 1950 to a woman of the Nsundi clan and a man of the Kimbanga clan, both freemen. During childhood she lived in her father's village and attended school for a few years. Up to her seventeenth year she helped with field and domestic duties, and her family recalled nothing out of the ordinary in recounting her early life. When she was seventeen she became romantically involved with Kitoko, a man of her father's clan. Her pregnancy by him provoked much discussion, not because of premarital pregnancy, since this is common, but because he was of her father's generation, in the relationship of a "father's brother" to her. Her mother opposed the union, but her father encouraged the two to marry. So, Kitoko made a small payment to her mother's brother, signifying intent to marry. He then left for Congo Brazzaville to earn the bride payment, where he stayed during the time covered in the present account.

Luzayadio gave birth to her child in November 1968 at the Sundi-Lutete Protestant mission maternity. Her pregnancy and the delivery were normal, but in January, after she had returned to working in the fields, she became weak and developed swelling of the limbs. Only with difficulty could she walk up the steep Manianga hill paths. She sought treatment from a retired mission nurse who gave her a penicillin injection. She also received treatment from what her father called *bambuta ku vata*, old men in the village, referring to a local curer. He made superficial razor scratches or cuts (*minsamba*), which he rubbed with plant substances. When she came to the Sundi dispensary, these small scarifications were evident on her right side. She was examined by Arkinstall, who found her to be very ill with limb edema, hepatomegaly (enlarged liver), swelling of her face, and an enlarged heart. At that time the main complaint was a cough. The laboratory examination revealed malaria parasites and an intestinal amoeba, but neither were present in serious degree. She was given emetine and chloraquin, but after a few days the treatment was terminated by the family and she was taken back to her village to "arrange family affairs."

This event was a typical step in Manianga therapy. She left the mission dispensary without the nurses' medical advice, but from past experience they knew that it would be futile to prohibit her going. The meeting of representatives of the Kimbanga and Nsundi clans was convened. We were unable to attend the first meeting, but her father later told us that his side had "examined kinship but they found nothing. Thus the illness comes not from man, but from God." The meeting sought to disclose whether hostilities, tensions, or malefic intentions among the kinsmen would indicate that the disease originated "by man." The official conclusion that it was "of God," and thus not due to human intent, probably did not convince everyone. It did not halt the Kimbanga representatives from asking the patient's forgiveness as a way of assuring that undisclosed evil intentions toward the sufferer were eliminated.

An examination by Luzayadio's maternal group under the guidance of her clan head followed in the same way, with the difference that Luzayadio herself was requested to ask the forgiveness of her clan (see Figures 3 and 4). Her mother's brother said, "She asked forgiveness, not for any sins of hers, but because it is the custom of the clan." The clan members in turn asked her forgiveness for any possible animosity or rancor they might have had against her. Although little was made at that time of unresolved debts over her bride payment, Luzayadio's forthcoming marriage to Kitoko was disapproved by her mother and several older women, and thus her mother and father were at odds. The significant structural issue at this stage was that as long as individuals within the groups could not agree on the marriage payments or even the desirability of the union, they would not be able to agree on therapy. The subsequent course of therapy depended on the analysis of this conflict. In the eyes of those who saw the union as basically sound, all that was needed was a quick payment of bride money to legitimize the birth of the child. For others the suspicion of "incest" had to be dealt with. An appropriate ritual could resolve this, if need be. Luzayadio's obligation to beg the forgiveness of her clan dispensed with this matter. But the discussion continued.

The European nurse at the Nsundi dispensary, who usually did not concern herself with the social affairs of her wards, said that Luzayadio's mother told her the union was "incestuous." The African male nurse did not share this opinion, saying that a union with even one's direct father's brother could be a proper "returned blood" marriage (*vutula menga*) in which the descent substance transferred from one matriline to the other in one generation would be returned in the next. These opinions reflected differences between Luzayadio's kinsmen. If she had not become ill, her marriage would probably have been approved, but without

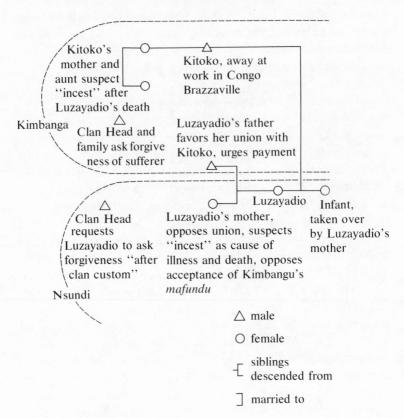

Kitoko's mother and aunt suspect "incest" after Luzayadio's death

Kitoko, away at work in Congo Brazzaville

Kimbanga

Clan Head and family ask forgiveness of sufferer

Luzayadio's father favors her union with Kitoko, urges payment

Clan Head requests Luzayadio to ask forgiveness "after clan custom"

Nsundi

Luzayadio's mother, opposes union, suspects "incest" as cause of illness and death, opposes acceptance of Kimbangu's *mafundu*

Luzayadio

Infant, taken over by Luzayadio's mother

△ male

○ female

⌐
⌐ siblings
   descended from

] married to

FIGURE 3. Kinship relations in Luzayadio's case.

a resolution of this issue the prospects for her recovery, in the eyes of her kinsmen, were not encouraging. Even so, they underestimated the seriousness of her illness.

Without medical care out in the village the patient's condition did not improve. She returned to the hospital after being absent for over a week. Arkinstall again examined her, finding peripheral dependent edema, cardiomegaly, heart murmurs, and other signs which indicated severe heart failure. She was not febrile, but had a moderate anemia. Although the precipitating cause remained unclear, Arkinstall suspected that she was suffering from rheumatic heart disease.[1] She was treated with the only available, but inadequate, medication. When she died several weeks later, the unresolved differences regarding her union with the father of her child took on a more serious magnitude.

	Paternal Clan	Maternal Clan
Examination within both clans reveals no malign affairs, but:		
Forgiveness asked by sufferer of clan	no	yes
Forgiveness asked by clan of sufferer	yes	yes
Before Death		
After Death		
Suspicion of "incest" as cause of death by	"Father's mother"	Mother, Mother's sister, Mother's brother
Acceptance of relationship as proper one by	Father	Mother's brother only after M.D.'s explanation of "medical" cause

FIGURE 4. Structure of confession and accusation in Luzayadio's case.

1. On this examination, Luzayadio was in severe heart failure with an irregular tachycardia, probably atrial fibrillation. She had a loud pansystolic murmur along her left sternal border and at the cardiac apex, plus a mid-diastolic murmur of moderate intensity. There was marked jugular venous distension with prominent pulsations along with an enlarged pulsating liver indicating tricuspid valvular insufficiency. Although she was dyspneic, orthopneic with a cough, pulmonary edema was not obvious on the clinical examination. There were no facilities for roentgenographic or electrocardiographic examinations.

Her body was taken to her clan home at Kintwala and was laid out before her uncle's house under a flower-decorated palm-branch shade. During the wake, immediate kinsmen from the Kimbanga and Nsundi clans came to mourn and to offer their gifts. The gifts were, in effect, ceremonial payments to maintain relations between persons and groups. At death they are expected from members of the father's clan, from the children's clans, from *bankwezi* (affines of the clan), and to a lesser extent from friends.

During the gift payments (*mafundu*) the disagreement between the paternal and maternal clans came to the fore. The Nsundi, Luzayadio's clan and possessor, refused gifts from her father's clan, whom they suspected somehow of being responsible for her sudden death. At first, only Luzayadio's mother had been against the marriage, but as her illness persisted, several elderly women of her lover's direct maternal line agreed that the patient's illness might have been caused by her "incestuous" mating. These opinions hardened when she died. Her father had continued until the last to approve the union and encourage the marriage payments to begin.

When we arrived in Luzayadio's clan village the day of her burial, considerable tension was evident in the people's silent grief at a time when they should be singing and drumming. Ill at ease ourselves, we were unsure about how well they understood our medical opinion about the cause of death. We chose to speak to Luzayadio's uncle, who was receptive but reluctant to admit that anything was amiss in the gift payment. We later discovered that at that time his family were refusing the payments. We explained that the patient had a mechanical heart defect even before it had become evident in her initial symptoms. Arkinstall suggested that this might have begun with rheumatic fever in

---

The presumptive diagnosis was rheumatic heart disease with damage to the mitral and possibly tricuspid valves. She was treated with the only available digitalis preparation, intravenous cedilanid plus an oral diuretic. She transiently improved, but it was impossible to control her rhythm and heart failure with available medication. Early one morning she suffered an acute episode of dyspnea and tachycardia. She was given an additional dose of cedilanid by the dispensary staff but died shortly thereafter.

infancy and that very little could have been done to prevent complications from developing. The childbirth had apparently brought on the latent tendencies in her illness. The uncle then corroborated our interpretation by recalling that Luzayadio had had a fever in childhood.

The influence of our intervention was not immediately apparent to us. However, her uncle spread the word of this heart defect, and the family accepted the traditional gift payments so that burial could proceed normally. Luzayadio was buried in her matrilineal cemetery and her mother took charge of the child.

The imputation of witchcraft, of "illness by man," was evoked by the disjunction of a "marriage of romance" in a clan-dominated society. The union could have become a "return blood" marriage. In these patrilateral cross-cousin marriages, a man "returns the blood" of his father by engendering children with a female of his father's clan. Though rare, this is a preferred marriage form. But Luzayadio's relation would not have been a true "return blood" marriage, although the union was of the father's side back to his wife's group. It was in fact more akin to a "mother's brother's daughter" (matrilateral cross-cousin) marriage in that it occurred between a man's daughter and one of his own clansmen (see Figure 5). Such a marriage can be contracted without transferring the "upbringing" or "child-rearing" payment (*n'sansu*) to the father, since the groom and father are of the same clan. Traditionally, this form of marriage was limited to marriage with one's slaves. In the case at hand, however, neither the father nor the mother's brother received payments beyond the original token. The father probably expected only a token payment, but the maternal side expected more. That Luzayadio died after giving birth to a child and without the payment was a serious confusion of complex relations between families that were allied by previous marriages. Normally, a young man will absolve his marriage debt within a year or two of the birth of his first child. Luzayadio's groom, away at work, no doubt intended to do this, but in his absence the death payments confused the ritual obligations between the clans. The family refused the death payment when it looked as if it was the overdue bride payment which

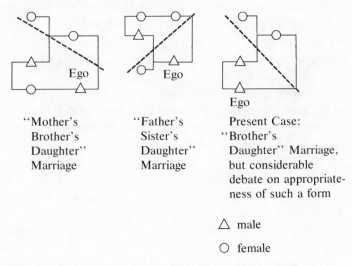

"Mother's
Brother's
Daughter"
Marriage

"Father's
Sister's
Daughter"
Marriage

Present Case:
"Brother's
Daughter" Marriage,
but considerable
debate on appropriate-
ness of such a form

△ male

○ female

FIGURE 5. Close kin marriage possibilities in Kongo matrilineal context.

would absolve the groom elect's debt. The custody of the baby was not so much at issue here—the mother's clan would care for it—as the rhythm of exchanges between the two clans.

Our involvement up until the patient's death had been minimal, consisting principally in Arkinstall's brief consultations at the dispensary about two weeks before her death. Typical of much Western medicine in Africa, information of a scientific nature was not communicated to the lay kin managers of the therapy by the dispensary staff. Nor was the nature of Luzayadio's illness explained to them after her death. Though in retrospect it seems callous of us, we explained the cause of death to the family more from personal discomfort at the paralyzed burial ritual than from a concern for the kinsmen. But despite our obtuseness, we learned from this act that the outside medical specialist could participate in the egalitarian group of kinsmen managing the concerns for an afflicted individual in their midst.

CHAPTER FOUR

Strife in the Family as Cause
of Child's Illness

In the present case the sufferer is an infant who takes no part in therapeutic decision-making; the mechanisms of negotiation and decision are thus seen in a pure form. The key figure in the story is the infant's mother Cécile, who, following parturition, was afraid her child would die. Fraught with anxiety, she removed her infant from the maternity ward to seek assurances from a prophet-seer. Her husband heard of her action and brought her back, but not before going through several other therapeutic efforts. These events were not necessarily "traditional," even though village healers and seers were involved. They illustrate the toll paid by individuals for the lack of integration of various aspects of therapy available in Zaire, as well as the inadequate understanding between the mother and the maternity staff. She was frightened and desperate and did not comprehend the illness of her child in the terms of the mission dispensary. Yet, in the end, the case indicates that full communication within the hospital between the therapy managing group and hospital authorities might forestall disasters.

The infant was born on a Thursday in March, 1969, in the maternity wing of a mission dispensary. She was properly cared for, but within a few days the mother thought the child was breathing with difficulty. Without discussing these apprehensions with the nurse, or notifying her husband, she fled with the baby to consult a prophet-seer ten miles away.

Axel and Cécile, the parents, were typical rural villagers of the area, although their situation was pathetic. Six of their ten infants had died shortly after birth. Like many other BaKongo women, Cécile had a contracted pelvis, which caused particularly difficult deliveries. It was clear that this infant had suffered some head injury during delivery. A serious complication of the mother's previous pregnancies was a fistula connecting the bladder and the uterus. Although it could have been corrected by surgery, the couple had not been able to afford the operation.

Cécile perceived her infant's "suffocation" with alarm, and feared the hospital staff were incapable of diagnosing and treating it correctly, for she suspected mystical causes. The prophet-seer she consulted was widely reputed in the region and had been invited to arbitrate disputes within the political party ABAKO when it was in power. He interpreted the choking as the desire of someone in the mother's clan to destroy her offspring. Just as her womb had been "tied" (*kangidi*) in the past, so she would proba-bly have future problems. Had she not already lost six of ten births?

Her husband was angry when he heard what she had done. No therapy had been recommended by the prophet-seer, and by Monday morning the child was considerably worse. Thus, Axel took his wife and baby to Masamba, a gentle herbalist also widely reputed in the region. Masamba had begun to work as a healer when, years ago, his wife seemed to die, and he received a vision of the plants needed to restore her life. The voice of God had revealed the nature of all plants to him, and he had practiced the healing art subsequently without demanding a fee. His specialty was *lubanzi*, a side pain not considered treatable in Western hos-pitals. Masamba chastised Axel for anger toward his wife and for abandoning her at the maternity. That is why she fled, he charged. When Cécile entered the courtyard a few minutes after Masamba castigated her husband, the curer went immediately to the forest, returning shortly with a handful of plants. Taking the stem of one of the plants, he rubbed a piece in his palm to make a pulp which he massaged on the infant's back. When the plant treatment was completed, he announced that a conflict in the family of Axel and Cécile would have to be resolved before the infant could be cured. This diagnosis concurred with that of the prophet-seer, who had emphasized that the infant's health depended on harmony particularly within Cécile's family. Masamba also gave Axel a plant that would prevent him from striking his wife's kinsmen. Then the party left with the infant to resolve the tensions in the family.

Although we did not observe the family proceedings, several people described them to us. The analysis hinged on Cécile's unique situation in being a member of a junior lineage (*mwelo*) of one of the two houses (*nzo*) of the local clan section (*dikanda*) (see Figure 6). In this house, three lineages were traceable back to a common ancestress, and were reckoned to be senior, middle, and junior daughters of this woman. The clan's analysis focused on the differential fertility in the three lineages. The senior lineage had many women, assuring them a plentiful progeny; the middle lineage had no offspring at all; and in the junior lineage, Cécile was the only childbearing woman. Thus, her fertility and the viability of her offspring greatly affected its survival.

The prophet-seer had located the problem between Cécile's lineage and one of the elder lineages, but he did not specify which lineage was at fault. An elderly woman of the middle lineage was clearly suspected during the consultations with Masamba. Postmenopausal women are frequently suspected of envy toward younger, fertile clanswomen.

Another explanation for Cécile's problem had been suggested on the previous occasions of her difficult deliveries. This was that her marriage was "incestuous," and the affliction a sign of ancestral displeasure. Axel and Cécile belonged to different lines of the same local clan section (*dikanda*), or closely related sections, but could not trace their genealogies to a single source. Cécile's lineage had formerly been enslaved, and while they lived with their masters, their genealogical link with the clan in their home

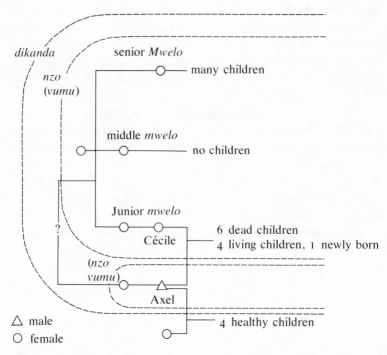

dikanda

nzo
(vumu)

senior *Mwelo*

○—— many children

middle *mwelo*

○——○—— no children

Junior *mwelo*

○——○
Cécile

6 dead children

4 living children, 1 newly born

(nzo
vumu)

○——△
Axel

△ male
○ female

4 healthy children

○

FIGURE 6. Skeletal chart of kinship dimension in case of Axel and Cécile.

community had been forgotten or suppressed. When they married, the union was not sufficiently "incestuous" for clan heads to oppose it. No term exists for "incest," and the line dividing a "nonincestuous" marriage from an "incestuous" one is not reckoned in a hard-and-fast way. In theory, marriage to someone of the regional clan (*luvila*) is wrong, but it is widely practiced. Marriage within the local clan is wrong, but sometimes permitted. And in such cases an untoward incident elicits talk about "incest."

So it was in the case we are considering. At Axel and Cécile's marriage, some felt it would have been wise to "kill a pig of kinship" (*vonda ngulu a luvila*), the ritual sacrifice that annuls blood ties. Each time Cécile experienced a difficult delivery, talk of "incest" and the need to "cut" the lingering blood stigma reappeared. The envy of the old woman was, in a way, an easier and more direct explanation of Cécile's problem. Rather than raise a lot of clan skeletons, it accomplished the same thing with less turmoil. In asking the clansmen to settle their differences so that the child could be healed, Masamba encouraged them to replace accusation by confession and forgiveness.

Yet, Masamba worked plants into his cure for an illness suspected to be due to witchcraft, and thus his option remained open. He worked now to correct one cause, and then to correct another. At Axel's first visit, Masamba had said the clan tension must be resolved before the child could be healed. He later told us that Cécile was suffering from a "faulty sack" which permitted water and body fluids to pass constantly. He said that she was not in a serious condition, but that he did not expect the child to live. At the same time, he "kept face" with the family by telling them to reconcile their differences so that the child could be cured. The following day he informed us that he had consulted his plants and they told him that Axel and Cécile had worked out their clan problems and were on their way to him to continue the herbal therapy. They returned as he predicted, and with many of the mother's kin.

To open the second séance, Masamba ground a piece of tree bark to a powder, moistened it, and massaged it over the infant's back. He placed a leaf under each arm, and with another plant he made a sort of sponge to massage the sides and chest of the child. The sponge was placed under the child's feet for a time to "draw down" the pain from the chest, and she seemed to breathe more easily. Despite the statement to us about the serious condition of the child, Masamba harangued the family and boasted about the efficacy of his treatment. He said his reputation was justified and that the baby was very satisfied with the treatment she had just received. But he concluded that the child must return to the maternity ward and remain there until its navel healed.

The child was taken to the maternity ward, but it died the next day. Cécile accepted the death with apparent resignation. The case remained inconclusive. She did not receive corrective surgery, nor was the "incest" problem pursued. Our diagnosis of the child's condition was that it had received serious injuries to the head at birth, and if it had lived, the birth injury might have damaged its maturation.

With hindsight, it is clear that Cécile compromised her child's limited chances of recovery by removing her prematurely from the maternity ward. But in her desperation, Cécile cannot be faulted for grasping at a straw, and the prophet-seer for offering her one. He gave her a definition of the situation that would provide a chance for some corrective action to save her baby.

Medical planners do well to recognize that what the prophet-seer and healer provided here—assurance, definition in the midst of despair, hopeful action—will either have to be accommodated as it presently exists in customary therapy beyond the doors of the ward, or it will have to be provided inside the ward.

CHAPTER FIVE

A History of Madness

We initially encountered Nzita Ann, the main figure in the present case, when she arrived deeply unconscious in a commercial truck at the Sundi-Lutete dispensary. Accompanying her were her husband, aunt, youngest child, and a brother who was pastor of a neighboring mission. We observed scars on her neck, which appeared to be due to abrasions, and some skin excoriations on her right hip and shoulder. We were told she had become so agitated that her husband was obliged to bind her to control her, and she inadvertently fell on some sacks wet with diesel oil in the back of the truck. She looked a mess, and whatever illness she had, the ride in the stiff-springed truck-ambulance bouncing over pitted late-rainy-season Maniangan roads certainly had done her no good.

An immediate examination on Nzita's admission was inconclusive because she could not be aroused. However, a moderate slap on the side to evoke some response caused her to move all limbs. One hour later, she woke up and sat on the bedside, still unresponsive to others. Arkinstall thought he detected some neck stiffness, which would suggest meningeal inflammation; however, her cerebral spinal fluid taken by a lumbar puncture was normal.

Subsequent examinations of blood, urine, and stool did not reveal any organic disturbance. Throughout her two-week stay at the dispensary she remained subdued, often severely withdrawn and appearing sedated. Displaying no physical symptoms, she was discharged after two weeks to go to her clan village, with the provisional diagnosis by the staff of having a "mental problem." Her case presented a challenging mystery to us, so we decided to research it more carefully.

Nzita's communication with kinsmen, hospital staff, and us was minimal, limited during this period and later to silence, a monosyllabic "yes" or "no," or just a nod or handshake. Thus, we were unable to talk with her about her illness. Nevertheless, we did learn a good deal about how her managing group had consulted various practitioners, and this process is interesting to follow. It shows the utilization of indigenous and Western medicine as a form of social control as the conflict-torn woman resisted her life situation and her tormentors by giving in to psychotic episodes.

She was about thirty years old and a mother of five children. Her husband worked in Kinshasa as a doorman at the Ministry of Foreign Affairs. She was thus responsible for feeding and caring for a family of seven on her husband's insubstantial salary. According to her brother, Pastor Makiadi, her psychotic episodes had begun several years before, following her near-fanatic participation in a prophetic sect. This may have had something to do with her present problem, he proffered, as well as the affair she was reported to have had with one of the prophets. Then too, he suggested, her husband had been unkind to her. Also, she had become very concerned about a favorite aunt, Muadi, who had been committed to a leprosy sanitorium. She had many worries and had become preoccupied with her illness, feeling abandoned by God and man and suffering a deep sense of guilt. She had asked forgiveness of her kinsmen in the home village and had asked forgiveness of God before prophet Kuniema, in Kinshasa, but her guilt persisted. Two psychotic attacks had occurred previously, but she had "recovered" in between. This was now her third. Her brother thought she would improve since he had prayed with her and told her to stay in the village, keep away from people, not brood on her illness, and go work in the fields with someone like her aunt Muadi, who was now back at home.

The present psychotic episode, according to her husband, had begun six months previously. He associated its onset with an abdominal pain she had developed, for which she received treatment in a Kinshasa dispensary. Two months later she began acting strangely, most noticeably at midday. Her condition deteriorated rapidly and within the span of a few days she was incapable of preparing the meals, and sat throughout the day making a "continual calling cry." She was taken again to prophet Kuniema in Kinshasa. He advised her that her condition was not serious, and was "caused by too many ideas in her head." She did not improve, and three days later she and her husband consulted an *nganga* who treated her with "traditional medicine."

Her bizarre behavior continued; she did not eat, she slept poorly, and was unable to relate to her family. One day she burned some of the clothes belonging to family members. She was thereupon taken to a Kinshasa dispensary and received a blood test. Medications by injection and an intravenous infusion were given her. The dispensary personnel determined that the cause of her problem was that she "was thinking too much." She returned home on medication, apparently improved, and remained well for approximately three months, when she again became ill. She was anorexic, apparently not eating for four days; she was insomnolent at night but slept during the day. She again visited the dispensary and received medication which included an intravenous infusion. She continued somewhat better for approximately four weeks when her difficulties returned once more. Following the latest exacerbation of her illness, her husband brought her to her maternal village in the Manianga, bound in the back of a truck.

Her brother and her husband told us that upon arrival in the village she continued to act strangely. She took notice of her brother and attempted to escape out of a window when she saw him. That same evening, however, he was able to talk to her. The day of her arrival the family had a brief meeting, and her husband, maternal uncle, and aunt Muadi were sent to prophetess Mama

Marie Kukunda. Mama Marie, a Protestant deaconness widely reputed for her insightful kinship diagnosis and counsel, told them that Nzita's problem derived from an unidentified young man in the family who was "playing with a fetish." She suggested that the family hold a full-fledged reunion to resolve the matter, and that a letter be written to clan members in Kinshasa asking them to hold a parallel meeting there.

The following day the clan reunion was held. The patient's brother had asked the senior pastor at the Sundi mission to attend and observe the meeting and to intervene if it became a discussion about "witchcraft." In the thinking of most senior Protestant pastors much influenced by missionary thinking, these kinship meetings to investigate and extricate the social cause of illness are regarded as sinful, exemplifying belief in witchcraft. Makiadi was uncomfortable about the meeting, but since the uncles insisted on it, he would go along with them, but guarantee it did not result in excesses or that he would be compromised in them. The maternal clan asked forgiveness of the patient, and the letter suggested by Mama Marie was written to Kinshasa. Several people said that Nzita Ann should be taken to an *nganga,* but Pastor Makiadi overruled them, persuading them to take her instead to the Sundi-Lutete dispensary, where we became aware of the case.

Her arrival at the Sundi dispensary in a state of unconsciousness constitutes one of the few examples we have of a therapy managing group—in this case her brother, uncle, aunt, and husband—acting simultaneously on two divergent therapies, one indigenous, the other Western. Her kinsmen in the clan reunion had suggested she be taken to Bilumbu, *nganga bilau*, specialist in cases of madness (*lauka*). Bilumbu had not seen the patient, but he had given her kin a liter bottle of herbal medicine, a dose of which had been given Nzita sometime prior to her arrival at the dispensary, causing her sedation. Her brother had then imposed his preferred treatment option, and Nzita was brought to the dispensary. None of the patient's kin revealed the treatment by Bilumbu to the nursing staff, much less to us. However, had we looked under the hospital bed, we would have found the bottle with the remaining portion of herbal medicine. She was administered a dose of this daily by her aunt Muadi who was caring for her in the hospital, and this accounts for the sedated, sleepy-unconscious state which so baffled us at first.

Bilumbu the *nganga*, who filled us in on these details, and whom we had come to know quite well by then, was a highly reputed elderly blacksmith and healer of the Kivunda region. The origin of his therapeutic practice dated back decades to when he was a labor emigrant among the BaZombo near Angola. While there, he learned one day that his wife had gone mad and sliced the head of a child with a machete. Bilumbu purchased rights to the cure from a fellow worker, returned home, and administered it to his wife. He continued to practice this specialized cure and over the years gained a wide reputation. He explained Nzita's illness in terms of the three types of madness: (1) those which "come from God," (2) those caused by clan problems, and (3) those caused by "touching a fetish." He treated illnesses from the first two causes and said that Nzita's affliction originated from the second, clan problems. He had treated her two years previously for a similar episode and felt she was sick from the inadequate and partial termination of the marriage payment (*longo*) and the envy and tension that ensued. He noted that she had not suffered in this way prior to her marriage.

Bilumbu's full cure constituted two stages, an herbal sedative and the "Kilambu Meal." The sedative consisted of the leaves of four plants (*kilemba-lemba,* 56; *kilemba-nzau,* 42; *kilemba-ntoko,* 75; and *kilembe-lembe,* 74)[1] mixed with water to form an oral dose of about one liter which he said could be repeated only twice, taken in small doses over a week's period, otherwise the patient might become permanently deranged. The second stage of the treatment contained the same four plants mixed with a peanut paste (*mwamba*) to make up the Kilambu Meal signifying the end of the cure and the illness. If the patient had taken only the first stage, a relapse could occur as it had in Nzita's case. In her

1. These medicinal plants are identified more fully in Appendix B where we list plants mentioned in the book, with their appropriate botanical names. The discussion on "The Art of the *Nganga*" in Chapter 11 elaborates the logical criteria by which these plants were combined.

earlier episode she had not taken the Meal, and he had declined to administer a third dose of the sedative, telling the family that he did not want her to become permanently deranged. He had advised the family that they must hold a reunion to resolve the affair before he would administer the Kilambu Meal. The Kilambu Meal, here as in other initiatory cures, signified the resolution of the social cause of individual symptoms and the identification of the patient with others who had gone through the treatment.

When Nzita was released from the dispensary, her therapy managers declined to go through with Bilumbu's Kilambu Meal. Rather, after informal deliberations they decided she must be taken to nearby *nganga mbuki* Madeko. Nzita's aunt Muadi walked with her and her small child the three or four miles to Madeko's village. Upon their arrival, Madeko briefly examined Nzita, feeling her abdomen, back, and chest. He prepared two separate potions from plants and water which he gave her to drink. He then completely annointed the upper part of her body, including her face and head, with the juice of leaves he held in his hand. Following this, he made a series of scratches with an old razor blade on the skin of her sides, back, shoulders, and chest. These scratches (*minsamba*) did not penetrate the skin or draw blood. He then squeezed more juice onto her chest and back, following which he rubbed a small amount of black powder into the *minsamba* scratches. He then looked into her eyes and noted that there were "worms" in them (*zinioka za meso*) which were causing the trouble in her head. He went to the forest behing his house and returned with a yellow fiber which he wrapped in leaves, and then squeezed the juice from this fiber into her eyes. Then he wrapped the fiber in a third leaf before discarding it on the firesite of the night before. At this point her treatment was interrupted while he treated another woman for back pain. Returning to Nzita, he brought a basin filled with clean water and told her to put her face into it and wash the medicine from her eyes. She did this dutifully. He then took the basin and with a small pointed stick extracted several gray, stringy strands of material from the water. These he showed everyone present—about 15 persons— and said they were the worms which had been removed from her eyes and they had been causing her "head to turn." The manner in which these "worms" had been created out of the coagula of the medicine was reminiscent of the way healers elsewhere in central Africa are reported to have removed intrusive objects such as ancestors' teeth, drops of bad blood, bits of cotton, and other "dirt" from the body of the afflicted person. When Madeko had removed the cause of Nzita's illness in the form of the "worms," he administered her a glass of another herbal potion, which she drank.

Nzita returned four consecutive mornings for Madeko's treatment, and on each occasion was given medicine to drink and had medicine applied to her body, thereby giving both an internal and external approach. The treatment of the first day, Madeko said, was intended to weaken the illness. Medicine rubbed on externally was intended to protect her, for her family would smell the plants and fear to touch or harm her. Madeko said she was not mad (*lauka*), but that there was some problem in her family about which she was thinking a great deal and this had made her ill. He asked Arkinstall if he had found any disease in her body. Arkinstall said he had not, whereupon Madeko said he, too, had found no disease. If a reconciliation could be achieved in the clan and in her relationships, the herbal treatments (*makaya*) could bring about her cure. Indeed, Nzita appeared much more relaxed as the treatments progressed. Though she was very quiet, she was observant of events and people around her; she was eating better, and she could manage the daily walk seven miles to and from Madeko's village.

We were unable to follow the quest for Nzita's therapy beyond this point. We learned however that the family was contemplating taking her either to another prophet-diviner with a technique much like Mama Marie's and Kuniema's, consisting of deft kinship analysis followed by confession, Bible reading, public diagnosis of dreams, and laying on of hands; or to the Croix Koma purification center near Brazzaville, where the entire local clan section would receive instruction and purification. As soon as the letter from Kinshasa reporting on the parallel clan meeting arrived, they would make their decision regarding the next stage of therapy. In the meantime, Nzita remained with her aunt Muadi, working with her in her gardens, taking care of her child, and quietly pondering her situation.

Our coverage of this case was similar to overhearing one side of a telephone conversation and inferring the words and thoughts at the other end of the line. Nzita's family members were faced with the same predicament, although they knew her character from earlier times. We were able to gain a considerable appreciation of her character too from their approach to her. We noted, for example, that they refrained from using the word *lauka* or any of its derivatives in her presence. It would be indiscreet to use this term before a suffering patient, although it may be used in his absence. Nevertheless, the kin showed that this was their diagnosis by consulting Bilumbu, specialist in the treatment of agitated behavior indicative of madness. In Kongo thinking, madness is a sort of epiphenomenon of a disorder at another level in the sufferer's life. Every therapist to whom she was taken distinguished clearly between symptoms and causes, and acted accordingly. Nzita was regarded by both her kinsmen and the therapists as situated somewhere on the continuum from well to deeply troubled to mad. Most held her to be temporarily deranged, but in danger of sliding into irremediable madness. It was apparent that although madness is feared and somewhat stigmatized in Kongo society, it is not sufficient grounds for kinsmen to abandon the afflicted or for a spouse to seek divorce. Quite the contrary, as we see in this case, as much concern is lavished on the patient of agitation and depression as in those cases where life is in immediate danger.

Nzita's affliction may be categorized in Kongo thought as "urban-derived insanity" which besets those who have succumbed to the temptations, threats, and contradictions of complex city life. She became converted to a sect, had a related love affair, was unhappy with her husband, and felt guilty about her relationships with others and before God. These expressions, and her periodic episodes of schizophrenic psychosis, represented a subjective response to deeply unsettling life circumstances. The annals of Kinshasa psychiatric treatment are filled with similar instances of women unhappy with their lot.[2] Despite the attractions of city life, a typical lower class urban woman in Zaire has less effective freedom and sense of reward than her village counterpart. She depends on her husband's inadequate salary for family meals and household upkeep, and for occasional new clothing. In the rural setting, by contrast, she would be independent in gardening, harvesting, preparing of meals, and marketing of small produce. The highly competitive and inflation-prone social and economic atmosphere of Kinshasa gives many women, as well as men, the feeling of being trapped. One solution for women is prostitution, either a steady liaison with a wealthy, well-placed man, or occasional street work—"tilling the streets," as it is called—which provides an extra income and a sense of greater independence, but often at the price of negative sanctions and guilt feelings. Another solution is petty merchandising, but this leaves the children unattended and frequently entails risky, semilegal trafficking. For others, adherence to one of the many prophetic sects of the city is a symbolic and religious solution. Where these solutions are impossible or unsatisfying, the result may be an escape into psychosis such as we have seen in Nzita's case.

2. This statement is based on examination of 1968/69 *psychopalavre* records provided by the Institut Neuropsychiatrie de Kinshasa.

CHAPTER SIX

The Professional as Kinsman

The first three cases were valuable in illustrating the role of second and third parties in the managing group. In those cases the status of the patient was that of subordinate: young unwed mother, newly born infant, and wife. Here the status of the patient in the society at large was that of adult male, professionally educated. In this case, in contrast to the previous three, the sufferer initially took an active role. On the other hand, as his case progressed and his condition became chronic, he accepted an increasingly passive role in which decisions were made for him by a managing group. The case illustrates the existing tensions upon workers in modern occupations in a country like Zaire. Nsimba was a nurse in his early twenties, an educated man, subject to professional values, achievement orientation, and salary dependence of modern society. Living and working on a mission station, he was exposed to a further set of challenges of family structure and behavior dictated by Western mores and loyalty to the foreign and indigenous authorities of the mission. The expectations of mission life did not take him completely out of the traditional demands with their kinship loyalties based on seniority and definition of roles by birth. This juxtaposition of demands was acute for Nsimba when he returned from nurse's training to hold his first job close to his paternal and maternal families.

The mission station at which Nsimba received primary and secondary training and to which he returned to work was established by the Swedish Covenant Mission in 1925. At independence in 1960 the Swedish foreign mission turned over de jure responsibilities to the African church. Thereafter, the work on the stations was administered by a board of African pastors and teachers and Swedish missionaries, and financed by local fees, the Swedish church in decreasing amounts, and governmental funding. The medical dispensary at the mission continued to receive many clients, on both an in- and out-patient basis, and it had recently been expanded to accommodate fifty bed patients in the dispensary and twenty in the maternity, with funds from Sweden.

After receiving two years of secondary school at this mission, Nsimba was sent by the board to the larger IME Kimpese mission post in the Lower Zaire to train as a nurse with the understanding that he would return to work in one of the mission dispensaries upon graduation. He worked hard and was well liked. His performance was above average in practical nursing, while his marks in academic subjects were only fair. His training was designed to give him a basis in general nursing and public health under the direction of a doctor. Nsimba expected to graduate as a registered nurse (*infirmier*), and although his training was the same as that of the preceding class, because of an upgrading in governmental regulations his class graduated with a lesser diploma of practical nurse (*garde-malade*). This was a disappointment to him.

Nevertheless, upon completion of his training as practical nurse he was appointed head nurse in charge of the dispensary at his home mission station. Although the Swedish nurse who had worked in the dispensary remained in charge of administrative responsibilities, Nsimba undertook the large responsibility for in- and out-patient care. This task was difficult, since there was no supervising doctor to whom to refer difficult cases. The Catholic hospital a half-hour's drive away was often without a doctor as well. The nearest hospital with a doctor at the time Nsimba entered practice was at Luozi, a day's drive away by rugged Land Rover vehicle over very rough roads. In addition to Nsimba and the Swedish nurse, the dispensary staff included an elderly male practical nurse who had been with the dispensary fifty years and three nurse's aides who worked on routine laboratory examinations and dispensed some medicines. The elderly nurse had become a powerful and influential figure in the community, even feared by some, because of his access to medicines. As head of his clan, and widely known because of his dispensary work, he had seen fit to open an unofficial private dispensary in his house in the village.

Nsimba handled the job of head nurse with apparent ease at first. The Swedish nurse stated "they would be unable to carry on without him." The elderly nurse however resented Nsimba, the first African to be in charge of the dispensary. Nsimba had criticized him for mistakes and malpractices. Then, a year after Nsimba's arrival, during his annual vacation, the elder male nurse was informed by the local mission authorities that since he was only a few months short of retirement and pension age (65) he would not need to return to work at all; the mission considered his term as fulfilled. This he took as an insult and an affront after fifty years of dutiful service. He held Nsimba responsible for this turn of events.

Apart from this relationship with the elderly nurse, Nsimba seemed to fare well in his career. He was married and had one healthy newly born child. His wife suffered from frequent abdominal pains and had a history of two earlier miscarriages, but these did not appear to disturb Nsimba.

Things took a turn for the worse for Nsimba in December 1968, at the time of the birth of his child, and about two years after he had begun work at the dispensary. He took ill with back pain and painful urination. Being a nurse, he submitted a urine sample for analysis and discovered a urinary infection which he treated with two antibiotics. But he felt he was not fully improving, so he requested a leave from his work to visit IME-Kimpese, the hospital where he had trained. In late January 1969, he left his wife and new baby behind and went to Kimpese where he received further treatment for his infection and had a biopsy performed on a swelling (*mumbutu*) in his groin which he stated had been present since 1961. He was slow to recover from his surgery. He continued to complain of abdominal pain and walked with a marked limp apparently due to pain following his surgery. No further diagnoses were made, and the biopsy did not indicate any specific pathology.

After recovering from his minor surgery, but still feeling unwell, Nsimba went to Kinshasa to be with his father and several maternal uncles. Shortly thereafter he began to suffer severe headaches, these kinsmen "feared for his life." They brought him back to IME-Kimpese for treatment, but when his headaches did not clear up, his kinsmen returned with him to Kinshasa for a consultation with *ngunza* Kuniema. This ritual practioner (already mentioned in Nzita's case) was a schoolteacher of Maniangan origin whose reputation was widespread in both the rural and urban Maniangan populace for the investigative and counselling therapy he performed. He examined Nsimba's case through extensive questioning and concluded that the illness was caused by evil acts (*mavanga mambi*) perpetrated on Nsimba by the people in his paternal village, those to whom he and his (maternal) clan section had been enslaved until 1958 (see Figure 7). In order for Nsimba to recover, these kinsmen would have to "remove their hands from him." The prophet had also mentioned something about a snake involved in the affair. When questioned about this, the only incident involving a snake Nsimba could remember had occurred a few weeks earlier when he was suffering a backache. A snake had entered the house while his wife was applying a hot compress to his back. The snake was chased out but not killed. Nsimba put little stock in the matter, although he acknowledged that in Kongo such snakes may be the familiars sent by an enemy or one's own familiar which, if killed, results in one's own death.

Nsimba felt uncertain about the problem with the paternal clan. But he suggested in no uncertain terms that he had had problems with maternal kinsmen. Shortly after he started work at the dispensary, those kin who lived nearby began to make demands on his earnings. He was expected to personally pay the hospital bills

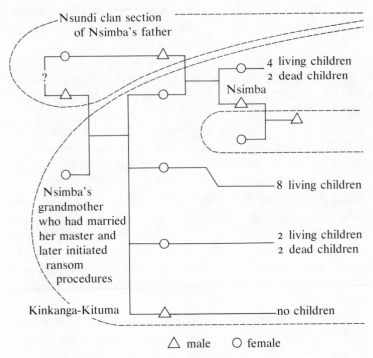

△ male   ○ female

FIGURE 7. Alliance and descent ties between the Nsundi and their former slaves, the Kinkanga-Kituma.

of any relatives treated in his dispensary. One month before he had become ill, a maternal aunt brought three children in for treatment and gave him the bill. He had paid for two children, but was unable to pay for the third, and his aunt had criticized him. Similar unpleasantries were becoming common. The demands were unreasonable. He was not earning much money, he complained, and was barely able to look after his wife and child and in addition meet these heavy outside kinship demands and responsibilities. This predicament is frequent among Zairian wage earners. It drives many to the conviction that they cannot both meet kinship obligations and benefit from the salary, and as a solution some move away or quit their salaried jobs.

The slave-master relationship between Nsimba and his father's group dated back to the time when his maternal grandmother of the Kinkanga-Kituma clan had been bought by the Nsundi clan section of his father's group. In 1958, she had initiated action to redeem the Kinkanga-Kituma slave section, but was unable to achieve this in customary fashion through ransom payments. She then took the case to the colonial court and won, forcing the Nsundi to accept the "pig" of ransom in the amount determined by the court. The Nsundi were not happy with this outcome, insisting on additional payment if the ransom were to be genuinely binding. One year later the Kinkanga-Kituma agreed to an out-of-court supplemental payment and final settlement of the issue. Thus the affair had rested until Nsimba's illness.

The relationship between this old slavery issue and Nsimba's illness had been raised and pursued by the prophet Kuniema, because it was noted that not only he of the former slave group was suffering, but other members of the group. One woman had frequent miscarriages and "children dying in her womb"; another suffered from tuberculosis and had two dead children. The Nsundi clan, *mase* ("fathers") to these persons, accepted the meeting recommended by the prophet to ask pardon of the sufferers. Nsimba returned from Kinshasa to his paternal clan's village in the Manianga countryside; a meeting was held. The paternal kinsmen went through the formal procedures of asking forgiveness of the suffering Nsimba and his clanmates, thereby extending their blessing. The significance of this act, in Kongo thinking, is that it withdraws any intentional or unintentional ill will from the relationship. Although the insinuation of witchcraft is present in this, a formal accusation of witchcraft is not necessary for this procedure to take place. Ill will, envy, backbiting and even gossip suffice to cause an illness.

The meeting may have laid to rest suspicions about the paternal kinsmen's role in Nsimba's illness, but it did not make him well. Quite the contrary. He began to feel dizzy. The aspirins he took made his dizziness worse. He became delirious and talked without making sense. He became frightened, fearing he would die. He sent a messenger to the mission, some forty miles away, requesting that the ambulance come immediately to take him home, for he wanted to see his infant child before dying. When he arrived at the dispensary with his wife, brother, uncle, and other family members, his panic had subsided somewhat, but he complained of dizziness and severe headache. Arkinstall examined him, but there were no physical findings. Nsimba improved slowly with symptomatic therapy at the dispensary, but his headache continued.

Nsimba did not feel he could return to work under the circumstances. He wished for a transfer to another dispensary within the mission, farther from his village and family. Failing in this, he would take another job.

Nsimba then went to seek relief for his headache from a regional primary school teacher reputed to heal a few specific head diseases, in particular *mumpompila*, a disease sometimes present in children from birth, whose main characteristic is a "separation of the skull." This problem may be caused, like "evil eye" in certain parts of the world, by the regard of an elderly woman, and it is manifested in children by sudden and unexplained crying. Among adults such as Nsimba, explained the teacher, it results in sudden intense headaches. The treatment administered in this instance was a head pack of several plants, one from the water and one from the savannah, crushed together and moistened into a pulp, and kept on the head for several days. After spending several days in quiet retreat receiving this treatment, Nsimba said he felt somewhat better.

But he did not return home, nor to work when the treatment had been completed. He went to spend several more days with prophet Luamba Zablon, accompanied by his father, his mother's brother, his mother, and a sister. Luamba, a self-styled prophet of Nsundi-Kinganga, received many people and maintained a supportive therapeutic retreat. He had originally had visions and was reputed to have done wondrous things. At independence in 1960 he had been coopted as provincial deputy and had served as one of several court healers for prominent BaKongo provincial politicians. Now he ran a small store in his village house and ministered to clients, often from the city, who would stay as long as several weeks or a month.

Luamba's standard regime, and the one which Nsimba followed, began shortly after arrival with a ritual bath in the stream below the village, an act Luamba required of all "serious cases." Luamba considered Nsimba's whole family—his father, uncle, mother, and sister, and Nsimba himself—to be sick; his father with "sickness of the stool," his uncle with cough and hernia, his mother, an old tuberculosis patient with "tight throat" (*nkangulu a malaka*), and his sister with difficulty in giving birth. Nsimba, he said, had "heavy head" (*nkatanga*), something he compared to "rheumatism," that is, "his intelligence disappears" (*nzailu imene*). After the ritual bath Nsimba received Luamba's blessing. He would not be permitted to take a bath again until departing.

When asked about Nsimba's illness, Luamba said, "Others will say it comes from his clan, or his father's clan; but here we do not analyze the origin of the disease, we just heal." He was reflecting an opinion voiced by some, but not all, prophets who refuse to become entangled in kinship conflicts. As illustrative of his approach, he quoted James 5:13–16 to us: "Is anyone among you in trouble? He should turn to prayer. . . Is one of you ill? He should send for the elders of the congregation to pray over him and anoint him with oil in the name of the Lord. The prayer offered in faith will save the sick man, the Lord will raise him from his bed, and any sins he may have committed will be forgiven." Luamba distinguished himself from other prophets who blame family members in searching for the causes of illness and provoke all kinds of arguments. He agreed that illness might come from the clan, but he insisted that he did not analyze cases in that way. To work out a conflict (*tengula mambu*) just causes too much trouble.

A further part of the treatment took place nightly in the village church. There Luamba would bring together his clients and hold a worship and healing service with them, singing hymns, teaching from the Bible, and eventually blessing, praying, laying on hands, and annointing each one individually with oil while intoning the following unique liturgy or some variation from it.

> Father! You have wisdom
> Sufficient to heal
>   All sufferings,
>   All illnesses.

> I do not possess herbs and medicines,
> But that which I have I give you.
> [laying hands on Nsimba]
> In the name of Jesus,
> Release the fount of health,
> Release it upon his thoughts,
> Release it upon his whole being.
> Give him peace.
> Open the fount of blessing.
> Open it upon you!
> In Jesus name I say:
>   Suffering!
>   All sicknesses!
>   Be still!
>   Be still in Jesus' name!
> Again I say:
>   All suffering!
>   And all sicknesses!
>   Release this person!
>   Release Gods's person!
> The possessor of this mind,
> And these, your thoughts.
> And your body and strength.
> Father, may the hand of God heal,
> And there where the pain is,
> May it vanish.
> If the health is choked out
> By the hands of evil ones,
>   May they release it!
> May you regain health at work!
> Oh, blessed Father,
> Father of peace.
> May your name be honored,
> May your Kingdom come.

Somewhat improved, Nsimba returned to the mission to take up work in the dispensary.

However, he experienced another setback. He found a bottle fetish in his house, containing a twist of tobacco, several peanuts, a few blades of grass, and a slip of paper with the name of a girl written on it. Although he discarded the bottle, he was afraid for his life by this gesture which had the impact of an anonymous threatening telephone call. The tobacco, which produces a feeling of intoxication when inhaled, was interpreted to mean he would continue being dizzy; the peanuts, a sign of fertility, meant he would no longer be able to have children; the grass, often a sign of life and hope, because it was cut, meant that his life too would be "cut"; and the girl's name, that he would become involved in a scandal, or in the revelation of a former clandestine act. Nsimba went back to the prophet Luamba with this new problem. Luamba told him the name of the person responsible, but Nsimba did not reveal it to us.

Shortly after this, a delegation of churchmen and mission personnel went on Nsimba's behalf to see the now-retired nurse who had given him trouble earlier. The delegation had taken the initiative in this visit, and Nsimba was in agreement with it. They asked the nurse "what he wanted," although they did not accuse him of having "planted" the fetish. He apologized for his ill will toward Nsimba and the delegation assured him that no ill will had been intended in his premature retirement.

After this reconciliation with the retired nurse, Nsimba seemed considerably improved so that he could begin work on a partial basis again. He still wished to leave his immediate kinsmen and take a position elsewhere in the mission circuit of dispensaries. He submitted a formal request to the medical personnel of the mission at a conference in June. The other nurses and station heads discussed his case and agreed to grant him a transfer as soon as it could be worked out. The meeting was a form of retreat with meditation and fellowship lasting several days, which Nsimba enjoyed greatly. Following the retreat he was back at work full force; his headaches had disappeared and he seemed happier.

Four years later we learned that Nsimba had not managed the move which he sought, but that he had continued successfully in the mission dispensary alongside the Swedish nurse. Mission leaders eventually decided he should become sole director of the whole medical installation in 1973. But as the time of his promotion to director approached, he developed symptoms similar to those he had had in 1969. The outcome was not obvious at the time of writing, but the relation of his special professional environment to his illness appeared clear. A person of sensitive character, Nsimba had shown he could barely cope with all the incongruous expectations and duties in the several professional and kinship roles he occupied. After an initial biomedical infection, he persisted in the sick role with a series of diffuse symptoms, enjoying the support of numerous kinsmen acting as his therapy managing group. It is noteworthy that the resolution of an important job-related conflict was managed by non-kin, providing evidence again of flexibility in the basic institution of Kongo therapy management.

CHAPTER SEVEN

Marriage and the Father's Blessing

We will now examine our most complex example of a quest for therapy. When we first met Lwezi Louise in 1969 she was 23, the unmarried mother of two children, living with her mother in her matrilineal clan village. While it is common, even normative, for Manianga girls to complete marriage procedures after being pregnant or having a child by the groom, those who fail to find a husband after having several children constitute a serious concern for their families. This situation is aggravated in the Manianga because male labor emigration has resulted in nearly three times more women than men between 25 and 40 years of age living in the countryside. Pressures for polygamy or concubinage are great. A "spoiled" woman has few chances of being the first bride of a man, and her elders are usually hard put to collect the bride payment. During the two years prior to our documentation of Lwezi's story, and during the time of the study, her behavior, health, and unresolved social situation caused her respectable Christian family with high expectations much anxiety and tension. The demanding and critical parents and siblings and the imbalance between the sexes caused social pressures converging into a troubled modern role that Western and African therapists had difficulty resolving, or even comprehending. With one or two exceptions, specialists of both traditions demonstrated rigid reactions to her case rather than adaptive responses to the problems.

Lwezi was born sixth in a family of seven children. The village home of her father and mother combined selected conservative traditional social values with those learned from the Swedish Covenant Mission. Her oldest brother completed secondary school and became a minister in the mission church. Another older brother became a talented primary school teacher. Her youngest sister was top in her nursing class. Other siblings felt somewhat resentful and complained that they were not as talented as these family members. One was a wage laborer; an older sister was married and lived in Kinshasa; a younger brother was just out of primary school. They were a close family, but prolonged and problematic illness exacerbated the divisions among them.

Lwezi's father was the only resident adult male in his clan village. As its headman, he was responsible for resolving problems of the clan and defending its interests in court. The major part of the clan lived in Kinshasa where a proxy headman from the junior clan section took charge of family affairs and maintained contact with his country counterpart. They shared many decisions, including those involving Lwezi. However, since she was not independent, Lwezi's quest for therapy was also managed by her brothers and their maternal uncles of a neighboring village. The maternal clan was less urbanized, with half a dozen adult males residing in the rural village. Its ranks also contained a number of army officers, craftsmen, prophets, and clerks. Thus, in the maternal and paternal clans, cleavages existed between village and urban residence, agricultural subsistence and salaried income, orthodoxy in regard to traditional social customs and rejection of custom under the influence of missionary teaching. Such divergencies clearly had an adverse effect on the ability of the groups to cooperate in time of crisis.

After finishing primary school in 1962, Lwezi took a job as nurses aide in a mission dispensary. She wished to continue on to school in nursing or attend secondary school, but her paternal kin discouraged this course, saying there were too many temptations and deceits in it. She was disappointed, but continued working as an untrained aide. She became pregnant through an affair with someone at the mission. The young man said he would marry her, but his family would not help him with the bride payment. He disappeared, leaving Lwezi with the baby. Although some of her family members wanted her to return to work, she left home to visit a maternal uncle and aunt in Congo Brazzaville. While she was there, her uncle introduced her to a man who had expressed an interest in marrying her. Lwezi consented, her new suitor paid the uncle the token "wine for the request of the bride" (*malavu ma ngyuvudulu a nkento*), and Lwezi moved in with him, the third woman in a polygynous household. The bride payment and marriage ceremony were deferred.

Approximately one month later she developed abdominal pains and returned to a mission dispensary in the Manianga for treatment. From there she was referred to the Luozi hospital, a distance of over 100 miles, where she underwent a dilation and curettage of her uterus.

Lwezi's father, Bola, had become quite upset by the behavior of his daughter. He was aware of the marriage negotiations initiated by her mother's brother in Congo Brazzaville. It would have been customary for him to consent to the union at this point with a paternal blessing in exchange for a gift from the suitor. No gift had been forthcoming, and he did not want Lwezi to return to the man, so he withheld the blessing. The maternal uncles in the village however were willing to let her return. Both groups, by custom, should have cooperated in the preparation of the marriage. Without her father's blessing, Lwezi returned to live with her suitor. When she became pregnant by him, the man finally wrote to Bola formally asking for his daughter's hand, but no gift accompanied the request.

Lwezi's pregnancy upset Bola even more. In her eighth month of pregnancy Lwezi received a letter signed "Bola" stating that her mother had died and that she should return home immediately. She returned home to discover that the letter had been forged. Bola denied having sent it, blaming the maternal side. Yet he was extremely angry over Lwezi, so that his wife Nkwelo felt constrained to remove Lwezi to the maternal village. There she stayed with her until the pregnancy reached full term.

The baby was born at the maternity in November 1968, without complications. Lwezi continued to reside in the maternal clan village with her mother and mother's brothers rather than rejoin her father. However, both maternal uncles and father were agreed that the marriage must be completed and that the payments be made permitting the blessings to be conferred before she could return to her suitor.

But no payments were forthcoming, and in this tense social climate Lwezi fell ill. Her maternal kinsmen brought her to the Sundi dispensary where we first met her. She had multiple complaints of periodic fever and chills, back pain which radiated to her neck, pain in her joints, loss of appetite, and general malaise. The dispensary examined her blood for malaria and her stool for parasites. Both were negative. She did have evidence of a moderate urinary tract infection. She had been treated initially with vitamins, analgesics, and stimulants and given a malaria cure.

Although at the time of admission she had been afebrile, one week later she had a sudden onset of fever of 40.5° C with neck pain. She was then treated with an intravenous fluid and two antibiotics. Approximately one month later when she had a similar spike of high fever and back pain, a diagnosis of acute nephritis was made. At this time she was treated with a third antibiotic. She then complained of pain in her arms and legs; a week later she spoke of a chill with back pain. After a month of care she was reported as "improved—can leave," with a final but very ambivalent diagnosis of "Rheumatoid arthritis?—nephritis?—ascaris and trichocephalia infestation." She had been given ten different medications: four antibiotics, two analgesics, a stimulus of ephedrine, an intravenous of glucose and electrolyte solution for two days, an intramuscular injection of quinine, and intermittent vitamins.

When Lwezi was discharged, she was taken immediately by her brother on bicycle—"because she was too weak to walk"— 40 kilometers to an *nganga* reputed for his handling of "psychological cases," as this brother put it. Her kinsmen had become increasingly convinced that the dispensary had not found the true cause of her illness. *Nganga nkisi* Bayindula, nicknamed "Mosquito," approached Lwezi's malady with daily treatments of razor-blade incisions over her body, rubbing a preparation of plants into the wounds and following that with cupping horn extraction of the blood. The *nganga's* court was large and contained several small huts for his clients. The dozen or so patients present with Lwezi, many from urban centers, would gather morning and evening for worship with Bayindula. For Lwezi he held private sessions, counselling her and the family members present—her mother, several brothers, and maternal cousins—that they must quickly complete the marriage formalities.

On the final day of her treatment with Bayindula, Lwezi received concentrated attention. After opening prayers and songs he treated her by making razor incisions at the knees, elbows, ankles, and back. Then he sucked these with the cupping horn in his mouth "to remove the bad blood," and rubbed a sponge of the fern *kuta-kuta* (1) over the cuts. He once more reprimanded her for "prostitution," telling her to go and marry properly and live like a Christian. With rosary in hand he chanted his eclectic adaptation of the Croix Koma Mass,[1] derived in turn from the Catholic Mass. Her clansmen joined in on the refrain as they had learned it.

> *Together* (Bayindula and sufferer's kinsmen): Yesu, Yesu, remove my sins from me . . .
>
> *Bayindula*: For we are strangers here below; Lord God Nzambi when he created us, what he made us, that we truly are. And so mourning and misery entered the world; so it is in all the world. The whites got their independence and we got ours; we reach old age and get even older; the body grows feeble and weak. Oh Zeladi, hear our supplications; out of the depths of suffering here in the world, our Lord we pray.
>
> *Kinsmen*: (Refrain) Oh Zeladi . . .
>
> *B.*: For suffering entered the world long ago; still Nzambi guards us, but those with *makundu* [evil, secret power] and *bandoki* [witches],

---

1. Derived from the Catholic Mass by Victor Malanda, founder of the Croix Koma purification movement and center near Brazzaville. The entire text of Bayindula's chant has been published in English translation in John M. Janzen and Wyatt MacGaffey, *An Anthology of Kongo Religion* (Lawrence, 1974), pp. 78–79.

their ways and actions are evil! For Yesu spoke these words: Truly the earth must have many people on it, it must be so. Oh joy, great joy in the hearts of the Christians when we pray to Him . . .

K.: (Ref.) Oh Joy . . .

B.: Now I give them [Lwezi and kin] two or three weeks [to see results]; and between the first and second week the Lord will heal her. In the name of

K.: the Father, the Son, and the Holy Ghost. . . .

B.: For palavers have a long history; we got our independence, and yet how we still suffer; still, Lord Nzambi truly protects us. We hope to gradually reach old age, and still older. The girl [Lwezi] has lost her strength, her arms are weak. The illness *will* disappear, I have saved many like this! Let no man challenge me, neither white nor black. We must all see each other as comrades. . . .

Bayindula requested and received 500 francs ($10) for his week's treatment from Lwezi's kin. He also asked them to return in three weeks after having settled the marriage formalities. Lwezi's maternal clan elders thought this a rather extravagant demand on Bayindula's part and refused to return to him. Lwezi returned to the maternal village with her mother where she spent her hours quietly and sadly pondering her situation. She spoke hesitantly with us, said she felt better now, but would not elaborate on her thoughts. She consented to a physical examination at this point, but Arkinstall uncovered no medical signs more serious than a suspected chronic urinary infection (cystitis), along with psychosomatic muscular weakness and musculoskeletal pains.

Her brothers, maternal uncles, and mother, now her therapy managers, maintained several diagnostic options about the cause of Lwezi's affliction. One brother was convinced that she had "psychological" problems. These might be due, in turn, to the same forces that were hounding other clan members in their varied problems such as the loss of a job on immorality charges, the undercurrent of mutual hostility in the clan, and chronic illness of several other members. Neighbors were beginning to talk about this clan, and something fundamental would have to be done. Lwezi might have stepped on or brushed against a fetish planted by the first wife of the "husband," or, being literate, she might

PLATE 1.–Out-patients at Kibunzi dispensary, Lower Zaire, waiting for treatment. Many are infants brought by their mothers.

PLATE 2.–Patients receiving medication at Kibunzi dispensary from graduate nurse (at left) and nurse's aide (at right).

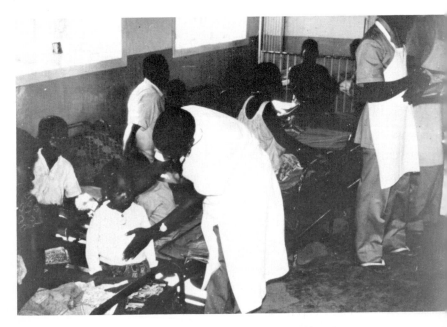

PLATE 3.–Nurse in Kibunzi hospital examining child while mother looks on.

PLATE 4.–Family therapy managers cooking patients' meals outside of ward. Institut Médicale Evangelique (IME), Kimpese, Lower Zaire.

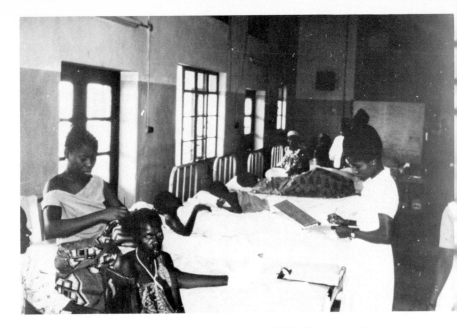

PLATE 5.–Nurse making rounds of orthopedic ward at IME-Kimpese, seeing cases resulting from auto accidents, palm-tree falls, and the like. Note coiffure of patient's acquaintance being done in ward while patient visits.

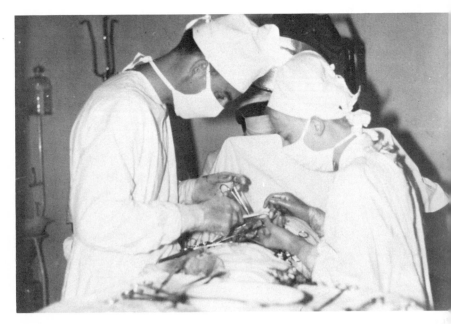

PLATE 6.–Dr. Arkinstall, M.D., wife Karen, R.N., and Zairian anaesthetist performing major sugery, IME-Kimpese.

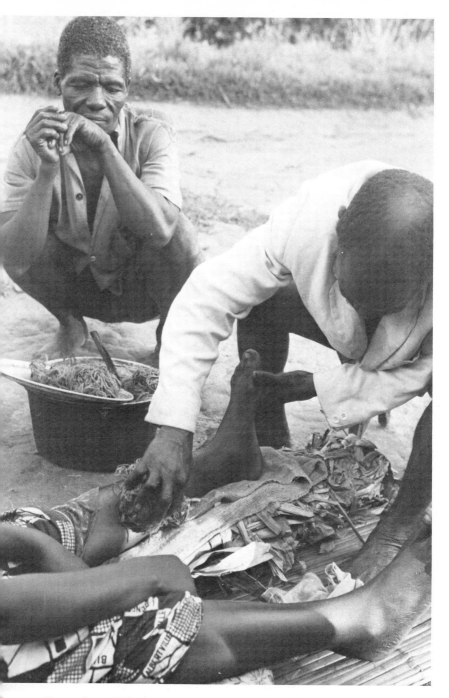

PLATE 7.–*Nganga lunga* Makunzu Zablon of Kinganga massages muscles around fracture with hot fibrous substance, a manual therapy he uses daily on fractures to keep muscles from atrophying. His apprentice, Davidi, observes.

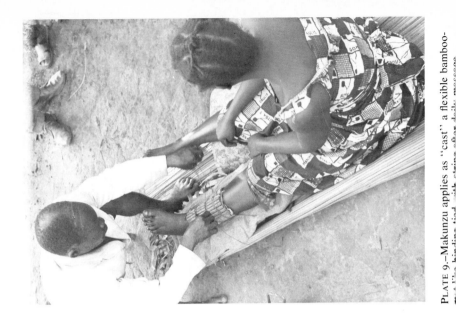

PLATE 9.–Makunzu applies as "cast" a flexible bamboo-mat-like binding tied with string after daily massage.

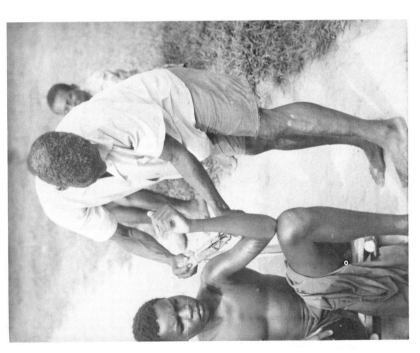

PLATE 8.–Apprentice Davidi asperges an oily herbal ointment

PLATE 10.–Mama Mankombo of Mbembe cuts a slit in her well-used finger cactus tree (see Appendix B, plant 124) to obtain white sap needed in her treatment for congestive swelling.

PLATE 11.–*Nganga* Tambwe (in coat and tie) purchases medicinal and magical ingredients from a Hausa merchant in big market of Kinshasa.

PLATE 13.—*Nganga nkisi* Nzoamambu applies ointment to lower back of client where heated machete (in fire) will be applied to treat "a kink in the back."

PLATE 12.—A traditionally trained herbalist, having accommodated to modern trappings, stands behind his vials and bottles of herbal medicines, preparing an injection for his client.

PLATE 14.–*N ganga mbuki* Madeko massages a disturbed patient over her whole body and head with an herbal bath (she also drinks a glass of the liquid). Full treatment requires about half an hour. Note therapy managing kin watching.

PLATE 15.–*N ganga nkisi* Bayindula applies cupping horn treatment to sufferer's arms and legs after having cut small incisions in skin. Herbal compact is then rubbed into wounds.

PLATE 16.–Bayindula, as *nganga nkisi*, has an eclectic set of acts and treatments including cupping horn, herbal massage, and a variety of ceremonials. Here he sings the daily Mass of the Africanized Croix Koma movement with clients and their kinsmen.

PLATE 17.–Mama Marie Kukunda, *ngunza*, conducts intraclan reunion. Sufferer is seated directly before her while members of maternal clan (the therapy managers who have accompanied sufferer) observe. Several other groups attend, waiting their turn.

PLATE 18.–Interclan reunion, with many hired speakers and onlookers, working out the denouement of a sickness in their midst. A prophet earlier identified several issues. Here formal gift exchanges, confessions, and curse revocations are being performed. Sufferer is within circle at right.

PLATE 19.–A severe case of psychosis is constrained in main thoroughfare of village. The method permits a community to restrain the psychotic, without removing him from its midst. Sufferer in this case was said, rather typically, to have gone to the city and experimented with magic too powerful for him. The result was that he went mad, *laukidi*.

PLATE 20.–This rite of the EJCSK-Kimbanguist Church at Nkamba-Jerusalem shows hundreds of pilgrims lining up for the blessing—by laying on of a hand—from one of the remaining four apostles of the original twelve chosen in 1921 by the prophet Kimbangu.

PLATE 21.–The rite of "Weighing the Holy Spirit" in an outdoor service of the Church of the Holy Spirit. This rite is taken over from traditional *dumuna* jumping blessings. Here it has become a spiritual evaluation as weigher grasps hand of weighee (jumper) sending him into ecstatic leaps three times because of "shock" of direct exposure to powerful spirit. If either the weigher or weighee fails to extend a hand and connect, the latter must confess (see left).

PLATE 22.–"The Healing" in Church of the Holy Spirit.

PLATE 24.–Fly whisk (*mfunka*) inherited by Nzoamambu from grandmother. Note characteristic "*Nsundi*" features in anthropomorphic statue. An *mfunka* commonly denoted chiefly authority and was used in certain healing rites to sprinkle holy water.

PLATE 23.–Nzoamambu, *nganga nkisi*, in forest, detaching bark of *nkuki* tree (see Appendix B, plant 130) for treatment of swollen stomach resulting from bad food or poisoning.

have picked up a talisman in Brazzaville which, when improperly used, overpowered her. Most of the clansmen believed the major problem was that her suitor had failed thus far to pay the bride money to her paternal clan and that resentment and malice instead of blessing measured the paternal relationship with Lwezi.

Indeed, in the weeks that had elapsed since the visit to the *nganga*, nothing had been heard from the suitor in Congo Brazzaville. This silence bred many rumors about what he might be up to: he had abandoned the relationship entirely; he was looking for a new and better job; he would arrive shortly to work things out. Lwezi's father refused to grant his blessing without the payment. She had cost him a fair sum through school tuition. The brothers, sensing their father's dilemma, made the unorthodox offer of paying the bride price and *lusansu* upbringing fee to their father on Lwezi's suitor's behalf, thereby compelling him to extend her the blessing. But the pastors on both sides rejected this, noting that it would set Lwezi free, with a blessing, to become a public woman. With the case stalemated, a delegation of Lwezi's paternal and maternal kin walked 20 kilometers to Prophet Marie Kukunda one Sunday in the rain to seek her counsel and divination.

Mama Marie, as she is locally known, had been hearing a series of minor cases earlier in the morning in her consulting "chapel" outside her house on a knoll away from the other houses in the village. Clients would enter the chapel and take a seat and listen to the case under consideration while waiting for their turn. When Lwezi's group arrived, she was finishing her last case and invited them in. She was well aware of this case and the whole clan with its many problems (see Chapter 8). Silwa, Lwezi's clan headman, knelt before Mama Marie and told her how the young woman had suffered greatly. After hearing Silwa, she motioned Lwezi and her mother, Nkwelo, to come forward, and the following divination ensued.

Mama Marie: Why are you here? (To Lwezi directly) Where does it hurt?
Lwezi: I'm in pain. I have come to ask forgiveness.
M.M.: Do you have many dreams?
L.: Many.

M.M. (after long searching pause, eyes closed): This is a very difficult case. (To Nkwelo) What about the marriage of this girl? How do things stand now?

Nkwelo: She left to go to Congo Brazzaville to her mother's brother who lives there. Her child stayed behind. I do not know whether she went to get soap or clothes or something like that from a suitor, or what. I was against her going to live with the man.

M.M. (to Nkwelo): Why did her father not send her with his paternal blessing? (Long silence ensues.)(To Lwezi directly) You think that God plays around with cases like yours? Your father isn't happy at all! He doesn't particularly want to make you suffer, but it's the law of the land that a girl must receive her father's blessing before going off to be married. What do you say about this?

Kula (Lwezi's brother): Let her get married! Her mother's brother in Congo Brazzaville was in charge, so there's no reason why it shouldn't work out!

M.M.: Well, how can this girl regain her health? (To Lwezi) Do you want to return to your man?

L. (quietly, in a daze): If you, my fathers want me to be married to him, alright. If not, I'll stay here.

M.M.: It would be a good thing to go through with the marriage [*kwela longo*, payment of bride price, the ceremony]. Your father who bore you, Lwezi, he deserves it. If you want to marry, your man will have to come here from Congo Brazzaville. Short of this, there will only be talk and more talk by the people about you.

L.: I don't want any great difficulty erupting on my behalf. I don't want to give my elders any trouble. My husband does want me, however.

M.M. (still sounding out various individuals to get a picture of the whole): Silwa, come here. What have you to say about the payment of the bride price and the marriage?

Silwa: According to the letter the suitor sent her father, he wants to go through with it. We, the mother's brothers, don't want to stand in the way. But she, Lwezi, has to act with her man, and he with her.

M.M.: But before the marriage it would be very advisable for the paternal family to give their child their blessing [*lusakumunu*].

S.: Let her marry! That's the important thing! (Rises and pretends to walk out in a huff. He feels the prophet is overdoing the blessing.)

M.M.: Why can't Lwezi be married in Congo Brazzaville then?

S.: We can't destroy this marriage, and we don't want to, but the ceremony has to take place here, either in the mother's brother's village or that of the father.

M.M.: (turning to Lwezi's father): And you Bola? How do you feel?

Bola: If the man already has other women in his house, I don't believe that he really wants to marry again. If he didn't already have other wives, I would agree to Lwezi's going to Congo Brazzaville. The others in the paternal clan, as matters now stand, might want to accept the money of this marriage, but as for me, never! Furthermore, the husband would be able to come here if he could find work. I thought the marriage would be in Congo Brazzaville. Perhaps he isn't coming to marry here because he is out of work, and therefore has no money. Last I heard he was at the coast in Pointe Noire looking for a job.

M.M.: Because your daughter was sick when she was in his house the first time, and again sick in your house later, this meant she was not happy.

B.: What are we fathers to do? We can't be expected to remain forever loving if we get no recompense for the child we have raised.

Having questioned and heard out first the maternal kin and then the paternal kin, Mama Marie then explored the relationship between Lwezi's parents, the focus of antagonism and ambivalence between the two clans. It is at this point where she then applied pressure of reconciliation.

M.M. (to Nkwelo): Come forward. What kind of conflict do you have in your house?

N.: Talk and more talk.

M.M.: You know that in the household the woman ought to be in a position of subordination before her husband, don't you?

N.: I've had stomach trouble, this is part of my problem.

B. (interjecting): My wife is a big gossip! If this kind of talking and bickering keeps up as it has, we'd be better off getting a divorce to end our own marriage.

M.M. (to both): Can you read? Do you know the story of creation. How God created woman from the rib of the man? Do you know what that meant? God made woman for a purpose. Man is first in his house, because woman is created from him. You should not have allowed talking and arguing and bickering to enter your home. The way to resolve Lwezi's problem is for both her maternal side [*bangudi*] and her paternal side [*mase*] to give her their blessing.

B.: I've been in great anguish [*mpasi mu ntima*, heart pain] over Lwezi's sickness. I poured out my heart in concern for her [*futa ntima, suka ntima*]. If she didn't die from her illness, it's because I prayed so ardently for her.

A Maternal Brother: True, the paternal side ought to receive a recompense for Lwezi's upbringing. But they ought also take what is offered them!

B.: No, I can't accept it.

M.M.: Bola, you and your wife must reconcile, and ask forgiveness of one another for the pain you have caused each other and your children.

N.: Satan entered my heart and created these problems for me. (Turning toward Bola with eyes downcast away from him, and on knees, she says) I ask your forgiveness for all the turmoil I have caused. (At the urging of surrounding persons, the two shake hands coldly.)

M.M. (to Bola who is stalling): Alright, Bola, are you going to ask forgiveness of your wife? You have brought all kinds of bad spirits into your life, and your wife is troubled. It's no wonder at all that your children aren't in good health, with all the gossiping and talking in your house.

B. (preparing to ask forgiveness of his wife): My strength is failing and I no longer have the energy to make my wife happy like I could when I was a young man. I cannot work like I could and I cannot buy her cloth and the things I should. I ask forgiveness of her now.

M.M. (to those surrounding the couple, as if in support of their mutual gestures): Are we going to forgive them?

Surrounding Group (loudly, in unison): Yes! (Mama Marie rises and lays hands on Bola and Nkwelo, prays briefly that God may bless them, and touches them with hands front and back, shoulder and shoulder.)

K. (after a pause of general relief by everyone): But what about Lwezi's marriage?

M.M.: As I said, the way has been shown. The paternal and maternal sides must both give their blessing to her. Then she should go to her husband if she wants to.

L.: (before prophet on her knees): I have suffered enormously. Sometimes I have great bitterness in my heart toward my parents. Father caused mother much suffering. And mother accused me of having used charms and learned magic from my husband. When I returned home to the village I wasn't happy there either. (She prepares to ask forgiveness of her mother.)

K. (interjecting): Before she asks forgiveness I have something to say. Since mother has mentioned charms [*minkisi*] and magic [*muyeke*] as possible causes for this illness of Lwezi's, shouldn't we look into that too? There are three possible causes, as I see it: she may have "walked on" a charm or medicine planted by the jealous cowives; she may have learned some magic from her husband and gotten overcome by it; or, it is the marriage problem and the absence of payments that are causing her illness.

M.M.: Nonsense! There are neither charms nor magic in this affair. If there were, she would have gone mad long ago, which she obviously has not. (Brushing off Kula's suggestions as out of place, she gestures to Lwezi to ask forgiveness of her mother.)

L. (to mother): Mother, in the name of the Father, Son, and Holy Ghost I ask for your forgiveness.

N. (to daughter): Daughter, in the name of the Father, Son, and Holy Ghost, I ask for your forgiveness. (Mama Marie lays foot on Lwezi's feet, and prays that she be cured.)

After this séance, which all considered to have been very helpful, Lwezi returned to her maternal village. Tension between her and her parents had appreciably lessened, but the fundamental source of the problem, that is the bride payment and the paternal blessing, had not been eliminated. Within a few weeks her pains set in anew. Her maternal family, principally a pastor brother and a few other siblings, took charge of her crisis. Having already consulted *nganga* Bayindula and the investigative prophet-seer Mama Marie, they decided to take Lwezi to Luamba Zablon, a prophet whose treatment (described in Chapter 6) consisted of soothing noninvestigative rituals such as baths, prayers, laying on of hands, anointment with scented oil, and counsel. But midway through the treatment her pains increased sharply. Against the wishes of the prophet, her family removed her by ambulance to the dispensary where she had been several months earlier. Two independent examinations by nurses in the dispensary established, similarly, that she complained of arm and leg pain, back pain, "heart pain," weakness and difficulty rising and walking, accompanied by fever. Laboratory examination of blood, urine, and stool were negative. The diagnosis by the nurse was that Lwezi had recurring joint-related rheumatism (*rheumatisme articulaire*). She was treated with a generous variety of medications, including 100 mg each of dolatine and gardinal (strong analgesics) by injection on arrival; intramuscular penicillin, two injections per day for a week; vitamins for a month; a five-day cure of nivaquine; timavon (a muscle relaxant); and finally, 50 mg phenergan (a sedative and antiallergic compound) twice for an itch.

After an entire month of dispensary care she had not improved appreciably. Her family then removed her to the large hospital at the IME-Kimpese 200 kilometers away. One brother expressed confidence that a "cardiogram" at IME would discover the source of Lwezi's true problem. A sister thought she should get together with an older sister in Kinshasa. This younger sister and an older brother managed her affairs at this time.

When Lwezi arrived at Kimpese by vehicle she had a high fever of 39° C. She was weak and apparently could not walk, necessitating her transport from the girl students' camp where she briefly stayed with a sister into the medical ward by stretcher. She complained of body pain and weakness, but she was now afebrile. She stated that her illness had begun in October of the previous year (1968) with arm and leg weakness and occasional loss of consciousness. Soon after admission she was examined by two American missionary doctors who did not find any abnormal physical signs. Her blood tests were negative; a nonspecific diagnosis of "polyarthritis" was made.

During the course of the ten-day hospitalization, an African nurse took the initiative to hold a conversation with Lwezi because he suspected she might be involved in some social problems. The typical attitude he had been taught to use in relating to patients was that they must forget about the past and think of the future, for with God's help one would become well. A short-term doctor had told him several months earlier that other dimensions of illness were important. He had asked Lwezi whether she were married, and she had replied in the affirmative. Many of the problems in this "marriage" that have emerged in the above account were also told to the nurse. He concluded that she would not get well with medicine alone but would require a solution to her marital problem. He told her directly, then, that there were two ways she could leave her hospital sickbed: "You can die and leave as a corpse, or you can get better and leave." She soon began to improve, he noted, and when she left she could walk without pain. She was diagnosed as having had "*rheumatisme articulaire*" and signed out by the doctor as having had "muscular rheumatism, cured."

The epilogue to Lwezi's story is as sad and complicated as the story itself. A query in 1973, four years after the original study, revealed that she had continued residing with a brother in Kimpese, refusing to return to the village because of all the problems. Eventually her "husband" from Congo Brazzaville had made the bride payment to her father and maternal uncles, and Bola had extended his blessing to her. But she did not join her husband. Rather, she moved to Kinshasa to stay with a sister.

CHAPTER EIGHT

The Clan as Patient

The sufferer is but a symptom of his family's sickness
DR. DÉNIS BAZINGA

This case takes us beyond the individualistic conception of illness and therapy to an instance in which a corporate group was seen as pathological and therefore in need of therapy. Mbumba, Mavungu, and Mukala, fellow clansmen of Lwezi (see Chapter 7), had been chronically ill with different apparent afflictions said to have been caused by one and the same underlying clan problem. Neighbors had gossiped about it, and collective action was due. The peaceful Manianga countryside dotted with neat red brick and thatched roof settlements, and people going to their fields to work and to market to trade or on errands and affairs to neighboring kinsmen, belied the latent tension that troubled this clan and surfaced from time to time. When we researched this issue, the structural dimension of illness and therapy engulfed the entire clan, the local church organization within that clan, a non-kin prophet community, and connections with local government.

Mukala had suffered persistent pains in his back, neck, and head. Mavungu complained of chronic stomachache for which routine intestinal parasite medicine had been of little help. Mbumba, whose case offers an individual perspective to this tangled collective affliction, dated his illness precisely to February 1953 when he was first attacked with asthma and coughing while assisting in the construction of the church building at a nearby mission.

Mbumba had been born in 1923, the youngest child of his family. Mavungu was his older brother. The two were the only males of the junior lineage of the clan (see Figure 8). They received sufficient formal education to learn to read and write following

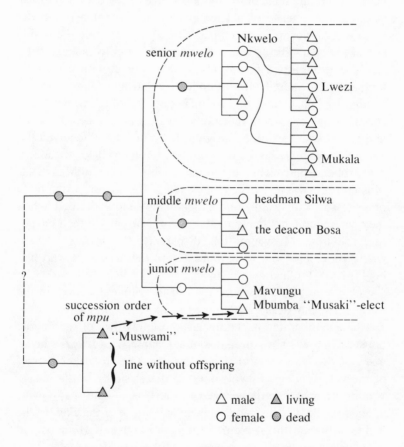

FIGURE 8. Partial genealogy showing names and relationships within matriclan of Mbumba's case, and Lwezi's case. Broken line indicates deceased clansmen.

which Mavungu became a cultivator and basket and mat weaver, while Mbumba, also a cultivator, learned carpentry as an auxiliary trade. Both men had settled in the matrilineal village, married, and raised large families. Mbumba's otherwise unspectacular career was marked by an important early distinction. In his youth he had been named to inherit the clan's ritual chiefship, the *mpu*, from his uncle Muswami. This ritual office appears to have passed from one male in the junior lineage of the clan to another in the junior lineage of a later generation, complementing the office of clan headman which passed frequently within the senior line of the clan. The *mfumu mpu*'s function was to safeguard the clan's spiritual interests and to maintain contact with the ancestors, a task he shared with the collective patrifilial children (*bana bambuta*). This clan's *mpu* insignia consisted of a bracelet and a cup, although elsewhere the additional symbol of ancestral bones in a basket was part of the insignia. If Mbumba had received the full office of *mpu*, his name would have changed to Musaki, a name scheme placing him in the succession of a line of Muswami, Musaki, Muswami, Musaki, and so on. However, Mbumba's predecessor, Muswami, and other clan leaders decided when they embraced Chrstianity to abandon this aspect of their corporate tradition. Muswami thus dispatched the insignia "there where they belonged, to be buried with the ancestors who had held them." He had died in 1957.

At the time of the abandonment of the ritual chiefship, in the thirties, the clan designated to the role of headman, an able slave. But he was liberated in the forties and left. Silwa of the middle house, whom we have already met in Chapter 7 as Lwezi's headman, succeeded to the office, and also became government chief of the village (*duki*). Silwa's only brother residing in the village was Bosa, deacon in the village church. It is evident that power, at least nominally, resided in this middle house of the clan, in the hands of two brothers. Neither the junior house of Mbumba and Mavungu nor the senior house of Mukala held any offices of authority. Many of the adult males of the senior line had received formal education in local grade and secondary schools and had taken jobs in education, church, government, army, or industry and had moved away. Several had sent money back to build large houses in the village, houses which either stood half completed and empty or housed other kinsmen. Mukala had the largest house in the village and spent his vacations there, although he had been absent much of the time as teacher and, since independence, as local communal chief, a demanding full-time task. An overall picture of this clan at the time of our research was, then, that its younger, better educated members had left to hold modern jobs, while clan leadership offices had gravitated to minimally educated elders left behind. The illusion of traditional authority concentrated in the middle line did not correspond to the traditional model of authority distributed over the several offices of headman, *mpu*-holder, men's hut chief, and others, held by individuals in several clan houses or lineages.

All this relates directly to Mbumba's quest for therapy of his chronic asthma. He sought treatment first at the Sundi-Lutete dispensary, but without results. He went from there to the nearby Catholic hospital at Mangembo, but with no improvement. He went to Kibunzi, the large Protestant hospital, but received no satisfaction there either. An X-ray taken at the state hospital in Thysville (Ngungu) revealed nothing. In fact, he had noted, these centers were unable to establish the real nature of his illness. He continued to suffer year after year with episodes of coughing and wheezing.

His quest took him eventually to Kinsumbu-Mutadi, a village situated in the hills near the Congo Brazzaville border, where prophet Muzandu Jacques lived. Muzandu had been a catechist for the Swedish mission, but when he became an active participant in the 1921/22 prophet movement, he was arrested and deported and allowed to return only in 1959. Upon his return he had opened a spiritual retreat center similar to that of Luamba Zablon and Bayindula, where he would receive as many as fifty pilgrims at a time seeking help. One pilgrim had called the cluster of dormitory huts, the prophet's compound, and the chapel "a grand city of the sick."

Muzandu ordered Mbumba to drink blessed holy water every time he coughed, and also counselled him about his other problems. As a consequence, Mbumba could state that he had been cured and had discovered the true meaning of his illness.

When, in about 1965, Mbumba returned to his home he had very explicit explanations of what had caused his illness, how he might remain well, and what the consequences were for him. In a week-night church service in the village he shared his insights with his fellow clansmen. The deaconness asked him to lead the singing and read the scripture and to sit on the platform with her. Following the preliminaries of the service, he told the congregation of the disease that, as they all now knew, had troubled him for so long. The quest for health in the hospitals had been in vain. Then prophet Muzandu had helped him. He had interpreted his dream:

> I heard the booming of the large *nkonko* slit drum announcing worship. I took my Bible and songbook and went to the church. When I got there I noticed I was late, for the singing had begun and the door had been closed. I wanted to enter, but on trying the door I found it locked, to my dismay.

Prophet Muzandu had interpreted this dream to mean that he had been refusing the call to become deacon, and this was the cause of his long illness. Before the small clan-dominated congregation in his village he announced his submission to the call and his desire to be their deacon.

The congregation responded enthusiastically, but the magnitude of the decision required a week's deliberation. Bosa, the first and only deacon, was ineffective in his job, and never led services. He suffered from epilepsy (*nzieta*) and was openly called a drunkard by the deaconness. The congregation had tried to replace him, but none of the designates had accepted the draft. Thus Mbumba's declaration was accepted with general acclaim. One week later an outside catechist came to help the congregation ratify his call. The catechist announced that Mbumba had stated his intentions and that it was now up to them to decide. Headman Silwa's wife spoke up ceremoniously, "God has chosen him, who are we to object?" Silwa seconded with, "If God has chosen him, we cannot disagree!" Without further discussion the catechist tapped her stick on the table and asked if all were in accord. *"Ingeta"* ("We are!"). One man added, *"tutondele"* ("Thank God"). As the gas pressure lamp hissed, the drummer set out the tempo for the song. In rapid Manianga musical style that frequently led to ecstatic outbursts the small congregation achieved at least temporary unity "in the spirit," granting their son the right "to be healed" and to become deacon.

Mbumba was consecrated with other new deacons at an annual church conference before several thousand persons. It was assumed by church administrators and the local congregation that he would replace Bosa as deacon. However, to their surprise, he returned to Mutadi with his wife and children to reside with the prophet, where he gradually took over the functions of deacon for the prophet's nightly worship services, leading the singing, reading scripture, and "officiating." He did not heal; that remained the prophet's prerogative.

Four years later, in 1969, Mbumba noted with confidence that his asthma had subsided markedly since his permanent residence with Muzandu. It had not completely disappeared, but he could live with it now. He had ceased eating rice, pepper, and bananas and had decided to return to his home village 30 kilometers away only to plant and harvest his fields and to attend urgent family matters. His house remained empty most of the time. When asked to explain this apparent breach with the understanding that he was to be deacon at his home village, he replied that "Bosa could still take care of things." "My spirit," he added, "tells me to stay here and to keep these rules; I am healthier living with the prophet."

It became apparent that his conception of his illness had shifted away from a specific personal cause such as resisting the deaconship to a more general cause such as residing too long in the home village. The cure, correspondingly, had shifted from personal acceptance of the deaconship to the general circumstance of residing with the prophet. Asthma and holy water receded, even in his thinking, into the background as symptoms of these more inclusive causes.

This expanded diagnosis of his affliction reflected the extensive counsel he and his fellow clansmen had received from prophet-seer Mama Marie. She had suggested that his asthma, along with his brother Mavungu's stomachache and his cousin Mukala's head-, neck-, and backache, had been willed by the clan's senior males and females (*bambuta ye bamama*). "All were actually one and the same affliction," although not one of these juniors had sought or deserved. The afflictions differed from the legitimate chastisement a clan headman might exercise upon an errant clan member through physical, social, or even mystical means. They were different, too, from the type of illness Lwezi, whom Mbumba identified as a prostitute, had brought upon herself by her own actions. The only common ground between the three types was their slow response to medical treatment.

The exact mechanism of causation in the three illnesses which were one remained shrouded in obscurity in Mbumba's mind, as his designation of the neologism "*mystères*" suggested. Pressed to offer a KiKongo equivalent, a flood of terms came forth: *mabanza mambi, nkadulu a mbi, kimfunya*. The first two mean evil thoughts and evil being, both euphemisms for witchcraft. The last term, though often used today in the same sense, harks back to a description of technical magical manipulations with wedges driven into wooden statues and spells uttered over intricate medicinal bundles called *mfunya*. There was no evidence for actual ritual revenge here, but where jealousies and uneven access to power, knowledge, and status existed, a fertile mind could easily create a concrete cause.

The events accompanying Mukala's illness were different from those in Mbumba's case, but in the way they were explained we shall see that they were held to have a deeper affinity with them. Mukala's diffuse pains in the back, neck, and head began to appear, in episodic manner, as he began his second five-year term as chief of a rural Manianga commune in 1965. His rule, by popular standards, had been successful and he had avoided scandal. But, as other communal chiefs, he was heavily burdened with a multitude of administrative tasks ranging from keeping vital statistics of his 15,000 constitutents up to date, maintaining public health and order in thirty villages and numerous religious, commercial, and educational posts, to serving as ex officio chief judge of the communal court which received a steady stream of civil cases. The staff of clerks, policemen, and officers needed to be coordinated in terms of central government guidelines, resulting in an endless stream of instructions, requests for reports, and memos to read, in keeping with the Belgian colonial norms of bureaucracy still very much in effect. Mukala had been philosophical about his chiefly role, and, as an educator, he had even written about power, witchcraft, and the judicial process in his land. But the sheer weight of work and the tensions of decision making, the deaf ear to reforms he proposed, and; most important, the recurring freeze on his salary, caused him much anguish. He would have resigned after his first term, but his constituency wanted him, and his council backed him, so he consented to a second term of five years.

When his headaches developed, he consulted both Western and African therapists, taking almost full decision-making responsibility upon himself. His main sources of care were Mama Marie Kukunda and Dénis Bazinga, a French-trained Kongo psychiatrist in Kinshasa in charge, at the time, of the Neuro-Psychiatric Institute. Dr. Bazinga had provided him with sedatives and sleeping pills for symptomatic relief, and eventually arranged a year's "sick leave" for him while a substitute took charge of his office. But, according to Mukala, the sedatives and sleeping pills did not prove effective; every time he thought of his job and the outside world his headaches and neckaches returned. Mama Marie approached his illness through an analysis of events in which his personal or family life had intersected with his professional life, leaving unresolved tensions. His affliction had originated in early 1967, she suggested, when he had "brushed against, or stepped on, a malevolent fetish, planted by a vengeful person out to destroy him." The agressor was identified by her as a member of a neighboring clan with land holdings adjacent to those of his own clan. During a boundary inspection by the communal court judges, in a land suit between his own clan and the agressor's clan, Mukala, acting as chief, had exchanged harsh words with the defendant for trespassing the boundary in planting his fields.

Mukala had tried to locate the buried fetish, but the brush had been too thick, and a year had already elapsed. Still, by his own admission, the exact definition of the event and the identification of an aggressor that Mama Marie had offered had helped him greatly to put his illness into perspective. It had given him a better understanding of how his private exchanges with persons, his clan relations, and his life as chief must not become confounded. Mama Marie had told him that sedatives and sleeping pills would do him no good, but that prayer and rest might. Indeed, he noted that his pains disappeared when he was in the village or in his forest garden, contemplatively cultivating. But any association with the outside world, his job, or even the pills, brought the pains back.

The illnesses of the three men consumed a great deal of time and energy in the clan and it was decided collective action must be taken. A general clan meeting was convened late in 1967 under the supervision of prophet Muzandu, his sister, and Mama Marie. The meeting opened in the church with many clan members present and an even greater number of onlookers, peering through the open church windows, to witness the chief's clan seeking to resolve its problems. Soon the meeting withdrew to the chief's large house, for embarrassing and private dimensions had been raised. The prophets, with Mama Marie taking the initiative, began to examine each member, beginning with headman Silwa. They asked him if he was a good family head, able to guard (*keba, sika*) the clan adequately. A headman is supposed to defend his clan in a crisis, but even more, he is supposed to guard against the occurrence of crises. The others said Silwa tried hard, but that he was ineffective. He had been responsible for the loss of several land cases in court, and he had permitted his sisters' daughters, for example, Lwezi, to marry into distant clans making it impossible to control them or their offspring, the future life of the clan. A sister in each of the three clan lines was in some kind of marriage trouble.

Mama Marie tried to establish lines of reconciliation between Silwa and his clan sisters over their daughters' marriage problems. Silwa and his sisters admitted error and forgave one another.

The next step of ritual reunification, again presided over by Mama Marie, consisted of all clansmen present asking forgiveness of the three suffering middle-aged men who should have been able to work and support the clan, yet who could not. Mbumba, Mavungu, and Mukala knelt down and their kinsmen filed by them, each in turn asking forgiveness of them individually. When the elderly mother of Mbumba and Mavungu, sole survivor of her generation, came to her sons, the prophets obliged her to repeat her plea three times, to "really and sincerely open her heart" to them. Confessions continued until all present had expressed their deepest concerns before the afflicted. Yet there came a point of resistance. The older clansmen, in particular headman Silwa and his brother, deacon Bosa, categorically refused to take the oath which Muzandu's sister urged them to make:

> By God on earth,
> By God on heaven,
> If I have engaged in witchcraft,
> May I be struck dead!

This oath is never taken voluntarily, for obvious reasons, except under extreme compulsion from a panel of judges or *nganga* to vindicate one's honor. In this instance it would have been utterly humiliating to Silwa and Bosa to take the oath, not to speak of it being dangerous for them. Rather, they countered that it was well and good to ask for confession of the afflicted, but they were not entirely innocent either. As an example, Bosa urged Mama Marie to resolve the problem of "the shirt" with Mukala. At first Mukala could think of no shirt affair. But as Bosa spoke, he recalled that Bosa had requested a shirt of him shortly after he became government chief. He had forgotten the matter long ago, although Bosa had not. Bosa envied those who could afford more luxuries than he. His house roof was of thatch and leaked, whereas Mukala's house was covered with metal and was weatherproof. In fact, it had been noted that all the metal-covered houses in the village belonged to the senior lineage! Mama Marie also raised the "affair of the curved ditch" which she had seen in the spirit, and which she said caused considerable misunderstanding in the clan. At first no one knew what she was talking about. Then an older woman mentioned that, indeed, a clan brother had traced the boundary in a curved manner restricting her holding for the year. A final detail emerged: the oldest grandmother in the village, a former slave who had stayed when her group had been ransomed, was taken aside by the prophets. They then reprimanded the clan for mistreating her in her dependence on them for land. "Love this sister," they admonished the group, "and let her work her fields in peace till death." This was intended especially for the other women with whom she shared land.

With that the meeting ended. At no point was the specific symptomatic illness of the three men mentioned. But on their behalf petty grievances between other clansmen were exposed and clarified to eliminate the diffuse common cause of affliction. This type of meeting is regarded as quite explosive, and it is usually not held without the guidance of ritual specialists. But it is a measure of the effectiveness of the meeting that when a year later other issues arose, the clan could hold another meeting without the experts. Again the clansmen asked forgiveness of the three sufferers, and the sufferers of the other clansmen.

Several years later the personal lives of Mbumba, Mavungu, and Mukala had become more stable. Mbumba resided with prophet Muzandu and served as his deacon; Mavungu remained at home, taking on an occasional court case for his lineage; Mukala retired from communal chiefship to the village and became increasingly involved in clan affairs and gardening. The inverse symmetry of Mbumba's and Mukala's cures is noteworthy in the light of their both being "part of the clan illness." Mbumba was cured by moving away with clan consent; Mukala was cured by moving back with clan acceptance.

Mbumba's asthma attack had been linked in his mind to the church. His dream, interpreted by the prophet as a call to serve the church, set the stage for his cure through becoming deacon. He was accepted as deacon by his own clan congregation and "given permission to be healed." In effect, they blessed his separation from them, and his allegiance to another symbolic community. The similarities with the ritual *mpu* chiefship are striking. In the past, the clan headman tended to come from the senior house or lineage. As a man of the junior house, Mbumba had almost no chance of asserting legitimate authority, except in breaking away from the clan to found another settlement. But he had no following. Had the *mpu*-ship been available for him in adult life, he would have fulfilled traditional structural expectations in an authority role complementary to the headman in the senior line. His calling to deacon replicated this same situation, several generations later, in a Christian idiom. For similar reasons, in other clans, the junior line becomes involved in prophet communities in Kongo society.

Mukala's return to the clan village was due more to his disparagement with public office, and exhaustion, than a clear call to assert himself in clan leadership. And yet he was structurally situated in the senior house of the clan to be a prime candidate for such a role. He understood clan and communal politics. In the end, he believed Mama Marie's analysis of the illness "caused by the clan": an alienation of grown men in the junior and senior lineages from authority held by the middle line, exacerbated by weak leadership and the tensions of modern life. Mama Marie saw that clan land politics did not mix well with higher governmental authority. Given Mukala's predilection to withdraw from power in the later years of his term as chief, she encouraged him to either cut his clan ties completely—a move which historic Kongo chiefly inauguration ritualized by the chief's murder of a kinsman—or reassert his hand in his own clan. Mbumba's case was the exact inverse. Given his structural alienation from clan authority, his withdrawal from the clan with their consent permitted him fuller life with the prophet—a move very similar to historic Kongo initiations to healing orders such as *mpu*, Lemba, and the rest.

PART III

THE LOGIC OF
THERAPEUTIC SYSTEMS

An Introductory Note

We turn now from particular cases in the quest for therapy to an interpretation of the quest. The multiepisodic character of these cases clearly indicates the need to follow the different lines of choice taken by decision-makers. Thus we can elucidate the logic of the therapy process. In tracing this logic we must be attentive to the contrast between statistically frequent actions and idealized norms. In Lower Zaire, most individuals with a common or simple problem such as a cold, fever, malaria, or accidental wound go forthwith to the nearest dispensary. But they may act less assuredly when they have suffered a more serious or chronic infliction attributed to nonnatural causes. People say, for example, that illness caused by an incestuous union between two sections of the same clan can best be alleviated by sacrificing a pig or goat in a ritual feast. Though incest is frequently considered to be a possible cause of illness, the performance of such a sacrifice is a major undertaking that no group under our observation ever performed. Indeed, it was recommended only once by a specialist in all cases we knew of. The logic of such choices must relate problem identifications to therapy techniques and specialists' unique roles. Only then do alignments of action and corresponding verbal categories become intelligible.

To analyze the coherent character of the medical system, we first examine how therapy managing groups arrive at their choices. We have tried to think our way into the decision-making process, and thus to formulate alternative therapeutic choices available within it. Diagnoses by the therapy managers and counselling experts rest partially on a culturally shared "anatomy" that makes the heart a focus of person, society, and natural world. A fairly standardized hierarchy of resort, based on this anatomy, propels the therapeutic response into one or another of several complementary therapeutic courses. The resulting "therapeutic systems" are complementary in the course of therapy in a single case, but mutually exclusive in their cultural logic.

References in parentheses are to chapter and episode as given in Appendix A. For example (3.6) refers to Luzayadio's case in Chapter 3, the January 26, 1969, episode (episode 6).

CHAPTER NINE

The Jural Status of Therapy
in Kongo Society

The Conveyance of Rights in
Litigation, Ceremony, and Therapy

Therapy as a social process in Kongo society compares with judicial and ceremonial institutions. All three are predicated upon an awareness of order and the realization that something has happened to create a situation at odds with what ought to be. If the problem is judicial, remedial action takes the form of litigation by a court of judges (*nzonzi*, from *zonza*, "to debate;" or *mpovi*, from *vova*, "to speak") who debate the issue (*vova nsamu, bula nsamu*) or hash out and resolve a dispute (*zenga nsamu*, from *zenga*, "to cut," "slice"). If the problem is ceremonial, remedial action takes the form of purification by a ritual expert (*sukula*, "to wash"; *vedisa*, "to cleanse") or initiation (*mpandulu*, from *handa*) to an *nkisi* or consecrated role in the context of a public ceremony (*nkembo*). If the problem is medical (*kimbevo*), remedial action takes the form of therapy (*buka*, "to treat"; *nyakisa*, "to heal," "raise") arranged and sometimes created by the therapy managing group. In each instance the protagonist's decision-making rights are transferred to second and third parties such as kinsmen and experts.

This chapter focuses on the conveyance of rights in the therapy managing group, and the extent to which it resembles the process in courts and cults. The therapy managing group may assume courtlike functions to resolve a conflict within the kinship community thought to cause the sufferer's affliction. Or, the therapy managing group may transfer its authority to a cult hierarchy or ritual expert. Finally, the therapy managing group may "release" the sufferer to plan his own affairs independently.

The process of conveying rights of therapeutic decision-making has been identified by a MuKongo writer in the following terms: "When an illness occurs, the person who is jurally responsible for the sufferer [muntu vwidi mbevo] quickly consults a doctor. If and when the consulting doctor has made his diagnosis, it is again this jurally responsible person who sends for the appropriate treating doctor."[1] The term vwidi (from vwa, "to have or possess") denotes the guardianship of a mother's brother, brother, child's father, parents, or slavemaster. It implies proprietary rights over the sufferer in keeping with the legal definition of a conveyance.[2] Thus, the lay therapy manager retains the right to choose the therapist even after a consulting doctor—diviner—has made his diagnosis and recommended action. No professional or bureaucratic referral enforcement is possible in this setting.

Our case studies show repeated instances of such conveyance of therapeutic decision-making, in both traditional Kongo and Western medicine. Decision-making responsibility is most frequently assumed by matrilineal kinsmen, for example, uterine or classificatory "mothers," "mother's brothers," or siblings in cases of adult sufferers (see Figure 9). Parents, or a joint set of maternal and paternal kin, care for infants and unmarried youths, as is evident in the study of Axel and Cécile's child, Luzayadio, and Lwezi. Spouses play a relatively insignificant therapy management role, although in the urban setting the spouse may take charge if no other kinsmen are present, as is seen in Nzita's case. Sufferers retain decision-making rights only if they are adult, usually male, capable of walking and travelling, and financially able to pay for care. Nsimba and Mbumba's cases indicate this.

1. Babutidi, Notebook 7, Laman Collection, Svenska Missionsforbundet Archive (Lidingö).
2. Henry Maine, *Ancient Law* (London, 1960), p. 185.

Specialists are frequently consulted for diagnosis and information, and thus have a place in the decision-making process, although their role is subordinate to that of kinsmen in charting a course of treatment.

Personnel in the therapy managing group shifts and varies from episode to episode within single cases (see Figure 9). This is hardly surprising in view of the burden of time and resources such management imposes. The shifting of personnel is also due to the requirements that alternative therapies place on particular role relations. Mama Marie, the modern diviner-counsellor, frequently requests an entire clan segment to be present for examination. Or, when the issue at hand is marriage, maternal and paternal representatives are both involved because both expect bride payments (7.5). By contrast, consultation with an herbalist (3.2, 7.2) requires only one or two persons to accompany and care for the sufferer. A restricted group, or individual, is often the only one in attendance in Western dispensaries and hospitals which expect families to provide meals for patients (3.3, 3.6, 6.4, 7.1, 7.7, 7.8). In the urban setting, therapy management is likewise usually in the hands of kinsmen. However, because of the kinsmen's scattered residences, job-related time obligations, and transportation problems, they are sometimes replaced in this function by friends, neighbors, more distant kin, political party peers, job peers, and religious associates (6.11–12).[3] Kinsmen's abdication of their therapy management obligation is regarded as scandalous in Kongo thinking, yet it is common enough in the urban setting to constitute a source of concern. The anxiety of a personal crisis without kinsmen was a recurring theme in psychotherapy sessions we monitored at the Neuro-Psychiatric Institute in Kinshasa. Expectations upon kinsmen were summed up in a role-playing comment of a "friend and neighbor" to a hospitalized "patient" whose recovery was slower than anticipated. When the crisis deepened, the friend therapy manager said

3. Dénis Bazinga, *Psychopalavre*, typescript (Kinshasa, 1968/69); Jean S. LaFontaine, *City Politics* (Cambridge, 1970), p. 131; D. M. Boswell, "Personal Crises and the Mobilization of the Social Network," in *Social Networks in Urban Situations*, ed., J. Clyde Mitchell (Manchester, 1969), pp. 245–96.

Decision-Makers	Chapter 3: Luzyadio									Chapter 4: Axel & Cécile							Chapter 5: Nzita											
Episode	1	2	3	4	5	6	7	8	9	1	2	3	4	5	6	7	1	2	3	4	5	6	7	8	9	10	11	12
Father(s)			x	x	x	x	x	x	x			x	x	x														
Father's Sister(s)					x			x	x																			
Paternal Peers																												
Paternal Kinship, Unspecified				x	x			x	x																			
Mother(s)			x		x	x	x	x	x	x	x	x	x	x	x	x								x	x	x	x	x
Mother's Brother(s)		x	x	x	x	x	x	x																x	x	x	x	x
Maternal Peers																								x	x	x	x	
Maternal Kinship, Unspecified				x	x		x	x	x					x	x		x	?	?	?	?	?	x	x	x	x		
Sufferer	x	x																										
Spouse																	x	x	x	x	x	x	x	x	x	x		
Professional Peers																												
Specialist														x	x	x									x	x		

FIGURE 9. Relationship of sufferer to person(s) taking over decision-making responsibility in course of therapy. This indicates the formation of the therapy managing group.

Case	Chapter 6: Nsimba													Chapter 7: Lwezi									Chapter 8: Mbumba										
Episode / Decision-Makers	1	2	3	4	5	6	7	8	9	10	11	12	13	1	2	3	4	5	6	7	8	9	1	2	3	4	5	6	7	8	9	10	11
Father(s)			x	x	x	x	x	x	x									x															
Father's Sister(s)					x																												
Paternal Peers						x																											
Paternal Kinship, Unspecified						x																											
Mother(s)									x						x		x	x	x	x												x	x
Mother's Brother(s)			x	x	x	x		x	x								x	x	x	x												x	x
Maternal Peers						x			x						x		x	x	x	x	x	x										x	x
Maternal Kinship, Unspecified														x				x														x	x
Sufferer	x	x					x			x		x											x	x	x	x	x	x	x		x	x	x
Spouse																																	
Professional Peers										x	x	x																					
Specialist						x										x		x								x	x	x	x	x			

to the patient, "Look, I'll go find your kinsmen. They must hold a family council and each one must confess that which they have against you, and we shall all cleanse our hearts. After that I'll go see the doctor, and we shall pay for strong medicines, and you'll be alright![4] While the urban setting has made it more difficult for kinsmen to fulfill the therapy manager role, it has not eliminated their normative obligations in this regard.

Therapy management, as developed here, has much in common with "lay referral" in social medical literature.[5] The lay referral system has been noted to demarcate the sick role and initiate consultation with a medical professional.[6] Similarly, the Kongo therapy managing group exercises diffuse sanctions upon the sufferer, organizes and channels information, and pressures the sufferer to consult a professional. But unlike the lay referral system in Europe and North America, which is described as discharging its duties after a professional takes over, the Kongo therapy managing group continues to exercise its authority and frequently even increases it while the sufferer is in the hands of a specialist. Other contrasts may be noted. The strongest lay referral system, according to some writers, is present in folk societies with an indigenous therapy tradition and in lower classes of society where knowledge of available professional medical services is not widespread.[7] BaKongo have their own indigenous therapeutic tradition, to be sure, and some are "lower class" in the modern economic setting, but at the same time they are quite cognizant, as well as supportive, of Western cosmopolitan medicine. Thus, other factors influence the strong institution of lay therapy management in Zaire. To explain this we may look at the pluralistic character of traditional and contemporary medicine in which loosely affiliated cults, services, clinics, and specialists must be mediated. The mediatory function served by the therapy managing group is situated within a broader structure of rights and or-

4. Bazinga, *op. cit.*, 1968.
5. See for example Eliot Freidson, *Profession of Medicine* (New York, 1970), pp. 290–97.
6. Talcott Parsons, *The Social System* (New York, 1951); more recently, Freidson, *op. cit.*, pp. 224–43.
7. Freidson, *op. cit.*, pp. 293–94.

ganization of decisions shared by therapy, litigation, and ceremony.

Kongo litigation is characterized by its decentralized courts which bring together litigants on the same shifting basis we see in therapy management. Although the colonial government and the national Zairian government have created modern appeal courts, traditional decentralized courts continue to provide a format for the resolution of conflicts in illness-related and other cases inappropriate for the state courts.

These traditional courts may either take the form of a clan council, an interclan (or intervillage) council, or a multiparty public council.[8] The clan council (*lukutukunu lwa dikanda*) is convened by a leading member for the purpose of arbitrating internal conflicts. It may entail diagnosis of clan members' problems and afflictions. For example, Lwezi's varied aches and pains precipitated speculations about "problems throughout the clan." Her kinsmen met in a limited council (7.4), analyzed the diffuse tensions, and determined that a prophet must be consulted. The clan council frequently has a more directly therapeutic function designed to expurgate mutual antagonism among contending members and to permit them to offer amends to one another. Meetings are usually closed to outsiders, since much embarrassing gossip and anecdotal animosity is vented. Ritual experts may be invited to preside over these meetings, for, as in the case of the clan council over the illnesses of Mbumba, Mavungu, and Mukala (8.10), issues may become very heated and nearly uncontrollable. However, the judicial process at the level of the clan council is dominated by a spirit of mutual compromise and reconciliation rather than by a need for the imposition of an abstract code of law. It is not always easy to distinguish litigation from simple decision-making at this level, but where the issue before the clan council is illness and healing, "court" becomes therapy managing, judicial action becomes kinship therapy (3.7, 4.4, 5.7, 5.9, 6.6, 7.4, 8.10–11).

8. J. Mertens, "La juridiction indigène chez les BaKongo orientaux," *Kongo-Overzee* 10–18 (1944–1952), p. 182 ff.

The interclan council entails the formation of judicial structures between conflicting parties over whom there is no higher kinship authority. If the conflict is between junior members in two groups, clan authorities informally impose settlement on them. If the conflict cannot be worked out informally, the two groups each hire professional advocates (*nzonzi, mpovi*) to debate the issue publicly until they reach a solution and an exchange of gifts to vindicate wrongs and renew bonds. Where contestants threaten to extend a quarrel into open fighting, third parties may convene a larger "*collège arbitral*," as one scholar has termed the ultimate level of traditional Kongo justice.[9] At this level all the richness of Kongo litigation emerges with brilliant oratory, proverbs, enigmas, sanction songs, dancing, and hard rhetorical logic. "Court" in this case consists of a panel of judges (also *nzonzi*) concerned with the prevention of violence, or the imposition of judicial solutions where violence has occurred. Fines include a pig for a drop of blood drawn in a fight, or "seven persons" or their equivalent in goods for manslaughter in the feud. Although state courts have assumed jurisdiction over capital crimes' prosecution, many features of the interclan council level of litigation survive. In two such episodes in our cases (3.4–5, 7.5) representatives of the paternal and maternal clans of the sufferer met to establish the basis for their inability to agree on formal marriage obligations—bride payments, blessings, residence, children. Where illness is directly at issue in litigation, as it was in these cases, the interclan court becomes a therapy managing group. Where its action entails the alleviation of illness, it becomes kinship therapy.

Ceremonial processes clarify other aspects of the conveyance of rights in Kongo therapy management. In traditional initiations, an acolyte submitted to a sponsor or priest for teaching, hazing, and consecration into a new commission. In Lemba, for example, the acolyte became a fictive "son" to his cult "father" (if he was not a true son to him already) who led him through the intricacies of full initiation and whose apprentice he became as a treating Lemba doctor. In the *mpu* order, the conveyance of rights was

9. *Ibid.*

reversed, and the candidate, usually an adult man, came under the sponsorship of his patrifilial children. He and his wife were secluded for a time from his matrilineal kinsmen, following which he would emerge as priest in the *mpu* order and guardian of his clan's insignia. Some of the case studies display similar transference of right to a ceremonial leader. Nsimba was dependent on his father in the same way a Lemba acolyte was dependent on a ceremonial "father." Even more strikingly, Nsimba entered seclusion in prophet Luamba's retreat and healing center accompanied by his father and other kinsmen (6.9). In the case of Mbumba, a permanent ceremonial dependency was created upon the prophet Muzandu, indicated by residence with the prophet and close personal loyalties. Both therapies were managed by recognized cultic figures who put the sufferer through a routinized process of "purification and initiation."

Therapy, then, dovetails on the one hand with traditional shifting arbitration courts, and on the other with ceremonial and cultic hierarchies. This comparison (of ceremony, litigation, and therapy) has been made in the sociomedical and anthropological literature on both small-scale decentralized societies[10] and complex industrialized societies,[11] using criteria of: degrees of freedom and constraint in the social structure, patterns of expression, and temporal arrangements of both these features. Thus, law or litigation, although it has been described as the withdrawal of individual rights and the imposition of obligations, is more accurately seen as an institutional setting in which rights and obligations are clarified. It is a course of events that brings about either the enhancement of rights or their clear curtailment; as BaKongo put it, *zenga mambu* ("*trancher une affaire*," or "cut the palaver") by eliminating verbal and social redundancy. Ceremony, and especially the ceremony of initiation, involves the temporary curtailment of rights and the long-range acquisition of other, even greater rights related to a new commission. The struc-

10. Charles Frake, "The Diagnosis of Desease Among the Subanun on Mindanao," *American Anthropologist* 63 (1961), 1:113–132; Frake, "A Structural Description of Subanun 'Religious Behavior,' " in *Cognitive Anthropology*, ed., Stephan A. Tyler (New York, 1969), pp. 470–86.
11. Freidson, *op. cit.*, pp. 203–332.

ture of an initiatory rite of passage typically increases the richness of traditional expressions during the middle "liminal" phase of seclusion to include many layers of redundant imagery about society and cosmos.

Therapy includes features of litigation and ceremony, as well as unique aspects. Kongo therapy entails the temporary surrender of the sufferer's individual decision-making rights. The sufferer and his advocates select from optional and alternative remedies that, in consecutive episodes, create a total course of treatment.[12]

12. Efforts have also been made to describe the therapeutic process in the formalist terms of mathematics, comparing it either to the stochastic process whereby prediction is possible only in a very limited way, or to the Markov chain whereby one can predict a process as accurately from a knowledge of the present state of affairs as from a knowledge of the present together with the entire past history. In the former case, the process would be "open," and random choice and combination would prevail. In the latter, performance would be entirely predictable, that is "closed," like certain aspects of language syntax, having the quality of a prescriptive institution. For further reference on these concepts, see "Time Series," and "Markov Chains" in *International Encyclopedia of the Social Sciences* (New York, 1968). Frake has attempted to apply these terms to his analysis of Subanun therapy, which is organized, he states, into four stages, one of which (X) is an "unscheduled frame."

    sickness / diagnosis / X / continued sickness
                         cure
                         death

This "description" blends the conditions of a "closed" or predictable sequence such as in syntax, with an open, preferential, or indeterministic description in which the probability of an event is a sole function of the outcome of the preceding event. The unscheduled frame is the "choice" of a large variety of therapeutic offerings: medication with 800 alternatives or religious therapy with numerous subclasses. The initial choice is made in relation to the anticipable outcome predicted by the diagnosis. Subsequent choices are made in relation to the results of previous choices which thus partially determine them. Frake, "A Structural Description of Subanun 'Religious Behavior.' "

Valuable though this description of therapy is, Frake, like all proponents of the new ethnography movement, blends social levels of action with classificatory and value levels, allowing no latitude for contradiction or interdependent domains of "society" and "culture," behavior and norm—a stance we prefer. According to Frake, "predictable," i.e., determined, events, become unpredictable or indeterminate only when alternatives appear. This appears to us to be tautological. "Scheduling," he states, "occurs only to the extent that no active alternatives exist." This "scheduled frame" analysis of action implies a perfect (impossible?) fit of values with actions, and commits the analyst to saying that what occurs does so because it has been scheduled by the culture. We would say that it occurs because actors, in concert and in a particular situation, consciously have decided upon it.

Consensus and Dissension in
Therapeutic Decision-Making

The therapy managing group must achieve internal cognitive agreement and social consensus in order to be an effective decision-making body. This does not happen by itself, for decisions reached by a minority among the sufferer's caretakers may be invalidated by a dissenting majority; resolutions made by laymen may be shifted after consultation with specialists; or, specialists' recommendations may be amended or ignored by laymen; and so on. Contrasting points of view within the therapy managing group tend to generate alternative courses of therapy. We thus need to examine the basis for shifting alignments of complementary and opposed, equal and unequal, symmetrical and asymmetrical roles, groups, categories, and personalities around a sufferer. This perspective is inspired by social field theory[13] and its successful application to central African social analysis.[14] In an article on the dynamics of therapy in the Lower Zaire, we have attempted to synthesize field theory, decision theory, small group analysis, and transactional analysis with social medical analysis of the clinical process.[15] These theories all emphasize the causal importance of social relationships upon decisions and actions in the therapeutic process. In our cases, the quasi-groups that emerge briefly in therapy managing acts align parents and children, siblings and generational peers, clan factions and interclan alliances, friends, neighbors, professional and job peers, religious associates, and doctors and patients (see Figure 10). Depending on how these alignments are brought to the fore in decision-making, the therapy managing group's configuration shifts from hierarchic and asymmetrical to egalitarian and symmetrical; its decisions vary in their inspiration from individualized to collectivized; the content of therapeutic proposals

13. Kurt Lewin, *Field Theory in Social Science* (New York, 1951).
14. Victor W. Turner, *Schism and Continuity in an African Society* (Manchester, 1957); *Drums of Affliction* (Oxford, 1968).
15. John M. Janzen, "The Dynamics of Therapy in the Lower Zaire," in *Psychological Anthropology*, ed., Thomas R. Williams. Papers of the Ninth International Congress of Anthropological and Ethnological Science (The Hague, 1975).

1. Self-treatment

2. Dyadic formation of group: sufferer and kinsmen

3. Kinsmen and specialist

4. Sufferer and specialist

5. Sufferer, kinsmen, and specialist

6. Sufferer and kinship factions

7. Sufferer, kinship factions, and specialist

8. Complex formation of therapy managing group: sufferer, kinship factions, non-kin factions, and specialist

a sufferer   c specialist or professional
b kinsmen   d non-kin
b₁ b₂ kinship factions   d₁ d₂ non-kin factions

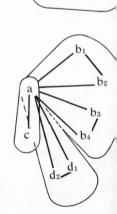

FIGURE 10—Schematic chart of social components from which therapy managing group is recruited, and typical configurations these components take in cases in Chapters 3–8.

varies from esoteric and specialized to popular and customary. Let us elaborate on this by discussing examples.

The simplest arrangement of therapeutic decision and action is found where an individual administers a remedy to himself. Nsimba the nurse, for example, upon perceiving and diagnosing his urinary infection, took antibiotics as a cure (6.1–2). Although this was individual action, later episodes of the case demonstrated complex social alliances.

A more common social alignment is represented when sufferers share their problems with other laymen or with therapists, creating dyadic relationships. In small-scale diagnostic meetings, several kinsmen confer with, or as a therapy managing group, on behalf of, the suffer (3.4, 6.3, 7.4). Such meetings, because they are sometimes convened in an emergency, reflect a practical consensus to facilitate rapid effectiveness of the therapy. They may however disguise deeper conflicts in the kin group or diverging opinions about etiology. If the sufferer is able, he may be involved in the decision. If no decision can be reached, extended kinship participation may be sought.

When the dyadic decision-making group consists of the sufferer and a specialist, an asymmetrical and hierarchical doctor-patient relationship comes into being.[16] In Lower Zaire, this type of therapy management dyad is usually limited to adult men or parents with children who consult specialists. When this is used in Western clinics the client's opinions may be sought to help discover diagnostic data on diet, work habits, previous treatments, marital status; but rarely is the broad-ranging counselling that occurs in the traditional setting carried out. The doctor- or nurse-patient relationship is frequently a one-way authoritarian or paternalistic flow of information with the patient being told what to do. The outcome of such treatment may be passive compliance

16. A much discussed concept, beginning with L. J. Henderson, "The Patient and Physician as a Social System," *New England Journal of Medicine* 212 (1935): 819–823; of more recent importance, M. Balint, *The Doctor, His Patient, and the Illness,* (New York, 1957); Samuel W. Bloom, *The Doctor and His Patient* (New York, 1963); Jean Pouillon, "Malade et médecin: le même et/ou l'autre? Rémarques ethnologiques," *Incidences de la Psychanalyse: Nouvelle Revue de Psychanalyse* 1 (1970).

with satisfaction. But frequently the outcome is bewilderment on the part of the patient and repetition of the same treatment elsewhere. Thus, in Mbumba's case, multiple visits were made to Western clinics for treatment of asthma (8.1–4). Initially he accepted the professional diagnosis but was not satisfied with the therapeutic outcome. He became a persistent "clinic shopper," trying different kinds and sizes of establishments. In due course he was offered an alternative etiology and accepted it.

When the dyadic therapy managing group consists of the sufferer's kinsmen and the specialist, a more egalitarian and bargained outcome results. Nzita's kinsmen, for example, consulted Mama Marie over what to do while Nzita sat in a drugged and agitated condition back in the village (5.9). They agreed, without Nzita's knowledge of the meeting, that a clan council must be held. Consensus between the kinsmen and specialist is quite common, and when this occurs the kin therapy managers are able to impose a doctor's prescription very well. But clinical prescriptions may be amended or rejected by the sufferer's kinsmen if diagnostic or therapeutic agreement is not reached. Cécile's action with her newly born infant may be recalled in this connection (4.2). As a result of the treatment she received from the maternity staff unaware of her plight, she fled the ward to seek help from a prophet-counsellor. Similarly, the kin managers of dying Luzayadio removed her from the ward to tend to family matters in the village (3.4).

The kin therapy managing group sometimes acts as independently toward traditional African specialists as they do toward Western clinics, amending and rejecting the specialist's expertise if they do not understand or cannot agree with it. When consulting *banganga* and *bangunza*, it is not uncommon for patients and their kinsmen to walk out if dissatisfied. But then, Kongo traditional therapists are not possessive toward their clients. Furthermore, it is the prerogative of the client to determine the success of the therapy and to make payment, where it is expected, only after satisfaction has been attained. We see this where Lwezi's kinsmen had been instructed by herbalist-magician Bayindula to return to his compound in ten days. They paid him, but rejected the return visit because his fees were deemed exorbitant and repetition of his therapy unnecessary (7.2). Lwezi's therapy managing group also acted on their own after she had been placed with the prophet Luamba to undergo therapeutic counselling with him. Her family removed her and took her to a hospital when she developed pains, totally ignoring his ceremonial schedule of baths, laying on of hands, anointment with oil, and prayer for ten days (7.6). The distinction is frequently made between "true" and "false" prophets, but in particular circumstances this corresponds with personal satisfaction and dissatisfaction, respectively.

These decisions and actions involving the dyads of sufferer and kinsmen, sufferer and specialist, and kinsmen and specialist, indicate that therapeutic action is usually motivated by diagnostic agreement based on shared information, worked out in the setting of structural congruence. Where information is not shared, or where differences appear, one part of the therapy managing group may break with the other, generating an alternative diagnosis and resorting to an alternative therapy. This leads to an even more complex combination of roles and categories in which the kin therapy managing group comprises opposed factions in the sufferer's social field (see Figure 10, 6.) Since kinship groupings are generally egalitarian sets of uncles, aunts, and parents representing lineages and larger clan segments, they are quite vulnerable to division by conflicting issues and events along existing structural lines of demarcation. In the case of Nzita, the therapy managers, who included her brother the pastor, her maternal aunt, and her mother's brother, were divided on religious grounds whether to patronize the pastor's mission dispensary or to go to a pagan healer specializing in treatment of madness (5.7). A measure of consensus was only obtained by satisfying both factions sequentially, first consulting the *nganga* and then taking the sufferer to the dispensary.

When differences are related increasingly to structural features of the clan, they cannot be simply resolved by acting sequentially on alternative therapeutic proposals. In the clan of Lwezi and Mbumba "troubles in the clan" had become a recurrent diagnosis. Because the parties involved in the therapy managing groups were themselves implicated in these deeper disputes, they abandoned issue-related solutions and sought collective help from a diviner (7.4–5; 8.10–11). The primary therapy managers in such a situation are often spouses representing allied corporate kin segments in important local and regional political networks. Luzayadio's parents and other close kinsmen who removed her from the dispensary, agreed in their deep concern over her severe illness that social causes were involved. But they disagreed with the wider clan groups on whether her unresolved, "incestuous," marriage had contributed to her illness (3.4–5). This and other examples suggest that couples who are drawn into interclan disputes in managing a therapeutic course find their marriages either victimized by the wider conflict (7.5) or utilized as a pivotal link in the resolution of the conflict (6.5–6).

These strategies of enforced reconciliation thus serve a task greater than just to facilitate consensus in therapy management. BaKongo abhor open violence and generally do all they can to minimize its effect on society. The tenet that "conflict may cause illness" is frequently exercised to rationalize the enforced reconciliation of conflict within a social circle because an illness has occurred there. On a small scale, with immediate results in mind, we see such actions as herbalist Masamba giving a distraught father, Axel, a charm to calm him so he would not strike his wife and in-laws (4.3). On a broader scale, the process is well illustrated in the case of Nsimba. There, time after time, the therapy managing group of his father, mother, mother's brother, and several other kinsmen had been involved in fractious cleavages in their own circle; they had undergone group therapy in the seclusion of Luamba's retreat (6.9). Later on, the non-kin therapy managing group of mission personnel sought out the senior nurse with whom Nsimba had been at odds, reconciling the conflict caused when he had resented being prematurely retired. In all these instances, the therapy managing group of a few kinsmen or peers expanded its scope to embrace conflicting second and third parties each related in their turn to the sufferer.

The extension of the therapy managing group to include second and third parties at odds with each other is an essential feature of Kongo therapy. It has been variously identified. We prefer Kongo psychiatrist Bazinga's term, the "triangle of truth." He defined it in his *psychopalavre* by cautioning participants to beware of contacts that related them to both a friend and an antagonist, who in turn have a relationship with each other. Only by discerning such a triangle in its totality can one avoid getting caught in society's "traps."[17] Customary Kongo wisdom develops similar strategies for dealing with alliances in terms of a "politics of oil" to smooth over tense relationships, and a "politics of salt" to add tactical tension to a relationship. Detractors of this process of raising awareness of latent contradictions in relationships derogatorily call it "a retreat into witchcraft." The charge, heard from some missionaries and old time African pastors, confuses conflict, which is the tension-filled confrontation of persons, with witchcraft, which is the willed or unconscious wish to do mystical and physical harm to another. All witchcraft is conflict, but not all conflict is witchcraft in Kongo thinking. Even the illness etiology "caused by man," which usually accompanies the expansion of the therapy managing group to second and third parties involved with a sufferer, may refer to conflict without the mystical element of witchcraft. Where this is the case, the extension of the therapy managing group into a troubled social triangle often has the salutory effect, as intended, of resolving psychosomatic illness. One perceptive medical observer of the phenomenon has called it "inverse psychosomatics."[18] To be sure, however, where confrontation and accusation occur, witchcraft suspicions readily emerge, adding to the tension if not properly handled. But this is why ritual experts exist in Kongo society.

Therapy in the "triangle of truth" confronts role contradictions playing upon individuals and groups. The most serious contradictions derive from modern conditions of labor migration, distribution of wages, and sources of prestige, which divide families on a host of daily issues in Zairian life. Nsimba came into conflict with the elderly nurse over the contrast of age-and-seniority-defined

17. Bazinga, *op. cit.*, 1968.
18. Don Bates, in comments developed in seminar at McGill University, 1971.

status on one hand and education-defined status on the other. Many of Lwezi's problems derived from the rural population imbalance due to labor migration. Problems arising in such cases can be resolved on an individual and episodic basis, but unfortunately too often the structural causes remain to resurface at a later date. Nevertheless, the rewards of temporary therapy are considerable. As the shift in etiology moves to "of man," questions are raised about shared ultimate values, justifying the sufferer's entourage in its reaffirmation of cultural wisdom or in its quest for original responses. Thus, when Lwezi's quarrelling parents threatened to bring relationships between their two clans into confusion, Mama Marie queried them boldly: "What does the Bible say about husband-wife relationships?" There was no need for extensive textual exegesis, everyone on hand knew that spouses had no business arguing like this. They agreed and made up, laying the foundation for the solution which included the paternal blessing for Lwezi. Conventional methods of therapy and conflict resolution work as long as all parties in a dispute subscribe to the same norms and value hierarchies. When contending parties' world views diverge, precipitating disputes over unshared norms, recourse to outside ritual help is likely.[19] In these situations it is the duty of counselling and divining prophets like Mama Marie and Kuniema, and *banganga* like Bayindula, to provide grounds for common and purposive action to the group. The popularity of Bayindula certainly lies in his ability to stimulate his clients' metaphysical urges. There is great comfort in knowing, for example, that despite the continuing injustices after national independence, the boisterous claims of science, and rumors that white men are inventing life, that "only God can create a person!" (7.2).

These efforts to cure social relations and to reinvigorate their basic ideas may be compared with the traditional cults. The cults too focused on pervasive contradictions and paradoxes such as the incompatibility of matrilineal descent rules and virilocal resi-

19. This follows a line of explanation for ritualization developed by Max Gluckman and Victor W. Turner, in Gluckman, *Politics, Law, and Ritual in Tribal Society* (Chicago, 1965), and Turner, *op. cit.*, p. 126.

dence norms; the predicament of the dynamic person in a structurally junior lineage house; and the philosophical problem of the two-in-one embodied in twins. Social roles were realigned through initiation to an *nkisi* cult so individuals could permanently deal with the contradiction; they, in the process, were transformed from the role of subordinate sufferer to superordinate doctor of the cult. Failing to eliminate the structural sources of anxiety, traditional cults devised an institutional system for coping with them. In contemporary cases, the contradictions are less clearly patterned because they are new or transitional, they are less well understood and less fully enshrined in the lore of particular cults. Having discarded most of the old cults, modern Zairian society is challenged to help individuals cope with the stresses of cultural change and strengthen customs that are beneficial in dealing with stress.

The significance of the therapy managing group in meeting these challenges can be summarized in terms of a set of propositions bearing on: (1) the scope of participation of individuals, (2) levels of agreement and disagreement, (3) the temporal order of events, and (4) the pattern of authority. It will become evident in the next section how these factors structure the choices made in the therapy managing group.

The scope of participation in therapy decisions is in part determined by the problem at hand. Simple, routine therapeutic undertakings require focal decisions of only a few persons in the therapy managing group. Issues entailing change of residence, habit, or mode of relationship and shift in role require a more extended participation, involving several persons and kin groups, and frequently a specialist. Issues that entail severe crises, impending death or debilitating disease, doubt over common values and norms, and other moral crises, will bring together a wide variety of laymen, specialists, and on occasion the public.[20]

Agreement or disagreement within the therapy managing group over these multiple levels of participation has its unique effects. Agreement at the lowest level over technical issues produces

20. C. M. Brodsky, "Decision-Making and Role Shifts as They Affect the Consultation Interface," *Archives of General Psychiatry* 23 (1970), 6: 559–65.

straightforward action. Divergencies in perception of technical needs will be worked out to accommodate all seriously entertained alternatives so long as broad moral diagnoses in a case are shared by the participating therapy managers. If a dispute engulfs moral norms and values that cannot be accommodated as alternatives, a shift of participation will result in quest of a consensus, or an outside specialist will be sought to reestablish common, agreed-on norms.

The temporal course of therapeutic episodes is determined in the alternatives that are entertained within the therapy managing group. Participatory therapy decisions often create majority/minority alternatives, the former acted upon immediately, the latter abstracted and projected into the near or indefinite future.[21] Alternatives may be conceived by individuals, dissenting lay therapy managers of kinship factions, dissatisfied clients in the hands of incommunicative professionals, or perplexed professionals referring difficult or complex cases to other specialists. Diagnostic disagreement, knowledge of alternative therapies, or conflicts within the therapy managing group will often generate subsequent action. Consensus, by these same terms, will tend to result in the conviction that therapy has been successful in the last therapy episode, and another episode will not be called for.

The structure of authority shaping the decision will also determine the outcome. An egalitarian context of decision, in which all parties are on equal status footing, will result in either agreement and concerted action, or major/minor alternatives. Dissatisfaction with therapy will, in the first instance, give rise to a new evaluation and another choice of therapist and therapy. In the second instance, the common consequence will be to follow through with the alternative proposal in a subsequent episode so as to maintain group harmony. In both instances therapy and therapist selected for the subsequent episode will tend to contrast to those of the previous episode (see Figure 11). A hierarchic context of decision turns out differently, especially if it is the relationship of a specialist to his patient and the latter's kin. Pa-

21. J. Kolaja, "Two Processes: A New Framework for the Theory of Participation in Decision-Making," *Behavioural Science* 13 (1968): 66–70.

	Social Context of Decision		
	Patient dominated decision	Lay managing group or person dominated decision	Specialist dominated decision
Selection of *same* therapist role as in preceding episode			
Luzayadio		1	
Axes and Cécile			
Nzita		2	
Nsimba	1		
Lwezi		1	
Mbumba	3	2	
Total	4	6	0
Selection of *different* therapist role from preceding episode			
Luzayadio		5	3
Axel and Cécile		2	3
Nzita		7	1
Nsimba	3	7	
Lwezi	1	5	
Mbumba	3	3	
Total	7	29	7

(left margin label: Choice of Therapist)

FIGURE 11—Correlation of the social context of decision with choice of same/ different therapist role in preceding episode. First episode of each case is omitted, as are: last three episodes of Luzayadio's case after her death; last episode of case of Axel and Cécile's case. Nzita's case is charted beginning with episode 3 because of scanty evidence, although we think husband made choices.

tients rarely negotiate openly with specialists in Lower Zaire. Diagnostic information is exchanged on an asymmetrical basis, the patient's being symptomatic and folk-informed, the specialist's systematic but esoteric, rarely fully communicated or communicable to the patient or his kin. This applies especially to Western medicine in Zaire, although it is true as well of traditional medicine where professional secrets exist. Successfully negotiated consensual therapy in this authority pattern need not accommodate the patient's or kin managing group's total understanding of the details of the professional's specialized explanation. Rather, sympathy and competence must be conveyed.[22] Dissension, on the other hand, arises if the patient is not given permission to return repeatedly with the same set of complaints. If this permission is not granted, he may generate new symptoms or go to a different clinic with the same complaint until consensus is found with another professional.

Because the Kongo therapy managing group is so frequently made up of an egalitarian set of lay kinsmen, situational and perceptual changes within the wider social field contribute to the proliferation of alternative therapies (see Figure 11). This also contributes to the unique integration of medical pluralism in Zaire and central Africa, permitting the study of all major therapeutic systems in so few cases.

Categories of Therapeutic Choice

Therapy managing groups who by their decisions enact their own therapy, or transfer rights of treatment to hospital staffs, traditional specialists, or prophets, establish a pattern of choice categories. By tabulating such choices in numerous cases we can see the general categories of choice and the logic of options and contrasts. Thus we have correlated therapy roles and techniques as they occurred in the case studies (see Figure 12), and we have analyzed cost factors (see Figure 13). Conceptual schemes used to interpret the symptoms will be examined in subsequent chapters.

22. J. D. Sapira, "Reassurance Therapy," *Annals of Internal Medicine* 77 (1972): 603–04.

The inventory of therapy roles and group activities elicited from the six case studies presents a strong sample of all major therapeutic types available to BaKongo. It includes the staff of a hospital, a dispensary, and the village nurse's clinic. The hospital staff includes a physician, several grades of nurses, and technicians. All except the physician are present in the dispensary. Village clinics are staffed by a single, sometimes diploma-bearing, nurse, and perhaps one additional aide. The inventory of *nganga* types includes the *nganga mbuki*, herbalist and general curer, the *nganga nkisi*, herbalist-magician, doctor of one or more *minkisi*, and the *nganga bilau*, healer of madness. The important role of the *nganga lunga*, orthopedist, and other *nganga* types not listed but current in the Lower Zaire will be described in subsequent chapters. Although Kongo therapist role terms do not identify different types of *ngunza* prophets, we noticed important typological distinctions in their functions and in the criteria used by therapy managing groups to choose an *ngunza*. One common role-related function is that of the prophet working alone in his compound, receiving clients on an individual basis with a few escorts. In contrast to such a consultative model of the prophet role is another we can best describe as "master of ceremonies" for clan councils. Thus, we have identified the interclan council with prophet, the intraclan council with prophet, and the nuclear family council with prophet. A final role category with greater significance in urban contexts than in our cases is the non-kin group, including work peers, neighbors, friends, religious associates, and the like.

As these therapists' roles and groups are correlated with therapeutic techniques, we can see better the intent of therapy decisions in the managing process. Techniques such as the dispensing of pills, injections, surgical procedures, X-rays, and so on, occur in correlation with the familiar roles of the hospital and dispensary staff and village nurse, constituting the cluster we have identified as particularly representing "Western medicine" (see Chapter 1). With almost equal discreteness, the *nganga* roles correlate with techniques of skin incisions, plant rubbings, cupping-horn applications, head packs, orally taken liquid medicines, magically prepared charms, and a variety of liturgical

Roles	Therapies	Pills	Hospitalization	Injection	Rehospitalization after interruption	Surgical procedures	X-ray	Plants on skin	*Minsamba* cuts in skin	Plant medication by mouth	Plant headpack	Charm prepared	Referral to hospital	Plant cure, nonspecified	Referral to settle conflict	Cupping horn
Hospital		6	6			I	I									
Dispensary		7	7	4	2											
Village Nurse				I												
Nganga mbuki								4	I	2	I	I	I	I	I	
Nganga bilau			I							3						
Nganga nkisi								I		I						I
Prophet (*ngunza*)															2	
Prophet with Interclan																
Prophet with Intraclan																
Prophet with Nuclear Family																
Interclan reunion																
Intraclan reunion																
Nuclear family (F)																
Non-kin (friends, neighbors, job peers, etc.)																

FIGURE 12. This chart illustrates the co-occurrence of therapies and specialist's (or group therapist's) roles. It is arranged to show incidence and type of co-occurrence of these two in terms of "smallest space," thus indicating numerical clusters of roles and therapies.

Singing, chants (liturgy)	Advice	Examination of maternal kin	Examination of kin, nonspecified	Examination, nonspecified	Retreat	Confession of kin to sufferer	Confession of sufferer to kin	Prayer	Prospective or actual move	Dream analysis	Holy water by mouth	Blessing	Payment refused	Referral to *nganga*	Examination of paternal kinship	Ritual bath	Annointment of oil	Laying on of hands	Payment	Return to village	Confession of third party	Confession of non-kin
	I																					
I	I																					
	2	I	I	2		I	I	I	I	I												
I		I			I	I		I								I	I	I				
I	I					I			I					I							I	
				I		I	I									I	I	I				
	5	3			2						2			I	I							
I	I	2			I								2		I			I				
																			I			
I				I	I		I	I	I													I

Cost

	Cash Payment	Gratis or Payment in Gifts
Vehicle (includes "at cost" rental fee)	Nzita: Nsimba: H, H, D Lwezi: H Mbumba: H, H	F Cter, PCter, Ctra, PF, NK, NK, NK PCtra, F
	Total 6	10
Two hours or more on foot	Axel and Cécile: Nzita: Nsimba: Nmb Lwezi: Nnk Mbumba:	P, Nmb PCtra PCter P, NK, P, PCtra, Ctra
	Total 2	9
Two hours or less on foot	Luzayadio: D, D, VN Axel and Cécile: D Nzita: D, D, D Nsimba: D Lwezi: D, D Mbumba: D, H	Nmb, Cter, Cter, Ctra, Cter Ctra, Nmb P, Nb, Ctra, Nnk, Ctra, Nb NK Ctra Ctra, Ctra
	Total 12	17

Distance (vertical label at left)

H	Hospital	PCter	Prophet with Interclan Reunion
D	Dispensary	PCtra	Prophet with Intraclan Reunion
VN	Village Nurse	PF	Prophet with Family
Nmb	*Nganga mbuki*	Cter	Interclan Reunion
Nb	*Nganga bilau*	Ctra	Intraclan Reunion
Nnk	*Nganga nkisi*	NK	Non-kin Group in Therapy
P	Prophet	F	Family

FIGURE 13. Correlation of distance travelled by client with cost and role of therapist consulted or therapy group which enacted treatment.

acts and counselling. This cluster we have identified as the "art of the *banganga*."

Remaining therapists' and groups' roles do not correlate with techniques into discrete clusters. However, the prophet's role suggests a pivotal distinction between two types of therapy: one emphasizing public investigation, confession, and social analysis, a category we call "kinship therapy," and the other emphasizing liturgies, anointments, baths, purificatory and exorcistic rituals without a corporate kinship component being as dominant. This we have called "purification and initiation." Both will receive fuller analysis in subsequent chapters.

The extent to which cost determines choices of one or the other of these categories deserves consideration, since fees, and energy and resource expenditures, enter into every therapeutic option. Western medicine in Zaire in the late sixties required a modest fee, varying from place to place. Although some missions and governmental institutions enjoyed subsidies, we found no free treatment. Nor was there health insurance in Zaire at the time. Western medicine was usually available in rudimentary form anywhere in the Manianga at a distance of a two-hour walk. But hospital care, less widely distributed, usually entailed the increased cost of both treatment and medication, the cost of motor transport to get there, and some boarding expenses while there (see Figure 13).

Many *banganga* charge fees as high as those of hospitals, or higher. Others, along with prophets, charge nothing. However, noncharging *banganga* and prophets regularly receive tokens of appreciation from clients. Treatment by an *nganga* involves lower transportation cost than does going to a hospital, because most *kinganga* specialties are found within walking distance. The same is true for prophets, although proximity of therapist type does not keep therapy managing groups from occasionally travelling far, by vehicle, to seek out a particularly highly reputed prophet-seer.

Kinship councils appear, on the surface, not to cost anything. However, gifts exchanged in the resolution of conflicts, and payments (prestations) made at marriage and death, entail either an expenditure of productive labor or an equivalent in cash. Furthermore, an assembly of dispersed kinsmen of one or two allied clans requires travel by vehicle. Vehicles used in the cases cited were merchants' trucks and mission ambulances, both of which were available only through payment of "at cost" rents. Kinship therapy may therefore be as costly as Western therapy.

Considering all types of productive and capital expenses, therapeutic alternatives in Zaire are about equal in cost. If distance travelled is added as "cost", then Western hospital medicine and consultation with prophet-seers for the analysis of social relations are the most highly valued (or perhaps scarcest) therapies. Our studies have not documented hardship cases in which the support structure breaks down entirely. Rather, we have seen the therapy managing system place collective resources at the disposal of individuals who need help. Within this framework, cost per se does not appear to be a significant variable in determining the selection of one therapy category over another.

In summary, this chapter has examined a number of variables that determine therapeutic choice: the composition of the therapy managing group within its social field; the role of the therapist or group enacting therapy; the technique; and the total cost of therapy. The configuration of the therapy managing group and the perception of the sufferer's problem both have a bearing on the type of resolution that will be sought. Diagnostic agreement and social consensus between all parties, lay and expert, guarantee maximum effectiveness in a course of treatment. Diagnostic disagreement and social conflict within the decision-making group requires this group to become the object of ritualized kinship therapy, conflict resolution, and reaffirmation of basic social norms and cosmological values. Such diagnostic disagreement and social conflict may generate alternative diagnoses and therapies, bringing into play a wide variety of secondary choices. The internal logic of these alternative ideas and institutions will be the subject of the final two chapters.

CHAPTER TEN

Interpreting Symptoms

Ultimately, worms can cause madness. NZOAMAMBU, *nganga nkisi*

Nzoamambu's Medical Cosmology

Few laymen—or even experts—can fully articulate their system of knowledge. In Zaire, where seventy years of colonial and missionary presence disrupted many traditional arts, ideas relating to symptoms and complaints were often opaque or had disappeared entirely from popular thought. Yet, therapy managers and divination counsellors knew how to manipulate traditional symbols and terms along with Western medical terms and had at their disposal an array of medical knowledge derived from both systems. For example, sufferers and close kinsmen could offer precise physical symptoms such as "headache" (6.4), "cough" (3.3-5), "asthma attacks while in home village" (8.9), "weakness in joints with pain" (7.6-8), "unconsciousness" (5.11, 7.8), or "the baby is suffocating" (4.1-6). As illnesses progressed, diagnostic meetings in the therapy managing group or consultation with specialists established diagnostic categories. A brother referred to his sister as a "psychological case" (7.4), a nurse referred to his patient's "nephritis" (7.1), a part-time herbalist described a patient as "a case of *mumpompila*, split head" (6.8), and an entire maternal clan became greatly concerned over a member's "odd behavior," incipient madness (5.1-12).

In order to lay bare the ideas which inspire and explain symptoms and diagnoses such as these in Zaire, we will take a look at the systematic thinking of Nzoamambu, master *nganga*, on the natural, physical, human, and spiritual worlds, his "medical cosmology."

Nzoamambu makes the heart a focus of the person (*muntu*), for the heart (*ntima*) embodies the principle of life (*moyo*). Other organs and functions, such as the abdomen (*vumu*, sometimes also *moyo*), head (*ntu*), blood (*menga, nkila*) and thoughts, carry on an existence partially independent of the heart. Affliction introduces anger (*mfunia*) into organs and functions, causing their impairment and congestion. If localized treatment is ineffective in restoring health, an affliction worsens along a predictable hierarchic progression of symptoms and diseases for each organ or function until the heart, "lord of the person," is also adversely affected. The heart is epiphenomenal to the rest of the body, both in health, where it is "calm," and in illness, where it is "agitated." The heart's afflictions, too, follow a patterned hierarchy of progression from simple "hard beating," to "very strong palpitations," to "fear in the heart," and then to "madness." These emotional afflictions must receive attention in their own right, but localized treatment simultaneously continues in other affected bodily areas. However, when the heart is touched by affliction, diagnosis must look beyond the body for an explanation, to spirit- or illness-invoked anger, a sufferer's own carelessness toward moral codes, or witchcraft emanating from the social environment. These secondary and tertiary dimensions of heart, society, and cosmos must be diagnosed and treated before an individual's health can be restored.

Lest too narrow a view be inferred of Nzoamambu's medical scheme, the configuration within which it exists will be shown before it is elaborated. This configuration consists of the domains of the person, society, natural categories, and related supernatural beings. Expressions are derived, and associations made, across these domains to create effective verbal images, chemotherapeutic cures, and spiritual powers. It is characteristic of cosmologies to provide the material by which dominant cul-

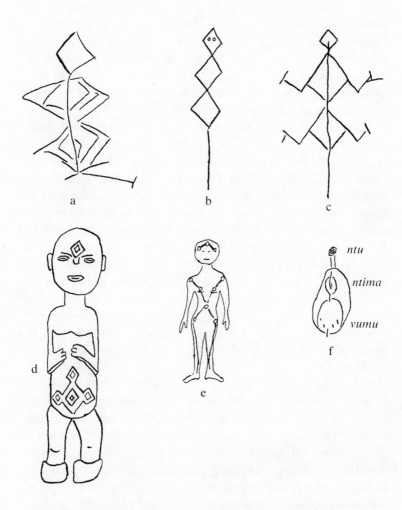

FIGURE 14. Diagrams of the body. (a–c) Inscriptions in caves and on rocks; (d) Sculpture, Kimpese Museum; (e) Ritual tracing with *mpemba* chalk: "medicine is smeared on . . . brow, temples, shoulders, and breasts, then lines are drawn from the navel to the breasts and from the navel round the hips, down the legs and round the ankles," K. E. Laman, *The Kongo III* (Uppsala, 1962), p. 46; (f) Nzoamambu's rough drawing of the human body.

tural metaphors are organized.[1] In Nzoamambu's case, he drew from this cosmology to inspire his *nganga*'s performances, to legitimate his calling to be *nganga*, to rule his clan village, and to compose an anatomy, pathology, and appropriate treatments. While we are here concerned primarily with his medical thinking, these thoughts are considerably clarified by noting how he organized his metaphors in the other areas.

Perhaps because of the heavy charge of symbols and ideas, Nzoamambu, like many another *nganga*, was a complicated character. Arkinstall had encountered Nzoamambu in 1965 when he was medical director at Kibunzi hospital, and Nzoamambu had entered the hospital to see patients. Arkinstall invited the *nganga* to his house for a meal, and in 1969 we responded to the return invitation. On April 19, 1969, Nzoamambu began his lessons to us with the preamble: "On this day, I show my plants to Dokotolo Bill and Professor Mr. John." The instructions, like his dealings with his clients, were couched alternately in tricks and truths. He was never a flat lecturer or clinician. Like other *banganga*, he was usually busy being his own public relations expert. His exhibitions frequently verged on the comic or foolhardy. But invariably, at some deeper level, the ludicrous front gave way to a scheme.

Thus, one day, Nzoamambu demonstrated a "thief trap" to several dozen onlookers. Public morality, anatomy, the power of nature, and his own skill were blended. "Take several corn husks," he began, "fold one over another so that they create a little pocket. Fill the pocket with three pinches of hearth ash and lay a leaf over it. For each pinch the apprentice snaps his knuckles—this gives it strength. If the thief does not confess immediately, he will begin to feel sick, and ultimately go mad." After this deft demonstration, Nzoamambu moved amongst the

1. Claude Lévi-Strauss's *La pensée sauvage* (Paris, 1956), remains the most stimulating treatment of the issue of how particular expressive symbols draw and manipulate from the cosmology's deeper structure. More recently James Fernandez has clarified some of Lévi-Strauss's major arguments and has added the notion of "metaphor" to clarify the theoretical issue of domains. See Fernandez, "Performances and Persuasions: Of the Beast in Every Body . . . and the Metaphors of Everyman," in *Culture, Myth and Symbol*, ed. C. Geertz (winter 1972).

crowd and asked several persons in turn, "Are you the thief? You? You?" His extemporaneous audience became rather concerned at this flippancy with serious magic. But abruptly Nzoamambu doubled over in laughter at the incongruity he had created, and all joined in with him. He had been joking, after all. Suddenly, as quickly as he had laughed, he turned deadly serious. "The ancestors," he warned, "had an even more powerful protection against thieves, a 'mystery stone' placed near the object to be protected." It was empowered by the *nganga*'s spittle and the invocation, "O God, Nzambi Mpungu, pursue the man or woman, boy or girl, who steals. Give him/her a bad hernia."

Nzoamambu, as *nganga*, had a passion for gimmickry, pervaded with connotations as intriguing as his inner thoughts. In addition to the wooden medicine ladle, carved fly whisk, and German crockery mug inherited from his grandmother, he kept all the teeth he pulled. His many-faceted art included simple dentistry. To convince his clientele that an abscessed or decayed tooth must be removed, Nzoamambu would dump the quart jar filled with teeth of former clients onto the table alongside his tooth-extracting tool acquired from some dentist. Disconcerted but impressed, the client would invariably submit to the painful extraction. Painless, and more impressive, was the full-sized grandfather clock in Nzoamambu's house which chimed every 15 minutes and struck on the hour. Against much negative advice— it would not arrive, it would be broken—he had mail-ordered it from Europe.

A part of Nzoamambu's style derived from his grandmother, Yakeba-Bote, from whom he had inherited his *kinganga* (*nganga*'s art). She had specialized in *nkisi na mayiza* (against fruit theft), *mpodi* (the cupping horn), and *madioma* (to remove the effect of a curse). Although her work had been disrupted considerably by the pressures of government, mission, and prophet to discard her work, she had been able to pass on to Nzoamambu a major part of her ancient lore. In this particular *nganga* tradition, the earliest recalled ancestor to have practiced was Mwe Bunzi of the Nsundi clan, who married into the Mbenza clan and crossed the Nzadi (Zaire) River from the south. He instructed Na Minlembo, a blacksmith in the same clan, who instructed a younger brother, Na Misenga, also a smith. From him the art was handed down, matrilineally, to blacksmith Kingwanda-Duma. He taught it to his sister, Mavengi-Nkombo, from whom it passed to her maternal granddaughter, Yakeba-Bote, Nzoamambu's grandmother. This genealogy authenticated Nzoamambu's knowledge. By our estimates, the lore and practice dated back into the eighteenth century, and Nzoamambu's instructions to us preserved some part of this past. His experimental approach to life may have been in the tradition, and it would thus be appropriate for him to add to his grandmother's teaching. Her instruction remained crucial, however, for she cured him of a serious illness in his youth. To be a good *nganga*, you have to have undergone such an experience, your knowledge coming from the person who saved your life.

As a boy Nzoamambu had had a swollen stomach and big eyes and often had been unhealthy. He disrespected his grandmother's work, especially after she had discarded most of her paraphernalia. "But God wanted me to be an *nganga*," he said, "initiated by my grandmother." In this initiation, symbols from anatomy, society, and nature come together to create a rich cosmology. To treat his big eyes she used an egg. For his distended stomach she made him drink medicine from the poisonous sap of the *diza-kia-nlembo* (finger cactus, 124). She then took him to the water, held his arms, and asked him, "Do you want to be healed, or to die?" "To be healed," he replied. So she took an *nlolo* fruit (127) and threw it over one shoulder, saying, "*Lolokolo mwana wau*" ("Forgive this child"), then she threw an *mfilu* fruit (126) over the other shoulder, saying, "*Fidimika mamonsono, buka nitu a mvimba*" ("Clarify all, heal the whole body"). Then she took a white chicken, held it up toward the sky and addressed God in heaven, "If this child dies, it will be 'the white chicken,' " thereby adjuring help to save his life. Three times she dipped the chicken under water and brushed his stomach with it; immediately his stomach "went down." Later he was required to eat the chicken. Because she had used *mfilu*, she told him, "*Fwa dia na ngembo, lumfukunia ufilanga dio*" ("The nest of the *ngembo* bat in the forest will be inherited by the *mfukunia* village bat''), meaning, "One day, you the 'domesticated village being' will understand these 'strange, powerful, wild' things.'' After they had walked a short way up to the village, he got the urge to defecate, evidence that his stomach was well. His grandmother began showing him plants and explaining their uses to him, a practice she continued until her death.

This condensed account of Nzoamambu's personal charter as *nganga* exemplifies, once more, the relationship of the anatomy to other domains in Kongo cosmological symbolism. References across domains are created to amplify and explain experience. Thus, initiation opened the body's passages and released powers from the "white" beyond the water. Here these powers were mediated by a white chicken and two plants, endowing Nzoamambu with purity and sight. The proverb about the bats, and the path of the rite from village to stream and back, brought into being and amplified a sacred space in which water, forest, and the mystical contrasted with land, savannah, village, and the temporal. Verbal punning (alliteration) over plant names endowed the fruits with power (e.g., *nlolo* fruit, means *loloka*, "forgive," "remove curse"; *mfilu* fruit, means *fidimika*, "clarify").

When Nzoamambu founded his new village in 1962, breaking away from Mbanza Mwembe with his immediate "house" (*mwelo nzo*) to relocate under the shadow of the old Nsundi burial grove, the same cosmology inspired his actions. Anatomical, social, and natural categories were associated to express the meaning of his new beginning. An *nsanda* fig tree (95) was first planted, following tradition, to determine whether the site would have adequate moisture for other trees and to receive the acceptance of the Simbi water spirits. When the *nsanda* grew, other trees and plants were put in: fruit trees, boundary-defining trees, shade trees, and the many herbs and shrubs needed in his practice. Nzoamambu said he disliked having to walk the Manianga hills to fetch plants, so he transplanted many essential to his treatments from the forest and savannah into his village. Some expressed traditional ideas. The tall *mpese-mpese* poplars (101) were planted to define the chief's enclosure (see Map 3); the circle of palms to provide oil, fiber, nuts, and wine; the outer ring of

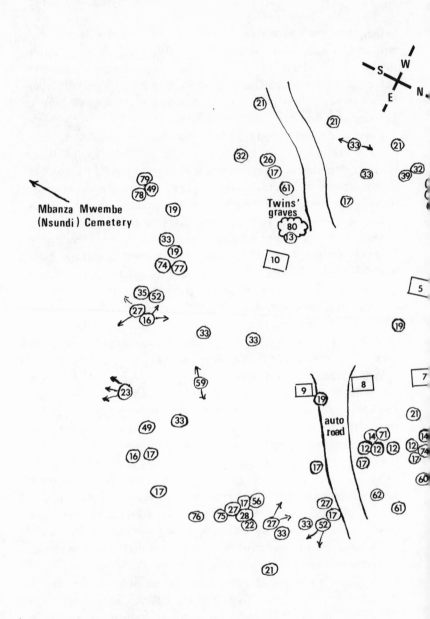

Mbanza Mwembe
(Nsundi) Cemetery

Twins'
graves

auto
road

MANSELELE, 1969
NZOAMAMBU, FOUNDER

(See Key to Plant & Residence
Numbers on Following Pages)

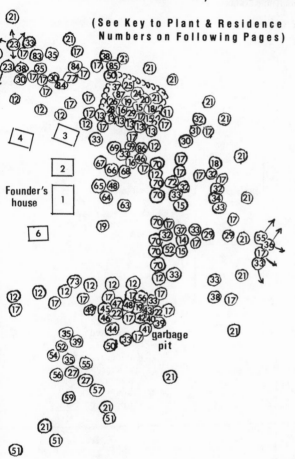

MAP 3. Manselele, near Mbanza Mwembe: Nzoamambu's garden village, its
plants and their uses

KEY

Residences
1. Nzoamambu
2. Nzoamambu's kitchen
3. Patient's guest house
4. Nzoamambu's son's kitchen
5. Nzoamambu's son and family
6–10. Nzoamambu's matrilineal kinsmen

Plants	Medicinal	Poisonous	Food	Other	Identification (Appendix B)	
11. nsanda	X			village-site marker	90, 95	"fig"
12. mpese-mpese	X			enclosure	101	poplar
13. diza dia kinene			X	enclosure	128	cactus
14. nlulukulu	X				94	
15. lubota	X				36	
16. nungu	X		X		97	
17. ba	X		X	cloth, fiber		oil palm
18. mumpala-mbaki	X				13, 115	
19. manga ma kongo	X		X			
20. mungye-ngye	X		X		116	
21. kazuwa	X			border	93, 98	
22. dinkondo			X			banana
23. mafubu	X		X			pineapple
24. luvete	X				117	
25. dioka dia 'cautchuc'			X			greens used
26. dioka dia kongo			X			manioc, roots used
27. sa kongo	X				125	also *ngai-ngai, nti a menga* (tree of blood, red)
28. mbala mputu			X			European potato
29. mfuluta	X				99	
30. nkondo				protect boundary		baobab
31. lubata-bata	X				47	
32. manga ma mputu			X			
33. nsafu	X		X			
34. votolo	X				118	
35. malala ma mputu	X		X			orange

Plants	Medicinal	Poisonous	Food	Other	Identification (Appendix B)	
36. *madeleine*	x		x			tangerine
37. *nlanga-nlanga*	x					
38. *mvuku-mvuku*	x				70	
39. *voka* (tea)			x			
40. *lolo ntumbi*	x				119	also *mvimbu, kienga*
41. *masonia*	x					
42. *tuvumvu*	x				96	
43. *nti wa babakala*	x				77, 120	also *lunsongi*
44. *ntima ngombe*			x			coeur de boeuf
45. *lemba-lemba*	x				56	
46. *nsadi*	x				105	
47. *wayeya*	x				106	
48. *bowa*			x			legume
49. *nung za mputu*	x		x			pepper
50. *wandu*	x		x			beans
51. *mfuma*	x				40	
52. *kilemba*	x		x		122	
53. *muinsi*			x			sugar cane
54. *tiba kia kongo*			x			banana
55. *nkama-nsongo*	x				107	
56. *payi-payi*	x		x			
57. *nsolokoto*	x					
58. *nsaka-nsaka*	x					
59. *nkalu*				container		gourd
60. *tiba*			x			type of banana
61. *diza-kia-nlembo*	x	x		ward off lightning, kill fish	124	finger cactus
62. *mpuluka*	x				92	
63. *bifulu*				decorative		red-flowered bush from European mission
64. *nkoyi a malonga*			x			
65. *tomate*	x		x			
66. *zangi bia nzi*	x		x			
67. *tula*	x				104	
68. *mbala za yangidi*			x			
69. *luyuki*	x				103	
70. *nsinda dia mputu*	x					

Plants	Medicinal	Poisonous	Food	Other	Identification (Appendix B)	
71. nti wa 'bonne année'				New Year's house decoration		
72. kimvumina	x				108	
73. nti wa mbandana				ward off lightning		
74. mansusu mankento	x				72	"female"
75. nsaku-nsaku	x			incense		
76. sofie	x					
77. mansusu mabakala	x				73	"male"
78. sa kongo			x	seasoning		"white"
79. makwiza landi			x			
80. (twin tombs)						
81. kinsimba	x					fiber
82. mpanga	x					
83. mbala nguvu			x			igname
84. bumi		x		kill fish		
85. nkamba	x				23	
86. mfundu	x				102	
87. nkomo	x				100	also *nzila-nzila*

kazuwa (93, 98), with its red and white blossoms, to mark the periphery of public village space, where, in the past, Khimba secret society acolytes ritually "died" and were "resurrected" back into society. Most of the plants expressed Nzoamambu's special cosmology, bringing together anatomical features with plants and powers needed for his work. *Mansiunsiu*, important in seasonings and medicines, had been planted so that the male (73) was to the right of his house (facing the square), the female to his left (72), consonant with Kongo tenets of bodily bisexualism. *Sa kongo* was differentiated into red and white (125), demarcating the edge of the village in the direction of the ancestral grove.

Sometimes Nzoamambu literally referred to his village, his clan society, and its inhabitants, as a body, or person, fusing his "medical" categories with social and herbal terms. Looking out over the village square one day, he asked, "Now why do you think I built my house here at the end?" "Because," he answered, "I'm chief (*mfumu*). If there is something bad in the village, it's up to me to remove it, just like the heart, lord of all else in the body, removes what is bad for it." Society, plants, and body merged in this metaphor, in the same way west African cosmographer Ogotemelli had defined the Dogon village as an exponential curve spiralling outward from a cosmic egg,[2] or the architects of Versailles had made the palace and its gardens a geometric expression of Louis XIV's absolutism.[3]

It is difficult, if not impossible, to abstract a simple physical "anatomy" from the *nganga*'s thinking, because in Zaire, organs, functions, and bodily symptoms are related to a more expansive unit than is the case in Occidental medicine, philosophy, or religion. This is why Nzoamambu's ideas about the body (*nitu a muntu*), which might be construed as such an anatomy, actually embrace constant reference to social relations, plants, and medicines. As has been suggested, the heart stands in analogous relationship to organs and functions, foods, medicines, human beings, spirits, and the whole universe, like a signal—calm in health, agitated in illness—for the *nganga*. Colloquially, Nzoamambu spoke of all this as his "plants." Kongo cultural categories would assign it to *kinganga* perhaps. We may call it Nzoamambu's theory of the person (*muntu*).

The *vumu*, abdomen, in Nzoamambu's theory of the person, is analogous to the lineage house in society, just as the heart is analogous to the chief. *Vumu* thus embraces both physical and social referents. It denotes vulva, uterus, pregnancy, mother's

2. Marcel Griaule, *Dieu d'eau* (Paris, 1948).
3. H. W. Janson, *History of Art* (Englewood Cliffs, N. J. and New York; 1964), p. 444.

breast, lactation, and abdomen, as well as family, or descendants of the same mother (see pp. 21–22). *Vumu* also refers to food substance or "ball of meat." It is a verbal category of congruent ideas, both physical and social, drawn from a dominant idea about subsistence, identity, and well-being.[4]

One important referent of this composite notion relates to the first months of an infant's life, during which time, according to Mzoamambu, the Kongo infant should receive three purges to cleanse the *vumu*. Before it can begin to nurse, it must produce its first excrement to get rid of *ndumba*, a problematic stomach condition. When the child begins to nurse it abuses its source of nurture. It sucks wildly about, getting too much air and milk, so that after two or three weeks its stomach is puffed up. It receives a purge made of the *vamu* plant (131) to make its stomach flow and recede. After another month has passed, the child may develop "elephant stomach." This is best treated with a purge prepared from *nsudi* tree leaves (105), again permitting the stomach to flow. In due course a third purge becomes necessary, because careless parents feed their child just about anything, or the child picks up and eats dirt or whatever else it gets its hands on. This time leaves of the *lubota* tree (36) may be used with good results.

In this series of three purges for swollen infant's stomach, an important anatomical idea that resounds through many Kongo symptoms and treatments is defined. Eating well and defecating freely are signs of health; obstructed bowels indicate self-abuse or ill-wishing and poisoning at the hands of others. The physical body is a channel through which nurture should move freely. In like manner, the social body lives from goodwill, generosity, and the exchange of gifts. Wherever obstacles appear, for example, during the child's entrance into society, they may be dealt with by cleansing the bowels.

Swollen stomach in the child, noted Nzoamambu, can also be a sign of hard spleen (*tadi dia mwana*, "child's hardness or rock,"

---

4. K. E. Laman, *Dictionnaire KiKongo-Français* (Bruxelles, 1936) offers this range of referents for *vumu*.

"le rat"). The stomach may hurt in various ways, causing further complications such as coughing and vomiting. Mothers often take their children precipitously to a European doctor who gives it quinine and aspirin. But tradition offers a treatment of pepper leaves (*nungu*, 97) taken from three plants, crushed with six peppers in a mortar. The pulp is rubbed into twelve *nsamba* incisions over the spleen and six on the opposite side "for protection." Then a toad is taken, its stomach is slit open, the pulp is rubbed into it, and it is buried in a path. The child is jumped (*dumunwa*) three times over the site as a benediction signifying the close of the illness, and handed back to the mother. The body symmetry noted is an underlying facet of Kongo anatomy, as is the demarcation of internal and external dimensions of the body.

A second major anatomical referent of the *vumu* has to do with descent identity and reproduction; the fetus, as well as the cognatic (maternal) line, is called *vumu*. Nzoamambu described the physical process of procreation as follows: "The liquid of the male hits or kills the egg of the woman, and she thenceforth misses her menses. The fluid [also *maluma*, semen] turns to blood, the blood becomes a child, and that ultimately turns into a person [*maza mana kituka menga, menga makitukidi mwana, zimunina muntu*]." This process is congruent with wider notions of descent and social structure which separate the "mother's side," the clan (*kingudi, dikanda, vumu*), from the "father's side," the blood (*kise, menga*). Nzoamambu believed the male to be the dominant partner in sexual intercourse, and that the "blood" created from the semen became the child, that is, "the child followed the paternal line." Still, the child belonged to the mother's clan. This dual belonging was explained colloquially: "The woman is like an envelope; the child sent by the father is the letter in it." Anthropologically put, jural membership of an individual rests with the matrilineal clan, and identity of origin with the patrilateral bond. In practice, father's father's clan, and mother's father's clan are added to father's and mother's clan, constituting the "four parts of a person's identity" (*ndambu ziiya za muntu*). The matrilineal *vumu* is analogous to a "company headquarters," according to Nzoamambu, "an organization with property." Witchcraft, inherited thieving, and incestuous unions exemplify troubles that characteristically develop within it. The paternal tie may resemble this if the blessing is not bestowed on children, but normally it is the channel whereby beneficent acts and spiritual and intellectual thoughts and appearances are transmitted from one generation to the next.

Fertility and lactation relate closely to Nzoamambu's understanding of the *vumu*. Although milk flow begins by itself, normally, it may be stimulated by washing the breasts with hot water and eating sweets. When a woman failed to lactate after giving birth, Nzoamambu recommended three glasses of clear sap of the *mudidi* vine (4), taken orally for several days. An even stronger treatment consisted of *mudidi* vine sap mixed with extract of *nzeka-nzeka* leaves (5, 82) and sugar into a drink given periodically.

Inadequate semen and eggs were seen as problems affecting conception. If the male's fluid could not reach the egg it could not produce a child. Semen could not by itself create a fetus, nor could the female blood of the menses, which carried the eggs, create a fetus by itself. After giving birth a woman should wait at least four months to have intercourse because of the soreness. Nzoamambu noted that conception could occur during the subsequent months a woman was nursing her child, even though she was not menstruating. The menses would begin after about a year. In Zaire, he noted, parents should space their children at least at two-and-a-half-year intervals, thus intercourse should only begin after two years. It might be done sooner, but cautiously, to prevent spacing children too closely. Also, intercourse must be avoided during menses. Men should sleep on different beds from their wives during this time, and the wives must not prepare the men's meals. To do so would invite bad luck, for, as he said, "menstrual blood is unclean."

Problems of conception could have purely "natural" bases, such as insufficient or weak semen, but mostly they were of another etiology, originating in incest, a woman's promiscuity, an affair in the family, the curse of a mother's brother "tying the sister's daughter's womb in a knot," or failure to receive the father's blessing in marriage. In Nzoamambu's scheme, as in Kongo culture at large, *vumu* functions were extremely vulnerable to breaches of social norm. They were classed, at the most general level, as "obstructed passages" (*nzila zakangama*), a sort of generic term for the effects of man-caused illness.

Nzoamambu's best known treatment for women's infertility— the most common affliction of "obstructed passages"—consisted of three spoonfuls of palm wine mixed with bark scrapings of the *lubota* tree. After drinking this a woman would be interrogated: "Do you want to have children? Have you been to another doctor? How long ago? Where? I'll treat you too. Wait three months, take three spoonfuls morning and evening. You should get a good hard stomach, and you'll be pregnant!" A stipulation of this treatment was that the child must bear the name Nzoamambu, the best possible publicity for his trade. (At last count he had 900 homonyms [*ndoyi*]). Although Nzoamambu offered this herbal treatment for infertility, he underlined repeatedly the futility of such, or any other, physical treatment without the simultaneous "calming of the woman's heart" or the elimination of the societal cause.

Chaude pis, a borrowed French term for venereal disease, itself of foreign origin, was an even more serious *vumu* affliction of obstructed passages. It was described as a disease of loose morals which not only led to infertility because of the confusion of various types of semen in the womb, but it also inflicted painful, bloody urination. A symptomatic treatment was possible with the roots of the vine *mumbala-mbala* (111), ground into pulp and mixed with six lemons, sliced into a pot and boiled. Patients should drink one cup, morning and night, for three days. Female patients should also use the medication as a vaginal douche. After three days the pus and blood would be gone.

The most serious of all "obstructed passage" diseases in the *vumu* region were "*hernie*" and "*appendicite*." Despite their being Western terms, and appendicitis being rare in Zaire, these terms had been incorporated by Nzoamambu (as Kongo medical culture at large) as powerful class labels for a variety of obstructed passages: internal, invisible hernia (*mpiki a mfio*); a slightly extended hernia (*madunga manketa*); a large external, extended scrotal hernia (*mpiki a luzamba*); and a uniquely woman's hernia (*babakala*). Although Nzoamambu did not have much to say about the treatment for various hernias, he noted that they could be caused by lifting too hard (i.e., physical causes) as well as social breaches. Accordingly, while local treatment was possible, the moral causes accompanying the disease must be removed before treatment could be successful. A neighboring *nganga*, Mama Mankomba of Mbemba village, used the *kanga-ngoyo* vine (141), chewed by the patient, to shrivel hernia swelling, and a pulp of *lubota* leaves to massage the hernia toward the same end. Combining the moral and physical causes for women's hernia, Nzoamambu stated it could result in a woman's incapability to give birth (*lembama buta*). This affliction is accompanied by difficulty or pain in starting menses, painful buttocks, and swollen labia. It being a "woman's problem," he did not have a treatment for this, but recommended the sufferer go to the hospital for a "dilation and curettage," or to a woman healer such as Mama Mankomba.

It is evident from Nzoamambu's discussion of the *vumu*, with its myriad of functions and qualitites, that multiple referents combine to create generalized, diffuse, and strongly emotional meanings. Specific physical functions, child feeding, reproduction, hernias, infertility, and related afflictions and impairments were combined into related statements about a single anatomical area. *Vumu*, more than any other part of the person, seemed to connote social legitimacy and illegitimacy. Perhaps this was due to the tie with social continuity through reproduction. The discussion on hernias, in particular, evoked overtones of the contrast between propriety and obscenity in society. *Mpiki* and *kibinda* were obscene words, in a general sense, but especially before someone of the opposite sex and before ascending-generation kinsmen. Nzoamambu had not been able to treat his mother's hernia, he could not even talk about it comfortably, for general social prohibitions forbade him from seeing her genitalia. The terms for hernia seemed to express the falseness, illegitimacy, of *vumu* fullness or the transgression of the sexes. "Woman's hernia" (*babakala*, "males") implied a disease of men which women sometimes get. Or perhaps it was a "false pregnancy." Similarly, *mpiki*, a men's disease, called forth the stigmatizing connotations of "a cluster of nuts or bananas hanging down, like 'false testicles.' " It was like the swelling of poisoning or of heart congestion, which made the afflicted person appear well nourished while being emaciated, or appear to have a healthy skin tone while having water under the skin. Such swelling was a "false roundedness" that superficially appeared to be a sign of health and well-being, but in fact resulted in death. All these *vumu* afflictions, especially those combining reproductive impairment with witchcraft connotations under the rubric of "obstructed passages," were so stigmatized. Considerable light is shed on the power of the multiple referent symbol *vumu* by recalling that in traditional Kongo thinking *kibinda*, the worst term for hernia, denoted a ball of strangulated meat or food just as *kundu* did, the sack in witches, verifying illegitimately accumulated nurturance. *Kundu* was treated by the most powerful purificatory purge known to BaKongo, the poisonous bark of the *nkasa* tree. This either killed the patient, establishing his guilt as a witch, or left him alive and exonerated. In either case it cleansed the society. The only legitimate fullness of *vumu* passages, to Nzoamambu and Kongo thinking, is pregnancy, which binds two clans together in mutual solidarity.

The anatomical region of the sides, chest, and muscle wall were subordinated in Nzoamambu's scheme to functions of breathing and the blood and corresponding afflictions. Some practitioners and laymen have seen breath (*kiwumunu*) as the principal manifestation of life in the person,[5] and its afflictions made apparent in choking, gasping, asthma, and pneumonia, all "obstructed passage" afflictions of the breath. Others speak of blood in this same way as the source or manifestation of life. Thickening, dirt, and pollution are its afflictions. In any event, sides, chest wall, lungs,

---

5. Fukiau-kia-Bunseki, *Kindoki, ou la solution attendue* (Kumba, 1973), suggests this idea, along with the *kidibidi* ("body"), and the *kini* ("spirit"), as principal components of the person, forming a human philosophical system, *kibantu*. See note 7 below for further comments on the Bantu "life principle."

breath, and blood are commonly associated in the disease *lubanzi*, or *mpanzi*. The term literally means "side," and is the word for rib. But it also refers to the disease and its symptoms. Sharp stabbing pains indicate the onset of *lubanzi*. Beginning symptoms are said to be due to "crossed ribs," "a drop of bad blood lodged in the side," or other abuse such as an accidental fall, too heavy exertion, and the like. These are "outer *lubanzi*" manifestations and are commonly treated with massages or *nsamba* incisions with plants rubbed into them. Sometimes the cupping horn is applied to "suck out" (*hola*) the object. *Lubanzi* may also move to the inside of the body, and it may appear elsewhere. Inner *lubanzi* is manifested by coughing, fever, bloody stool, or other serious symptoms. For this reason it is alleged that Western therapists do not understand the disease, and that a patient risks dying if he goes to a Western hospital.

Nzoamambu spoke of a case of "neck *lubanzi*" which required massaging, so the patient could again look up and around without pain. If massaging did not free her from symptoms, then she had serious *lubanzi*. In another case Nzoamambu diagnosed *lubanzi* in the side and lower back. He took *tula* tree leaves (104) and three palm nuts and mashed them into an oily pulp which he massaged over the sore spot. Meanwhile, he had heated a machete red hot over a fire of *luvete* wood (117) and had squeezed a few drops of the juice into the fire to make it pop and jump with great effect. The red-hot machete was pressed firmly but very quickly, in crisscross pattern, over the site of the ache. "Momentarily painful, but effective," he observed.

The progression of *lubanzi*, and corresponding treatments, from external to internal, and from mild to serious, follows a fairly patterned course. In one source, from 1915, this is characteristically shown. The *nganga* neutralizes the ill will (*mfunia*) engendered by the disease in the patient's body. If this does not relieve the symptoms, he takes *nkisi* NaKongo, a raffia cloth sack containing pungent plants, and holds it under the patient's nose for him to inhale. Then he massages the *lubanzi* ache with the same sack. Finally, the patient is given a potion of *lemba-lemba* extract (56). Thus, the breath, the side ache, and the mouth are brought together in a single cure, as a song is sung over the patient. In characteristic hierarchic progression, the source continues that if the *lubanzi* persists and manifests itself as the more serious internal variety, *nkisi* Misambu (*nsamba* incisions) is resorted to. This too is a raffia bundle containing numerous plants and mineral objects crushed together with an oily palm nut. This substance is rubbed into the incisions, and a potion of the above plants and objects, together with *lemba-lemba* is administered to the patient. If this treatment is inadequate, and the patient has *lubanzi* of the side as well as bloody stool and sore liver, he needs *nkisi* Mbumba, consisting of additional plants mixed into a potion, but without the *nsamba* incisions. For the disease has internalized itself and is no longer accessible from the outside.[6]

Nzoamambu did not provide a synthesizing anatomical or organic concept to explain *lubanzi*. His treatment in one case and his discussion demonstrated that he handled it as "outer *lubanzi*" (i.e., muscular spasm or pain). Others dealt with it as a disease object just beneath the skin which could be removed "as a drop of bad blood" by incisions and cupping horn. "Internal *lubanzi*" has been likened by some to pneumonia which accounts for the coughing and fever. As such a composite disease or category *lubanzi* remains a definite research problem in Kongo medicine.

After his explication of the *vumu*, Nzoamambu developed the symptomatology of the head, *ntu*, and the heart, *ntima*, most completely. In both areas the hierarchy of progression of diseases and treatments was vividly clear. This concept offers the foundation for his general view of the person.

Head affliction (*yela kwa ntu*) was described in terms of a number of illness types—such as, ache, dizziness, dissociation, unconsciousness, ranging from mild to serious. Ordinary headache (*ntu tatika*) can be treated with the reddish extract of *mawandu* bean leaves (see Map 3) taken orally, three spoonfuls morning and night. If the headache persists despite this treatment, it might be *ntu lukika*, diagnosed by Nzoamambu in one case where a woman complained of "something walking about in

6. Babutidi, Notebook 7, Laman Collection, Svenska Missionsforbundet Archives (Lidingö).

her stomach which went up to the heart and out the fingertips, again other times going up into the head accompanied by dizziness as if she had drunk too much wine." One treatment for this utilizes *sesa* broom straw charred over a fire, made into a black powder, and rubbed into three *nsamba* incisions over each temple and on the neck muscles at the back of the head. If the treatment is ineffective, *ntu lukika* may be the beginning manifestation of convulsions (*mbadukulu lembama*), for which a more potent treatment is needed, such as that utilizing an extract of bark scrapings of *mangeke* and day-old leaves of *munkwinsia* (114) as nose drops. If the headache at this stage is accompanied by red spittle, it is contagious; the spittle should be buried in a hole in the ground.

Although Nzoamambu understood "contagion" as communicable disease, he attributed headache caused by it to a kinsman's curse or ancestral displeasure. For this, an *nganga* must continue local treatment while driving off the curse with magic, initiating a reconciliation meeting of the patient's clan, or recommending a sacrifice by the patrifilial children to the tombs of the patient's clan ancestors. It is appropriate for an *nganga* therefore to investigate the specific animosity at the origin of headache threatening to grow into convulsions.

For continuing *ntu lukika*, specific therapy alongside the clan meetings and sacrifices might include a treatment from the extract of the soft stringy inside of *mwindu* bark (81) and *munkwinsia* juice, given morning, noon, and night, as a drop in each eye through a leaf cone. If the patient feels better after this treatment, well and good. If not, an *nganga* should check other lines of etiology. Does the patient have eye pain in connection with headache? Ringing of the ears? Stomach worms? Has he been receiving treatment for anything else? Nzoamambu noted that headache might be brought on by parallel diseases elsewhere in the body. If eye pains accompany headache, causing "eye worms" (*nioka zameso*), a treatment with pepper and tomato plant extract is effective. (Nzita's treatment, episode 5.12, follows this exactly.) Earache and stomach worms causing headache each had their prescribed treatment, in Nzoamambu's scheme. These headaches caused by parallel diseases were like dizziness, but not that of drunkenness or that of tobacco, rather like the dizziness (*nzieta*) of anemia, extreme hunger, or nausea.

A wide variety of simple headaches can, according to Nzoamambu, progress into a headache of convulsions, called *sansa, bebama, sisuka,* or *maladi ma ndeki* ("bird illness"), terms sometimes translated as "epilepsy." They are all very dangerous, noted Nzoamambu, because the sufferer may fall into the hearth fire and burn himself severely, or even die. An elaborate treatment for all these diseases consists of taking the patient behind the house, to the place of the hearth, and rubbing into groups of three *nsamba* incisions on the forehead over each eye, the back of the neck, shoulders, elbows, wrists, knees, over the big toe (letting him lick the blood from the knife), extract of boiled male and female *mansiunsiu* leaves. The raw extract from these plants follows the cooked, and is rubbed into the same incisions. Finally, the extracts are given as nose drops. There are other treatments resembling this for convulsions, which deal with the problem locally. But *sansa*, the most severe of them, alone touches the heart, causing heart pains which may result in madness.

Nzoamambu's understanding of the heart (*ntima*) constitutes the integrating link in his medical cosmology. The heart is "lord of the person" (*mfumu a muntu*), which at once reflects or "echoes" afflictions elsewhere in the body and responds in caution, alerting the whole person to dangers that may beset it. The heart is life (*moyo*), will, soul.[7] Normally the heart is tranquil (*ntima dingalala, ntima zeeza*), but when danger arises or illnesses afflict, the heart warns. As Nzoamambu stated it:

> The heart may go "ko! ko! ko!" This is *madikitila* [heart palpitations]. An even stronger beat, indicating severe disquietude, is *ntima diata mu ngolo* ["heart pounding very hard"], or *ngongo zeti budika* ["the

7. Laman's *Dictionnaire, op. cit.*, itself a compendium of definitions, ideas, and customs, identifies the term *moyo* ("life force"), as synonym for both *vumu* ("abdomen"), and *ntima* ("heart"). Other parts of the person than the heart may be utilized to symbolize this life force in rituals and religious cosmologies. All formulations of this important central African (Bantu) metaphysical principle point to its physical and symbolic embodiment. Misused or gone awry, it can destroy; therefore, it must be handled circumspectly, preferably by consecrated specialists.

beat on a calabash"]. Fear in the heart [*wonga mu ntima*] is the strongest stage of reaction. "Heart palpitation" can be caused by someone surprising you, or someone shouting at you with a loud voice when you do not know what is wrong. Or you have a nightmare and wake suddenly, heart beating hard. Or you see others fighting, or someone threatens to kill you, or people run around excitedly. Or, you are walking alone, suddenly you hear a whistle, yet see no one. Or your hear strange voices and sounds. The palpitations last as long as you have thoughts on the subject.

A number of widespread treatments exist for *madikitila*. Nzoamambu begins with one already noted in episode 5.8 of Nzita's case, entailing two leaves of *lemba-lemba*, three of *lemba-ntoko* (140), and grains of *lemba-nzau* (42). These are pounded into a pulp on a mortar and mixed with water and an egg. The result is a good oral sedative, to be given any time in doses of half a glass morning and evening. All three plants "calm the heart" (*lemba* or *lembikisa*, "to calm").

If this treatment fails to heal the heart palpitations, to calm the heart permanently, another, utilizing the root of the *kanga-ngoyo* vine (156) may be used. The treatment is in good part psychological. The *nganga* fetches still water from quiet pools in a leaf or a rock, brings it to the patient, quietly, and drinks it with him; he is given portions of the root of the vine to chew.

Another treatment, in case the above does not work, utilizes leaves of *wayeya* (106), two to three leaves of *lemba-lemba*, and two of *malulukulu* (94), mixed with water until it becomes dark. This potion should be effective even for someone suffering palpitations of long standing. If not, it is an indication that his family or clan is implicated in the illness; they must be sent for, and the treatment repeated in their presence.

Nzoamambu drew a fundamental distinction between heart palpitations leading to "fear in the heart" (*wonga mu ntima*) and "heart pain" (*ntima tatika*). This latter term refers to nausea (*ntima funduka*), the urge to vomit (*ntima vuzinga*), or a sharp, stabbing pain in the chest (*ntima kanduzuka*). These sensations may be caused by stomach worms, stomach gas, or other lower abdominal illnesses, including "woman's hernia" and infertility.

A variety of food prohibitions may be necessary to relieve these symptoms, including a ban on using too much palm oil. Leaves of *wayeya, lemba-lemba,* and *malulukulu* may be taken orally to relieve the symptoms.

Heart palpitations, again, frequently indicate the effect of magic upon a person, according to Nzoamambu. For example, a thief may be pursued "in magic" after an *nganga*, upon a client's commission, has prepared medicines for this purpose. (The example given at the outset of this chapter illustrates what Nzoamambu means by this.) Both the magic prepared by the *nganga* and the theft victim's anger are at work in this. If the thief returns the stolen items, the *nganga* must neutralize the magical charm to stop the palpitations. Failure to do so would lead to the thief's incurable madness (*lauka*) from fear. Many variations on this topic of magical charms and thieves exist, some with magical objects and ingredients, others with spells predominating. The *nganga* understands both symptoms and causes well, for he inflicts, for a fee, as well as uncovers and heals.

When an *nganga* receives a sufferer with "fear in the heart," he explores simple matters between family members, the possibility of a disturbing dream and its meaning, or some hidden secret in the sufferer's life. Simultaneously, he may pursue a treatment such as *lemba-lemba, lemba-ntoko,* and *lemba-nzau* to calm his heart. But the true fear in the heart can only be eliminated by getting to the root cause: finishing the affair, disclosing the secret, or interpreting the dream. Many families take sufferers with "fear in the heart" to hospitals, but eventually they end up at an *nganga*, who understands these things best, and can uncover the cause. Nzoamambu gave an example of his own work in this area.

A hunter was brought to me complaining of "fear in the heart" and "harassment by demons." I treated him with *lemba-lemba, lemba-ntoko, lemba-nzau,* and an egg [see above], but there was no change in his behavior. Bystanders thought him incurably mad, because of the way he spoke—having heard monkeys and wild pigs crying in tall grass. But I thought there was more to it. For as the search team went out with flashlights at night to see what was out there, his heart was going "ko! ko! ko!" despite the tranquilizer he had received. Then they discovered the body of another hunter whom he had shot by mistake. The police commandant asked me how I knew, before they found the body, that he was not mad. Well, he didn't respond to treatment.

It is axiomatic of Nzoamambu's scheme that "fear in the heart" not dealt with appropriately progresses into madness. Few BaKongo ventured a definition of madness because it related to the loss of control, the emergence of total chaos in a person's life. Loss of coherent speech was for some a crucial symptom of incipient madness. Inability to cook meals, make beds, or perform other role-designated tasks were indicative symptoms for others. As has been suggested in the case of Nzita, madness is total illness, epiphenomenal of all other physical and social problems. In Nzoamambu's scheme it was the ultimate illness that affected the dominant organ, the heart. And yet, it was not, apparently, cause for abandonment of the afflicted individual. Government files relating to action against "fools," as well as observed cases, conveyed the impression that families and clans keep and care for their own, even though the colonial government and its post-independence sequel remove "fools" from the population by force, isolating them in prisons or other asylums.

Nzoamambu's treatments for advanced madness once more indicated both a local symptomatic understanding as well as a concern for deeper causes. One treatment utilized *mawandu* bean leaves and tobacco juice as nose drops, along with with scrapings of *mumpala-mbaki* bark (151) as eye drops. If the patient responds to these, he may be given on the following day a drink extracted from the *makinda-ngolo* vine leaf (145) with water. The *nganga* drinks some along with him and gives him the vine to wear around his hips as a reminder.

Many cases of madness received by Nzoamambu were young men and women who had "played with charms" (*minkisi*) or "walked on a fetish" (*diata va nkisi*), meaning they had consulted or purchased magical devices and had either not observed the rules or had gotten involved with medicines too powerful for them and had "burned their fingers" as a consequence. Nzoamambu, having received instructions from his grandmother in the enigmatic area of magical power, relished his understanding of its problems and mastery of the techniques. He illustrated his understanding of madness by showing us three types of *nkisi*-related afflictions, and the cures for them as he had administered them.

A young man who contracted a charm to protect himself against thieves accidentally killed the long black *ndimba* snake (familiar) specifically mentioned as a taboo in the oath. He was brought to Nzoamambu babbling incoherently, hands and feet bound. Nzoamambu tells how he cured him.

> I boiled down into medicine a sliced bulb of the *dinkondo dia kimbiti* bush [112]. I approached the young man, remembering that he was my comrade. I took some of the liquid, and played "politics" with him, faking that he had something else—in his eyes. I squeezed tobacco juice into his eyes to distract him, then gave him a glass of the liquid to drink. He went to sleep. Whenever he awoke, for several days, I continued giving it to him.

The strong sedative and Nzoamambu's "politics" sufficed to release the young man from the uncontrollable fear of the consequences of killing his familiar.

In another case the cure was exclusively symbolic. A young man had ordered medicine from France, said Nzoamambu, to make him into a *"petit Wallon"* (French-speaking Belgian), and it drove him mad. He could be cured only by throwing away his cherished European possessions—into the river, before the ancestors. This cure echoes Fannon and Mannoni's analyses of the self-effacing psychological effect of colonization, and how it may be cured, sometimes painfully, through violence against the colonizer.[8] It also reflects some of the cultural symbols of postindependence nativistic movements elsewhere in Zaire.[9]

Finally, Nzoamambu demonstrated how a skillful *nganga* intrigued first to ward off witchcraft and then to dominate and cure the kinsman upon whom the magic had backfired. His sister's son had contracted with another *nganga*—whom he derogatorily called a *"féticheur"*—to deliver up in witchcraft Nzoamambu, an

---

8. Franz Fannon, *Les damnées de la terre* (Paris, 1961); O. Mannoni, *Psychologie de la colonisation* (Paris, 1950).

9. Herbert Weiss, *Political Protest in the Congo* (Princeton, 1967); Benoit Verhaegen, *Rébellions au Congo, I* (Bruxelles, 1966).

aunt, and his mother in order to become a famous carpenter.
When he came to get his victims, Nzoamambu was warned in a
dream, and confronted him, asking what he wanted; putting him
to work; telling him to bring his parents; and standing up to him.
Three times the nephew returned, each time "overpowered" by
Nzoamambu. The *féticheur* became angry, and the young man
fell ill with "sickness in his heart." He visited prophets and healers, but to no avail. Finally he came, with his parents, to
Nzoamambu, wishing to be healed for "incurable fear in the
heart," accompanied by headache. His parents feared he had
broken some kind of prohibition. Nzoamambu got him to reveal
the *féticheur* whom he had consulted to take others' lives. In a
description of the ritual cure of his nephew's heart fear with
headache, Nzoamambu related:

> I took him down to the river and asked him whether he wanted to live.
> He said, "Yes." So to dominate my nephew I took leaves of *nlolo,
> mfilu, munsangula* [12, 173], *mvuka* [168], *nsonia, seesa,* and pineap-
> ple. Because he had paid one *nsengi* to the other *nganga,* I asked him
> for the same coin. He entered the water and I asked him:
>   "Who's your mother's brother?"
>   "You are."
>   "Who should be the chief?"
>   "You."
>   "Do you want to be healed?"
>   "Yes."
>   "Then come to me, do not do stupid things like you've just done.
> From this day on . . . [putting one leaf of each plant into the water,
> calling out its name]:
>   *N'lolo*: forgive him (*lemvukila lolo*);
>   *Mfilu*: conclude it so he realizes (*fidika kuna yamona*);
>   *Munsangula*: bring it into visibility (*sangumuna*);
>   *M'vuka*: put him back together (*vuka mo*);
>   *Mfuba*: cause his nefarious acts to fail (*fubisa fu babio*);
>   *Seesa*: [holding it in air] God in heaven, [holding it down in water],
> [sprinkling nephew with it]. What gets purchased with money, is not
> taken back [*kiasumbwa na nzimbu: kiatabika*; i.e., what I am
> performing, is legitimate].

In a scene reminiscent of Nzoamambu's own cure long ago, he
related how he then threw the money into the water to wash away

his nephew's sins. They quickly bathed. He took him by the hand, jumped him out of the water, and ran up to the village. There he jumped him three more times (*dumuna*) to bless him, and passed him three times between his legs to pronounce the illness over.

Nzoamambu's summarizing statements on "heart afflictions" summed up his whole medical cosmology. An *nganga* must have many remedies for the heart because the heart has many reactions. When the heart reacts to something negatively it is not content. If one treatment is given for an illness and the heart is not content, another is tried. If a person cuts a finger, blood spurts out because the heart suffers; if there are worms in the stomach, the heart's suffering causes vomiting. If the illness is not treated soon enough, something as small as worms can ultimately cause madness. Foot sores can cause madness. When the heart suffers it warns the eyes, ears, and brain just as a hunter is alert when he stalks an animal, or when an *nganga*'s heart tells him to be cautious when he hears tell of a plant remedy.

Nzoamambu concluded his presentation on the heart and summed up his medical views with these words: "The heart suffers from all illnesses, and the death of a person results from the death of the heart. The heart possesses the entire body [*yandi vwidi nitu a mvimba*]; he is lord of the body [*nkuluntu a nitu*]; the heart is the person [*ntima i muntu*]."

This medical scheme and theory of the person may not be the only one of its kind in central Africa, but its validity is borne out in the striking similarities between it and exposés of disease concepts and therapeutic practices in cultures as widely dispersed as the Lunda of southern Zaire, Zambia, and eastern Angola,[10] and the Xhosa-speaking peoples of southern Africa,[11] to name a few. It offers considerable analytical leverage in the understanding of symptoms and complaints in medical cases in the Lower Zaire.

10. Victor W. Turner, *The Forest of Symbols* (Ithaca, 1967), especially Chapter 9, "Lunda Medicine and the Treatment of Disease," pp. 299–358; *Drums of Affliction* (Oxford, 1968).

11. G. Jansen, *The Doctor-Patient Relationship in an African Tribal Society* (Assen, 1973). Chapter 5, "Introducing the Anamnesis Among the Bomvana" is a good discussion of symptoms and their meaning from the patient's point of view.

Diagnostic Ideas

General principles may be derived from Kongo diagnosticians, whether they be an *nganga* like Nzoamambu, a divining expert such as Mama Marie, a therapy managing group, or a practitioner of Western medicine. Analysis of sufferers' presenting symptoms and later imputations of etiology in terms of these principles establishes the cultural forms and values in illness as well as the cultural perception of ecological determinants of disease.

To begin with, Kongo diagnosis is as capable of empirical observation as any other tradition. Sufferers and close kinsmen offer precise and localized symptoms of strong, painful afflictions like a broken leg or kidney infection. The empiricism of Kongo diagnosis produces poignant, easy to grasp, imagery. Thus, boils pulsate (*zubu-zubu*), a child's stomach turns "elephantine," dread produces a heartbeat that "pounds like a drum," and madness causes a person to "thrash about like a bird." Such symptom labels are perhaps as numerous as there are individuals with complaints and are thus almost impossible to organize. This feature has led one early-twentieth-century observer of Kongo medicine to note that "illnesses are as a rule cured with a medicine . . . specifically indicated for each case."[12]

The specificity of such symptoms may be misleading, for some refer to disease entities or diagnostic categories of greater inclusiveness. The label may appear descriptive of a physical sensation, but its referents may also be conceptual. *Lubanzi*, for example, denotes pain in the side; yet, as a diagnostic category the term also denotes the internal complications of cough, fever, "bad blood," and internal bleeding. Even the adoption of *pneumonie* as a French gloss for this disease entity or category has not altered its reference to both the external pain, treatable by an *nganga*, and the internal lung infection, today believed to require penicillin and hospitalization. *Kosa-kosa a menga* ("coughing with blood") is a similar descriptive term that has taken on diagnostic value. It is used to refer to tuberculosis. The KiKongo term would be used to describe the condition of someone who

12. K. E. Laman, *The Kongo II* (Uppsala, 1957), p. 62.

perhaps had a cough, was losing weight, and appeared generally unwell and suffered bloody spittle. But with the earlier diagnosis of tuberculosis by X-ray and laboratory examination, many patients now would say they suffered *kosa-kosa a menga* even though they never had bloody cough. The term has taken on diagnostic value of its own, and is used interchangeably with *la tuberculose*. *Kinsuba-nsuba* ("pissing-pissing"), in a similar fashion refers specifically to diabetes mellitus, a diagnosis introduced by Western medicine. These and other descriptive symptom labels denoting a disease entity suggest that diagnostic classification may occur without verbal generalization. The context of the term's use, and the user's interpretation as seen in therapeutic choice, are required to discern its meaning.

Other diagnostic categories derive from general principles evident in an anatomy or theory of the person such as Nzoamambu's where anatomical functions are related to areas of society and culture. Thus, "suffocation" was an accurate description of a child's difficulty breathing (4.1-6), but in the light of Nzoamambu's interpretations, this term could also have been descriptive of "choking, knotting, binding, interfering" in social processes. A "lump in the groin" was a growth, arrested long ago (6.2); from Nzoamambu's discussion it seems plausible to relate it to the category of "obstructed passage" afflictions and to other symptoms in the case such as "abdominal pain" and "urinary infection" (6.1-3). "Bad blood" might have been a local interpretation of anemia (3.2), but since the diagnosis emanated from an *nganga*, it may have been intended as a suggested ritual pollution evaluation. "Rheumatism of head" and "loss of intelligence" (6.9), "split head" (6.8), and "dizziness caused by eye worms" (5.12) could be related to the series of head afflictions in Nzoamambu's scheme, culminating in convulsions. "Heart pain" (7.7) and "fear of death" (6.7) were expressions of extreme anxiety, which, according to Nzoamambu's key idea and the implied diagnosis by the therapy managing group in Nzita's case, could progress to "madness" (5.8).

Other diagnostic ideas evident in the cases, in Nzoamambu's scheme, and in Kongo medical culture at large impose principles upon the anatomy from a variety of sources. Some appear to have a physiological basis, others definitely echo religious symbolism. One of these ideas, which has already been noted in the case of *lubanzi*, is the inside/outside dichotomy of the human person. It permits the doctor to manipulate "empirically" from the outside through massages, cupping horn, incision, nose drops, and the like, all the while the sanctity of the "inner" person is left to mysterious powers within the body and the outer world. Thus, in one treating song, the *nganga* addressed the *nkisi*, "*E Nkumba na Nayama*, who has given me power to treat, you treat internally, I will treat externally."[13] A host of diagnoses such as "drop of bad blood," "an object crawling around inside me," "noisy abdomen," "pounding heart, lord of the body," serve to define the inner person. Frequently these concretized disease objects are credited with having a degree of anger, expressed in terms of their "biting," "crawling," "voraciousness," or "pounding." *Nganzi* and *mfunia* are used to denote the anger of the illness. At other times the inner person is defined by the use of a "double" or mirror-image alter-ego of the sufferer. Every individual may have a homonym (*ndoyi, mbanda*), or double, who is either human or animal. In the conceptualization of medicines, this feature extends the life force of the protagonist out to the double, or familiar, with the prohibition of eating, killing, or touching it. Thus the probe for a snake familiar in Nsimba's case (6.5). Various religious theories of the wandering, night-flying witch, or the spirit that enters a prophet, help define the enigmatic inner person in sickness and health.

A related cultural principle applied to diagnosis is the symmetry, or complementary opposition, within every person. The most frequent idiom in which this is expressed is one of sexual dualism in every person, the left side being "female," the right, "male." A disease can wander, it is thought, from one side of the body to another, if both sides are not treated simultaneously.

The anatomical notion of "closed passages" has implications, in Kongo diagnosis, of ritual pollution and purification. What is

13. *Ibid.*, p. 73.

expressed at the anatomical level in choking or suffocation of breath, infertility of reproductive organs, thickening of the blood into "drops of bad blood," tends to define a situation of ritual pollution, a general condition of closed, clogged, tied, dirty human life. The prevailing treatment for such conditions, correspondingly, involves purging, opening, clearing up, confessing, and other purificatory symbols. While not all such diagnosis has these religious connotations, there is a cultural history of purification ritual in Kongo, and frequently in these rituals the body becomes the expressive battleground for warring forces in human society.[14]

Beneath most Kongo medical diagnosis there is an etiological structure that Nzoamambu's scheme has clarified considerably. Several aspects of body, the sufferer as a person, and his social and natural environment are dynamically linked. Parallel processes in these domains are monitored by the diagnostician, whether that be healer, diviner, sufferer, or therapy managing group. For Nzoamambu, afflictions such as headache signalled ailments elsewhere, ailments such as stomach worms or earache. The heart, similarly, signalled well-being and sickness in all other areas of the person, including social surroundings and mystical connections. This makes it evident that Kongo etiology consistently draws the effective boundary of the person differently, more expansively, than classical Western medicine, philosophy, and religion. The outcome is usually disconcerting or unreal to Western medical observers, although completely logical within the terms of Kongo diagnosis.[15] The syllogism used is the same as in Western medicine: If symptom (or disease) A is not cured by medicines W or X, then the affliction must be disease B, for which medicines Y and Z are appropriate. At some point in this

14. Mary Douglas has developed a paradigm of pollution and purification systems in which the body is seen as the arena of conflicts. This is especially true, she notes, in societies in which role and status norm boundaries are poorly defined or in contradiction. See her *Natural Symbols* (New York, 1970) and *Purity and Danger* (London, 1966).

15. The reader may wish to consult Robin Horton's excellent discussion on the comparability of West African divination and Western science, in "African Traditional Thought and Western Science," *Africa* 37 (1967): 50–71, 155–187.

hierarchic progression B becomes the social and mystical surrounding of the sufferer. Causal assertions are made which relate them to anatomical conditions, for example, "the mother's brother's curse causes his sister's daughter's tied womb," or, "conflict in the family causes the child's illness." The outer boundary of the afflicted person includes these social and mystical factors.

To see the inherent logic in this definition of the person, it is necessary to understand the hierarchy of symptom progression that links parallel domains. In Nzoamambu's diagnostic framework, external causations came into play at that point where the anatomical progression of symptoms reached the heart. His theory of "contagion," exemplified by the headache accompanied by red spittle, caused by a kinsman's curse or ancestral displeasure, illustrated the causative connection mediated by the heart. Other diagnosticians offered that "germ illnesses" or "microbe" infections could be caused by witchcraft. Mama Marie, for example, stated that "the healthy body passes bad food or poison without ill effect, but the body that is bewitched will allow poison and bad food to lodge in it and enter the blood." The definition of the person, as drawn in the typical Kongo hierarchy of symptom progressions, creates a framework within which all of the physical diseases in Western medicine (e.g., pneumonia, hernia, malaria, tuberculosis, diabetes, germs) can be added to the diagnostic repertoire without abandoning the wider etiology of gossip, mysteries, evil acts, curses, "threads of social connection," "being in someone's hand," and "strange death," the usual euphemisms for witchcraft.

And yet, few symptoms or diseases are immediately and categorically relegated to social and mystical causes. It is an analytical error to draw up mutually exclusive lists of "natural" and "supernatural" diseases in Kongo.[16] When a disease is diagnosed as having a social or mystical cause, the therapeutic tradi-

16. Most efforts to classify symptoms and diseases in African cultures, which come up with mutually exclusive lists of natural and supernatural diseases, are done in the context-free tradition of componential analysis. Our own approach to this dichotomy, in a context-sensitive theoretical framework, has been proposed

tion prescribes simultaneous treatment for localized symptoms and wider causes. The apparent abuses in traditional therapy, as well as the drawn-out, objectified, statuses of certain diseases in concrete cases result from the inability of a managing group to deal with the problem at both, or several, levels simultaneously. The therapeutic course frequently extends to serially related episodes after specific symptoms have abated or others have developed.

The identification of diagnostic ideas, as it has been attempted here, is not only of importance for the cultural analysis of a medical tradition, it is of significance to medical care. A movement has emerged in medical nosology (a branch of medicine dealing with classification of disease) emphasizing linguistic meaning and cultural form in presenting symptoms and complaints. An assumption made in this movement is that care may be improved if the patient's expectations are understood. "Symptoms" refer, as in traditional medicine, to subjective descriptions of an affliction; "signs" to objective concrete evidence of disease; and "diagnoses" to the assignment of disease concepts to signs and symptoms so as to account for them causally in terms of a disease entity. This emphasis has permitted medical research to understand how presenting symptoms, complaints, and problems portrays the body, pain, person, and their relative importance in the culture of diseases.[17] It has also shed light on difficulties inherent in diagnosis arising from the cultural embeddedness everywhere of symptom and disease language. The discovery has been made,

as a semiotic of Kongo symptoms, presented at the Annual Meeting of the American Anthropological Association, November 28–December 2, 1973, New Orleans, entitled, "Signs, Symptoms, and Symbols: A Semiotic Interpretation of Kongo Illness and Therapy."

17. The trend is marked by editorials, articles, and major works such as Kerr L. White, "Classification of Patient Symptoms, Complaints, and Problems," *World Health Organization* (December 1970); "Problem-Oriented Medical Records," *The Lancet* (February 5, 1972); Lawrence L. Weed, *Medical Records, Medical Education, and Patient Care* (Cleveland, 1969); S. T. Bain and W. B. Spaulding, "The Importance of Coding Presenting Symptoms," *Canadian Medical Association Journal* 9 (1967): 953–59. This movement in medical record keeping and classification has given rise to the widespread "Weed method" of records. Parallel to this, in the social sciences, has been a series of culturally sensitive symptom and disease studies, such as I. K. Zola, "Culture and Symptoms: An Analysis of

for example, that only 55 percent of the entries in the World Health Organization's widely used "International Classification of Diseases" (ICD) are "scientifically diagnosible" entities, that is, reducible to single, universal and duplicable, sign-symptom complexes. Remaining entries of the ICD are independently varying signs and symptoms classified somewhat arbitrarily according to body parts and problem focuses.[18] In other words, cultural assumptions, rather than laboratory experiments, pervade much of the ICD. The obvious conclusion to be drawn from this, and one in keeping with our analysis of Kongo medicine, is that many symptoms and complaints can only be understood by grasping concepts latent in a culture and in conditions affecting sufferers.

Patients' Presenting Complaints," *American Sociological Review* 31 (1966): 615–30; David Mechanic, "The Concept of Illness Behavior," *Journal of Chronic Disease* 15 (1962): 189–94; I. H. Pearse and L. H. Croitar, *The Perkham Experiment* (London, 1949); R. Duff and A. B. Hollingshead, *Sickness and Society* (New York, 1968) especially Chapter 7; H. J. K. Kupferer, "Couvade: Ritual or Real Illness?" *American Anthropologist* 67 (1965): 99–101.

18. *World Health Organization, International Classification of Diseases,* 8th ed. (Geneva, 1965); "A Classification of Disease," *Journal of College of General Practitioners and Research* 6 (1963).

CHAPTER ELEVEN

Contemporary Systems of Popular Medicine in Lower Zaire

The contemporary therapy systems in Lower Zaire—"the art of the *nganga*," "kinship therapy," "purification and initiation," and "Western medicine" each have their own historical past. Here we will look at these therapy systems in terms of their specific techniques, the place of their specialists in society, and the criteria of referrals from practitioners of one system to those of another. The resulting picture of Lower Zaire medicine offers a unique pattern of integration with all therapy systems required in meeting expectations of complete care.

The Art of the Nganga

A clear continuity exists from the diagnostic ideas of Chapter 10 to the therapeutic assumptions in chants sometimes heard at the outset and close of the *nganga's* séance. The opening is addressed to God.

Nge Tata Nzambi,	O Father God,
Vo kedika kedika	If it is truly You,
Nge waveni maladi kwa mbevo,	Who gave illness to the sufferer,
Kansi vo muntu wa nza wa mbi	Or another person in this evil
Mu kiena wa veni kimbevo:	World (who gave it to him),
Mono nzolele yandi kaniakisa	May he be healed.
Nge Tata Nzambi ku kati	You, Father, the inside,
Mono ku mbazi.	And I the outside.

The closing is addressed to those accompanying the sufferer, the therapy managing group:

Luendo kweno,	Go in peace,
Ka mfun'a mona wonga ko.	There's no need to fear.
Kadi, kimbevo ka kien'andi ko.	He is not really sick.
Vo balanda, balanda,	Though they harass,
Kieno ye batakwa.	They'll be put to flight.
Balanda, balanda,	They harass,
Kieno ye batakwa.	They'll be put to flight.

The *nganga* and God Nzambi work as a pair on the case, the *nganga* devoting his attention to the visible, external person, God to the inner person. The cause of illness may be "of God," direct and natural, or it may be of someone in the "evil world," "those who harass." Arousal of fear, calming, and defense of the patient are present in every *nganga's* therapy. His art is at once empirical and magical, traditional and experimental, physiological and social.

The public role model of *nganga* distinguishes between the *nganga mbuki*, herbalist (from *buka*, "to treat") and the *nganga nkisi*, magician (from *kisi*, "knowledge" or "consecration"). Herbalists use raw plants to treat simple problems without imputations of human or supernatural cause. Magicians take on the same illnesses, but are said to be especially competent with "anger illnesses" in which the physical manifestation must be treated as well as the anger calmed.[1] Anger illnesses are not distinct illnesses, rather they are those diganosed to be difficult to heal because of this dimension. An example, swelling (*nitu kwiza*), illustrates this distinction.

Swelling may be caused either by heart congestion or by poisoning, according to Mama Mankomba of Mbemba village. Only the latter type of swelling is an anger illness, growing out of the animosity of one individual for another. Therefore, it requires a different type of treatment. Simple swelling (from heart congestion) was dealt with by an initial emetic from the drops of sap of the *diza kia nlembo* cactus with a soapy base to keep the poison-

1. Fukiau-kia-Bunseki, *Kindoki, ou la solution attendue* (Kumba, 1973).

ous sap from harming the body. This was followed by a potion made from roots of six savannah plants (127, 151, 152, 153, 154, 173) taken three times daily. Dietary restrictions against sugar, salt, and pepper were also imposed. Poisoning cases received the same initial purge, but were followed by a second purge of *munsangula* bark scrapings with salt and palm oil to provoke diarrhea and vomiting, instead of the above follow-up. Although Mama Mankomba treated the physical manifestations of an anger illness, she refused to deal with deeper causes which must be resolved by judicial or other means in order for the afflicted to become well. Her kinsmen called her an *nganga mbuki,* an herbal therapist of simple illnesses of natural origin, but she modestly shied away from calling herself *nganga* at all, preferring to be called simply "one who treats."

The distinction between herbalist and magician is not always clear in practice. There are intermediary *nganga* types, like the healer of madness, *nganga bulau.* Also, some healers, such as Mama Mankomba, diagnose anger illnesses but shy away from dealing with its deeper causes.[2]

Banganga who fully accept the role of magician, pursuing it with relish as Nzoamambu did, evoke the symbolic more fully than their colleagues the herbalists. They work with some symbolization of the ill, the "illness's anger," carrying on the tradition (somewhat thwarted by colonial and missionary repression) of encapsulating the anger in *nkisi* bundles called *mfunia* ("anger").[3] Bayindula of Balari, for example, is identified as an *nganga nkisi,* magician. In addition to his herbal treatments for constipation, difficult urination, anemia, foot and eye pain, he wields the cupping horn with skill, removing the illness (i.e., bits of dirty cotton) from his patient's bodies. He has framed this

2. Fukiau suggests that the *mbuki* handles illnesses that are "inside the body," but refrains from dealing with those of "outside" cause. *Ibid.,* p. 46.

3. *Mfunia* refers to the wedge, bundle of hair, or other object in the *nkisi* which "angers" it and "makes it attack"; it also refers to the abstract nature of evil, malicious action, injustice, or violence. Human aggression, in Kongo thought, may be both concrete, couched in symbols, or highly abstract, formulated in words and ideas. Matunta, Notebook 306, Laman Collection, Svenska Missionsforbundent Archives (Lidingö); K. E. Laman, *Dictionnaire KiKongo-Français* (Bruxelles, 1936).

technique in the neo-Christian idiom of the Croix Koma purification liturgy in dealing with anger illnesses. The *nganga nkisi* is moved by a strong public calling and superior intelligence into the treatment of complicated cases of poisoning, psychosomatic pain, ancestral wrath, and witchcraft-caused afflictions. He is a public morality engineer, usually on the side of the good.

One factor in an *nganga*'s career which indicates where he will be situated on this range from treater of simple physical ills to magician is his recruitment to the role. Having a visionary encounter with the spirit world during a personal trauma, being an apprentice to a master *nganga*, purchasing treatments, and, once in the role, experimenting with cures, are all acceptable modes of becoming *nganga*. In practice, the recruitment of a particular *nganga* entails several of these modes. An orthopedist may have fallen from a tree and broken numerous bones before seeking apprenticeship to this speciality, *nganga lunga*. A woman may have been obliged to purchase a treatment for a sick child and then have begun practicing it on others as a favor. In Nzoamambu's case, traumatic illness. its treatment, and apprenticeship to the kinsman who healed him merged into an intricate sense of calling. Frequently an *nganga*'s calling is confirmed by a vision couched in symbols of death and resurrection, with help offered from supernatural beings. An *nganga* specializing in women's reproductive problems entered his career as follows.

> I was a young man with two children. Then, in one month, four deaths occurred in my clan. In the next month there were five deaths. I became ill next, and when I died, I found myself at the bank of the Zaire River [*va simu Nzadi*]. Across the river several people appeared and said, "You must not die; there are too many orphans to care for." They told me about three plants which cure women suffering from barrenness. When I awoke from my death, I vomitted peppers, which to this day I do not eat.

Plants, in this *nganga*'s vision, mediated the world of the living and the beyond, realm of the ancestors. Here they provided a promise of clan continuity. Pepper, a common ritual barrier between the two realms, became a personal memento for the *nganga* of his vision. In another *nganga*'s vision, trauma, death, plants, and the call were presented differently.

I was out tapping palm wine when word reached me that my wife, away at a funeral feast in a nearby village, had succumbed. I was dumbfounded, and in disbelief I set out to fetch her body. Suddenly a voice—like the voice of God—spoke. I beheld a beautiful garden, and beside the path, three plants. The voice told me to take the plants, for they would raise my wife. I took them, and raised her with them. Suddenly, I knew all the plants of the forest.

For these two *banganga*, plants constituted the vital sign of their religious calling. They and others who enter such a career through visionary experience without much prior training, are comparable to Arctic shamans. The medium of their vision—in the case of the *nganga*, plants, often three in number—continues to speak to them and guide them. Such *banganga* are fearful of divulging their plants lest they betray the source of their power and die. None named their plants for us.

Banganga who acquire their knowledge through apprenticeship have a more matter-of-fact relationship with their plants and techniques. A fully established tradition such as Nzoamambu's, reaching back generations, may have little tie to the mystical, but more emphasis on technical mastery and the remembered lore of the ancestors. Such a tradition is perpetuated through an apprentice, often a kinsman, though not invariably. Patrilateral succession (from father to son) is the expressed preference as a mode of apprenticeship. It avoids the characteristic jealousies between sister's son and mother's brother, but still binds kinsmen together. Over several generations such a mode of succession works much like the "returned blood" of the preferential marriage tie, linking two clans permanently. Alternate generation apprenticeship, as was seen in Nzoamambu and his grandmother, solves the same problems. *Banganga* who have experienced a vision sometimes take on an apprentice; their art thus becomes an inherited craft. Although the original visionaries detest dilution of their knowledge, their apprentices normally augment it by purchasing additional treatments until a sizeable herbarium has been built up.

The apparent role of the mystical in Kongo medicine—just as in architecture, metallurgy, writing—has led some observers to suggest that there is little experimentation in Kongo culture. In practice, there is abundant empiricism and experimentation, but it is subordinated to the supernatural, as a way of legitimatizing it. Simply pragmatic treatments exist in Kongo medicine, such as this one for snakebite. A bandage is bound around the limb so the venom may not spread. The limb is smeared with *minkwiza* juice and *dinsusu* herbs, and massaged. This is followed by incisions and sucking with the cupping horn at the bite. *Nsaku-nsaku* grass is finally rubbed into the incisions.[4] We also found testing with plants and techniques. Kitembo of Muyeni, a dynamic *nganga nkisi*, who had trained as his father's apprentice, experimented in this manner. If he found that plants did not live up their promise, he replaced them with others or discarded them outright. He had used *kuluba* (58) and *kienga* (170) to treat diarrhea, but they did not work as indicated. He had also abandoned the purificatory use of the cupping horn (to remove "objects" from patients' bodies) because it had become increasingly difficult to convince patients of its validity. Removal of a "piece of dirt" was effective only, he mused, if the patient believed in it. But even here, where the empiric/symbolic distinction was self-consciously related to an experimental approach to healing, the healer subordinated his work to the mystical. When confronted with difficult cases, Kitembo dreamed of his father who would show him appropriate cures.

The subordination of the *nganga*'s empirical plant science to the mystical, while not preventing experimentation and pragmatism in making effective chemotherapeutic and manipulatory cures, does remain central to the *nganga*'s art. Consecration of individual ingredients (*bilongo*, "medicines") produces an altered, inviolable, treatment (*nkisi*). Activated by spells or songs, the combined ingredients take on a life of their own which may not be modified in use or in transmission from one practitioner to another.[5] The purge of 1921/2 had the effect of temporarily secularizing the *nganga*'s activity. Colonial and missionary efforts to promote "nonmagical" treatments amongst herbalists and

4. K. E. Laman, *The Kongo, II* (Uppsala, 1957), p. 64.
5. Nsemi, "Sacred Medicines," in *Anthology of Kongo Religion*, comp. Janzen and MacGaffey (Lawrence, 1974), pp. 34–38.

laymen resulted in such projects as "Tata Paul" Verstig's book, *Makaya ma Nsi masadisa Nitu* (*Medicinal Plants for Bodily Healing*), and encouraged rejection of *banganga's* exploitative tactics.[6] But new medicinal consecrations emerged which were either Christian inspired, like Bayindula's, or followed the old cosmological structures.

Rules by which plants and symbols are associated remain, in contemporary *banganga's* art, those derived from the cosmology of ceremony, myth, and society. Many treatments draw one plant or object from the forest (or water), associated with the spirit world, and another from the savannah, (*ku nseke*), associated with the village and the human world. The spirits represented in medicines proper are usually *bisimbi*, believed to inhabit deep pools, waterfalls, ravines, or other locations in nature.[7]

The basic forest/savannah contrast is amplified, in many medicinal recipes, by association with other complementary oppositions. In a common treatment for agitated behavior ("madness") the following domains are brought together under the general rubric of "calming" (*lembikisa*) the sufferer. Mixed together are: *lemba-lemba*, a domestic village plant, with *lemba-ntoko*, a wild plant of the forest; and *kilembe-lembe kia mpembe* (176), "white," "male," with *kilembe-lembe kia mbwaki* (177), "red," "female," both growing wild (as weeds) in a domestic savannah field. The contrast of wild and domestic is associated with the forest/savannah contrast. In this particular case, it is further amplified by its connotation of the contrast of madness and civility. The two *kilembe-lembe* plants, one male and white, the other

6. Paul Verstig, *Makaya ma Nsi masadisa Nitu*, 9th ed. (Matadi, 1966).
7. Manianga healers were not able to develop this notion for us, nor were they prone to discuss *bisimbi*. Perhaps this was due to the aggressive defamation campaigns conducted by missions and the colonial government against them. The best explanation of the exact role of *bisimbi* in *minkisi* medicines is by Buakasa, who writes: "The constitution of the *nkisi* object is a mechanism and a mode of domestication, of caging, or better, of capturing the *simbi* in a material object that represents and even surpasses it. This mechanism assures the suppression of sentiments of hate or hostility which animate the *simbi* since primordial times. This guarantees the elimination of destructiveness weighing on subjects of the new society and imposes peace and bodily health. The *simbi* are thus made beneficent." (Our translation.) From Gérard Buakasa, *L'impensé du discours: "Kindoki" et "nkisi" en pays kongo du Zaire* (Kinshasa, 1973), p. 295.

female and red mediate these oppositions in a treatment for agitation, effective both symbolically in that it calms "wildness," and empirically in that it is an effective chemotherapeutic tranquilizer (see treatment of Nzita for severe agitation, p. 85).

The male/female and white/red contrasts reappear as major principles of association in many recipes. Gender distinctions are explained in the following ways, among others.

	Male	*Female*
Kunata's general explanation:	works instantly	takes effect slowly and endures
Kitembo's identification of *mpuku mwifi:*	(65)	(63)
—flower color	purple (*ndombe*)	white
—fruit color	black	white and red
—fruit cluster	small	large
Kitembo's identification of *makangaya*	(7)	(8)
	hairy	clean skin
Diakebwa's identification of *bumi*:	(135)	(134)
—leaf size	small	large
—relative strength of poison	stronger	weaker
—flower color in dry season	white	yellow
Kongo cosmological and anatomical organization:	right side	left side

In the foregoing definition of the male/female contrast, it is noteworthy that colors have been used as if they possess cultural significance. Red, white, and black are pervasive ceremonial colors in Kongo as in some other central African societies.[8] White, represented in chalk or river clay, seeds, flowers, and cloth, symbolizes the serenity of the beyond, of purity, of death, spoken of as "going to the white" (*ku mpemba*); it is the color of mourning. Red symbolizes danger, transition, marginal status, and boundaries. It is represented in the ground bark of the *tukula* tree, in

---

8. Victor W. Turner, "Color Classification in Ndembu Ritual," *The Forest of Symbols* (Ithaca, 1967), pp. 59–92.

paint, cloth, and other medicines. Black, less frequently used, represented by charcoal, symbolizes chaos, guilt, witchcraft. The use of these colors to define gender is not entirely consistent, as is evident above. White associates with male in one case, with female in another. This is however, entirely in character with the *nganga*'s expressive liberty in his culture and the power that comes from shifting and even inverting conventional relationships.[9]

The notion of complementarity is not expressed only in terms of gender and color. As if to illustrate the dictum that "what can kill can also heal,"[10] the *nganga*'s formula, frequently combines a poison with protective, neutralizing, substance. Thus:

	Poison	*Neutralizer*
In Mfwemo's treatment for dizziness (*nzieta*):	roots of *luhete* (167) and *kilembe-lembe* (176, 177)	never without lemon (*lala dia nsa*)
In Dianzenza's treatment for diarrhea (*vumu luta*):	mango bark	never without egg
In Mankomba's purge following treatment of congestive swelling (*nitu kwiza*):	three drops of *diza kia nlembo* cactus sap (124)	never without mixing it into cup of soapy (*savon bleu*) water

All of these treatments are taken internally by mouth, and particularly the poison of the third treatment is lethal if used unadulterated. It is used to kill fish. A drop in the eye will blind, it is said.

The distinction between inside and outside the body, as we have seen it in Chapter 10, is also a type of complementary opposition in the *nganga*'s technique. Inside/outside the body are defined by a number of associations, including color, plants, and geospatial domains. Many treatments introduce plant (or other

9. This point is repeatedly emphasized in Lévi-Strauss's works. It is absolutely essential in understanding the *nganga*'s ability to utilize an orthodox cosmology yet innovate within it.

10. J. Kusikila, *Lufwa evo Kimongi e?* (Kumba, 1966).

substance both orally and through incisions in the skin. Impurities are extracted by these paths, internally through purges, through the skin with the cupping horn. The skin's surface is conceptually organized in the *nganga*'s therapy to correspond to a number of other classificatory domains. Thus, the treatment of boils, some of which are hidden beneath the surface of the skin, others of which are open at the surface, is done with the *loko* palm fungus. This fungus appears in white, red, and black varieties, used to cure boils hidden under the skin and those that are at the surface, respectively. The use of *mpuku-mwifi* ("rat thief") male and female, with black and red/white fruit respectively, for rheumatism treatment, follows the same order. Ashes from the plants are rubbed into *nsamba* incisions at the point of the pain. In both treatments the inside/outside contrast is coordinated with the color triad in the following way:

inside	white
	red
outside	black

Blood ideology and the theory of conception follow this same principle: "[White] semen turns to [red] blood, and this to a [black?] person." In birth, the person moves from inside to outside, from white, through the red of birth transition, to personhood.

The distinction between inside and outside the body is associated with other domains in the *nganga*'s art. Kitembo's cure for inner *lubanzi* requires "corpse raiser" (*munkula-mvumbi*, 41), a tree growing near the forest border. Its leaves are prepared for a drink and as a pulp to be rubbed into *nsamba* cuts to join the blood. The disease, which is by the plant's name associated with a corpse, is drawn out or reduced. The following associations are made in this treatment:

inside	the dead (corpse, disease?)	forest (water)
outside	the living	savannah

The plant, drawn from the edge of the forest, is applied in the medicine to both inside and outside the body, to attack the disease inside the body.

A few rules of contrast and similarity permit us to see the structure within which *banganga* compose their medicines and inspire their techniques. Some analysts of central African traditional medicine have concluded that the treatments created along these lines have little empirical derivation and are based on mystical ideas.[11] We would be at a loss to explain the *nganga*'s dissatisfaction with his own work, his experimentation, his effective tranquilizers, snakebite treatments, abortions, and above all, poisons, if he had no knowledge of the effective workings of plants. The categories brought out in the foregoing observations merely provide broad criteria—forest, village—for the choice of plants. They do not dictate exactly which plant is to be used in a cure; rather, they indicate the symbolic realm through which an experience is given meaning. We prefer to see the *nganga*'s art as possessing a logic as careful as any other therapy system, directed however toward unique aims, namely, dealing with the so-called "anger" illnesses which affect not only the body, but the total person.[12] *Banganga* study the effects of plants, and they observe the world around them. They signify the boundaries of their art's competence by referring sufferers in the modern context to Western dispensaries, diviners, and kinship councils for conflict resolution (see Figure 15).

Kinship Therapy

The heart of kinship therapy is the clan meeting, *lukutukunu lua dikanda*. Several cases exemplify diagnostic meetings followed by therapeutic meetings (3.4–5; 5.9–10; 6.5–6; 7.4–5). Clan meetings are usually delayed until cases are perceived to be very

11. See, for example, Turner's early writing on Ndembu therapy, *The Forest of Symbols, op. cit.*, p. 356.

12. This is the argument of Robin Horton, in "African Traditional Thought and Western Science," *Africa* 37 (1967): 50–71, 155–187, and one we share. It commits us neither to dismissing the *nganga*'s art as bad science based on faulty logic, nor to saying it is just religious symbolism.

Problems	Plants rubbed on body	Plant medicine by mouth	*Minsamba* cuts	Plant head pack	Nonspecific plant cure	Cupping horn and incisions	Charm prepared	Singing, chant (liturgies)	Advice	Referral to settle conflict	Referral to hospital	Treatment in hospital
Birth injury	X										X	
Unconsciousness		X										X
Swelling of limbs	X		X									
Suffocation	X									X	X	
Odd behavior	X	X	X		X							X
Headache					X							
Unfinished marriage									X			
"Worms" in eyes	X	X	X									
Mumpompila			X									
Head turning	X	X	X									
Lauka (madness)	X	X										
Bad ("black") blood	X		X			X						
Loose living	X		X			X		X	X			
Too many ideas					X							
Envy in maternal clan	X						X			X		
Lack of blessing	X		X			X		X	X			
Psychological case	X		X			X		X	X			
Clan problems	X	X	X									
Desire to move				X								

FIGURE 15. Correlation of therapy actions and problems in case episodes handled by *banganga*.

serious, or until several cases can be dealt with sumultaneously. Meanwhile, a sufferer is not being neglected in his quest for care. Kin therapy managers will already have taken early therapeutic steps, in the course of which they have decided that a particular case does not respond well to treatment for "natural" causes; research into human causes is required.

Etiologies considered by diagnostic clan meetings are witch-craft (*kindoki*) and magically caused illness (*nkisi*). They are almost always imputed through a rhetorical screen of euphemisms. "Talk, talk, and more talk" (gossip) is considered a destructive force that erodes community harmony. Malevolent intrigue, lies, machinations, and ill-wishing are summed up in the term *kimfunia*; explicit evil action is distinguished as *mavanga mambi*. Although these modes of negative interaction are only semi-intentional outgrowths of excessive anger, they are believed to cause illness and misfortune. Stronger and more destructive are explicitly uttered curses (*n'loko, m'finga*) believed to destroy individuals and collectivities unless revoked. These etiologies re-flect a considerable awareness of social rules and moral codes. "Social relations" are consciously invoked as an etiology in the term *n'singa*, meaning a "cord" or "string" binding persons to-gether. Possessively "holding" or "having one's hands on" another similarly indicates a social cause of illness. Social con-tradictions are sometimes understood by kinship diagnosticians, but usually only in an idiomatic sense. No KiKongo term exists for incest, to our knowledge, although clan endogamy is identified as a problem by the prohibition of persons of the "same blood" marrying and by the existence of a ceremonial sacrifice to "se-ver the blood" of a couple married in the clan.

Magically caused illness is discussed more openly than that believed caused by witchcraft. Such terms as "walking on a fetish," "playing with magic," or "having medicines in one's house" denote magic as the cause of illness. Here, as in the case of witchcraft, a distinction is drawn between self-inflicted illness and other-inflicted illness. Individual responsibility is determined by the diagnostic kinship meeting to permit appropriate action to follow. Frequently, a clan member having "burned his fingers on magic," will be allowed to suffer the consequences if no one else is affected. If others are to be hurt by the consequences, appropriate neutralizing and protective therapy is undertaken. The diffuse aura of perplexity in this whole area of diagnosis and therapy frequently generates the etiology of *mystères*. Some say this is an equivalent of the older KiKongo term *kimfunia* ("anger") illnesses, brought on by oneself or others. Others suggest it has to do with foreign, badly understood, illnesses. In either case it is discussed at length in the diagnostic kinship meeting.

Moving from diagnosis to the kinship meeting involves several strategies. If the sufferer is not responsible for his illness, he must be protected from the forces inflicting it. This may entail consulting an *nganga*. If indications are that witchcraft is involved in the illness, then the meeting may move directly to action. Diagnosis and therapy are two sides of the same process here. In the past, there were techniques for the identification of an individual witch. Since the 1910 ban on the poison ordeal, and the promulgation of slander laws in government courts, clans avoided the isolation of an individual witchcraft perpetrator whenever possible. Many clans avoided even committing themselves to a "roll-call" oath on this question, preferring to handle it as a pro forma round of confessions before the sufferer, and he before them. Kinship investigation has the potential of leading not to confession but to open accusation liable to prosecution as slander. The line dividing controlled inquiry of social cause from the innuendo of suspicion and accusation is fine indeed; our informants offered willingly that it was difficult to deal on one's own with envy, jealousy, and competition in a clan.

Two further therapeutic procedures to kinship diagnosis entail the engagement of hired speakers for a public conflict-resolution debate to "settle the palaver" (*nsamu*) and the consultation of a diviner-prophet (*ngunza*). These procedures may be combined into one event or resorted to separately.

In a public debate (referred to thus far as an "interclan meeting") therapeutic techniques such as blessings, gift exchanges, sacrifices, and food distributions drawn from Kongo social reciprocity, are utilized. A meeting is usually scheduled after the two contending parties have, through their advocates, agreed that an end of hostility is mutually beneficial. Patrifilial children may need a blessing, and have agreed to pay amends to their offended "fathers." A clan may be in need of an ancestral prayer, but has offended the patrifilial children who alone can offer such a prayer. Clans may have become entangled in a complicated fabric of marriages, land exchanges, misunderstandings, and curses so that their perceived need of peace is greater than their sense of injury. Or, illnesses may flare up, prompting urgent action on the human causes. A grand kinship therapy council is a work of social art and organizational skill. A public is always on hand, numbering up to a thousand individuals. Many of the features of a festival (*nkembo*) emerge, evoked by the anticipation of the end of a serious tension. Wherever gifts are exchanged and food distributed, the attraction of a free meal draws others.

As in the festivity of a marriage, funeral, lifting of mourning, or inauguration, so in a kinship therapy council the general rules of etiquette, debate, exchange, and public order apply. The two contestants come bearing palm wine, pineapple wine, or other in-season wines and liqueurs, garden produce, goats, pigs, bottled beer, bolts of store cloth, sugar, tea, coffee, and cash. A church service may serve as prelude to the debate, presided over by a local catechist (Catholic or Protestant), a prophet, or any other trusted public figure. Hymns underline the virtues of godliness, peace and goodwill, and the sanctity of the site of reconciliation. The sermon further exhorts restraint modeled after Biblical figures. The sermon and last-minute divination often has the effect of diffusing tension in the gathering. The sufferer may be made responsible for his illness at this time for having dabbled with bad medicines or misused powers. The prophet may, alternatively, invoke mystical causes for the illness having to do with the offense of twins, ancestors, and *simbi* spirits. Such divinatory strategies cool off the heat of witchcraft suspicions and accusations, laying the groundwork for the debates of reconciliation.

The debates open after everyone has gathered around a circle before the men's hut or urban compound. The host, usually one of the contestant headmen, announces the purpose of the gathering with such words as "We are here today, not for the fun of it, but because we wish to resolve the affair that has made one of our clansmen ill." Debate between the advocates proceeds in a quid pro quo manner, confession offered for withdrawal of accusation, blessing against the revocation of a curse, debt payment against sacrifice, goods for forgiveness, and the like. Each party must withdraw after every offer to agree to accept the terms. Public etiquette described in previous chapters finds its highest expression in these reconciliation debates, with every cup of wine, every animal, every proverb and sanction song suited exactly for the occasion and the case. The exchange of goods solemnizes the contract that has been cleansed. The general redistribution of food and follow-up feast makes the contract publicly binding. Collective symbols are invoked to affirm the success of the reconciliation. In one kinship meeting, after the last offer had been accepted, the curse revoked, and the blessing extended, a brother of the sufferer arose and fired his gun into the air in a salvo of rejoicing, and led the whole crowd in the hymn "The doors of heaven have opened wide." Another man arose and announced that "the *kodia* has descended! The affair is over; may the ill be healed." *Kodia*, the spiral snail shell, container of medicine, symbol of authority and power, brings conflict to an end. As a symbol of healing it appeases inner tensions and discloses secrets.

The prophet's role in kinship therapy proceeds at the individual and the collective (public) level. As certain public *banganga* of old, for example, the *nganga* Lemba, or the *nganga ngombo* diviner, the prophet nowadays facilitates group reconciliation. As other *banganga nkisi* who worked with individuals suffering from "anger" illnesses, the prophets nowadays remove the sufferer from the social setting that has caused the illness. The prophet convinces the clan to permit the sufferer to move away to detach himself from their midst, as in the case of Mbumba. The prophet may take the sufferer to his neutral retreat, or minister to him and a restricted set of kin for a time, as in the case of Nsimba. Intervention of the prophet into kinship therapy separates the sufferer from the kinship setting believed to be destroying him and encourages the correction of that condition for the sufferer's, and everyone else's, benefit.

Purification and Initiation

Purification and initiation therapy, as some kinship therapy, is handled mostly by the prophet (*ngunza*), either as an individual operator or as part of a movement such as the Munkukusa purificatory rite, its more permanent outgrowth Croix Koma, the independent Church of the Holy Spirit, or a pagan cult such as Nkita. This diversity of movements and cults is however united in a common set of ritual techniques such as purificatory baths, anointments, isolation, laying on of hands, prayers, and songs (see Fig. 16). The sufferer is usually given a new role that is accompanied by a stronger identification with a sacred object or holy figure, and perhaps a new place of residence.

Purification therapy defines the termination of the illness, an important motif in central African healing. After the sufferer and his surroundings have experienced pain, tension, anger, and accusation, purification expurgates this "dirt," allowing a sense of healing to pervade. Patients who submit to such therapy often say they feel better. Although the theme of purification—*vedisa*, "to cleanse"; *kusa*, to rub—is commonly dealt with nowadays by prophets, it is also present in the symbolism of *banganga* and dominant in certain historic cults. Many *banganga* as a matter of course add brief termination rites to their cures to designate the purification of the sufferer and an end to the illness. The persistence of specialized purificatory rites may actually be enhanced by the lack of recognizable closure in Western medical care, where patients often do not know what has transpired in their bodies, and although clinically "well," may still consider themselves sick, polluted, and in need of cleansing.

Practitioners whom we situate in purification and initiation therapy minimize, or even avoid, the investigation of social relationships as the cause of illness. Coincidentally, they thereby

Sufferer has talisman, etc.					X			X	X	X						X	X								X	
Interclan conflict					X				X	X						X	X									
Nkatanga (''heavy head'')						X					X	X	X	X				X								
Whole family sick						X		X			X	X	X	X		X	X	X								
Pain in joints						X					X	X	X	X				X								
Incurable headache								X							X											
Evil actions of sufferer								X							X											
Snake (familiar)								X							X											
Psychological case								X	X							X	X								X	
Abdominal pain				X	X																					
Limp				X	X																					
Continued ill health				X	X																					
Headache						X	X							X				X								
Desire to move						X	X							X				X					X			
Swelling limbs								X							X											
Improper alliance								X							X	X	X									
Concern for kin's health				X				X																		
Indecision over illness of Man/God				X				X													X	X				
Wish to be deacon				X			X													X						
Others have ''hands on patient''															X	X			X					X		
Cash demands															X	X								X		
Accusations																					X					
Rheumatic fever																						X				

FIGURE 16. Correlation of therapy actions and problems in case episodes handled by kinship groups, and *bagunza*.

The following matrix cross-tabulates **Problems** (column headers) against **Actions** (row labels) and **Roles** (right-hand grouping).

Lack of blessing	Clan problems	Unfinished marriage	Asthma in home village	Resistance to "call"	Asthma	Cough	Envy of maternal kin	Suffocation	Too many ideas	Odd behavior	Young man playing with magic	Does not recognize kinsmen	Non-kin conflict in job	Fetish in house	Actions	Roles
											×	×	×	×	Referral to settle conflict	Prophet with individual client
										×	×	×	×		General examination of situation	
			×	×	×										Holy water by mouth	
													×	×	Nonspecific kinship examination	
×	×	×							×	×			×	×	Advice	
			×	×	×										Prayer	
	×			×											Move suggested or taken	
×	×				×	×	×	×	×						Examination of maternal kinship	
×	×	×	×	×	×										Dream analysis	
×	×	×													Confession of third party (kin)	Prophet with kinship groups, clans
															Laying on of hands	
															Anointing with oil	
															Ritual bath	
															Singing, chants (liturgy)	
	×			×											Examination of paternal kinship	
×	×	×													Confession of kin to sufferer	
×	×	×													Confession of sufferer to kin	
															Religious retreat	
×															Blessing bestowed on sufferer	Kinship groups (clan, clans) and other non-kin groups
			×	×											Recruitment to new role	
															Payment offered, rejected	
															Payment (Mafundu) accepted	
												×			Confession of non-kin to sufferer	
									×	×					Referral to nganga	
	×	×													Referral to prophet	
									×						Return to village	

share with those who engage in kinship diagnosis the conviction that conflict leads to disease, and are universally aware of the investigative mode of divining. But they say they prefer not to follow it, regarding it as dangerous, "red." Luamba, the prophet who appears in two of our cases (6.9, 7.6), explained his approach by saying, "I do not analyze the origin of disease, or blame family members and conflicts for illnesses, I just heal." Another prophet who avoided the imputation of conflicts and malicious intentions in his treatment of illness, allowed that "human sin, conflict included," could cause illness. But his own unique gift for prayer and laying on of hands (*sambila*) differed from the gift of questioning, examining, and researching (*fyongunina, fimpa*) human conflict. Still others had the gift of prophesying (*bikula*) and healing (*nyakisa*). Luamba's ten-day therapy of isolation hardly considered a sufferer's kinsmen. He preferred that the patient, having taken his initial purificatory bath, remain alone in his care with prayer, meditation, worship, anointment with oil, and a final bath. Thus, these practitioners held that while kinship conflict indeed caused illness, healing was not synonymous with the analysis of conflict.

The strong identification with a cult figure, for instance, the prophet who diagnosed the illness, an ancestor who had been a member of a cult in life, or a patron spirit of the cult, helps the sufferer overcome his anxiety in a troubled situation. Mbumba, for example, moved from a difficult structural position in his clan into a favored relationship with a prophet, becoming his right-hand helper. Role changes accompanying this type of therapy frequently redefine the patient as a well person, or even a "doctor." In some traditional cults of affliction, the sufferer became a priest through initiation. Thus, a Lemba song, "That which was a 'stitch' in the side [*lubanzi*?] has become the path to the priesthood! *E yaye!*"

Still, such a role shift from clan to cult is not as easy as it might seem. The accentuated cathexis to a cult object or figure is often interpreted by the acolyte as disloyalty to kinsmen over which a sense of guilt develops. Kongo custom is resourceful and provides that the clan bless the sufferer at this juncture. Mbumba received the permission of his clan to become the prophet's deacon. Nsimba was at the point of obtaining consent from his kinsmen to move away from their petty demands. The release from guilt may be shrouded in a dream of an ancestor who had belonged to the cult, calling the sufferer to join that cult, thus permitting the sufferer a way out of a stressful situation while at the same time preserving the clan's legitimacy.

In the Lower Zaire Nkita cult, devoted to *bisimbi* spirits and twins, Nkita sickness is directed, it is believed, by clan ancestors seeking someone amongst the living to exert influence (*yala*, "govern"). Since the sickness is sent by water spirits, through the ancestors, to those in the village, the cure, according to one Nkita priest, must consist of an anointment of the seed of the waterside *mpebe* tree and the domestic village papyrus *nsaku-nsaku* (158). Guilt, pollution, and perhaps marginality in the clan is transformed into recruitment to leadership, as the herbs (*nsaku-nsaku* standing for blessing, *sakumuna*) are rubbed onto the body of the suffer and chief priest.

The modern purificatory rite of Croix Koma, founded by Catholic *abbé* Victor Mandala in Congo Brazzaville, features the purification of the corporate matrilineage (*dikanda*). The entire group, or a delegation under the direction of the headman, journeys to the site of purification. There may be some confessions, but the main features of the rite are a liturgy and an oath, followed by a laying on of hands and the issuance of a "certificate of purification" by the priest. Croix Koma grew out of a mass purification movement, the Munkukusa (from *kusa*, "to rub," "to cleanse," the face in ancestral mud), that swept through the Lower Zaire from 1951 to 1953. Its principal features were the bringing of tomb earth into the village church, into a crosslike trench, where this earth was mixed with palm wine. The resulting mud, symbolizing the ancestral presence, became the vehicle of purification as clansmen rubbed their faces in it. Hymns and other liturgical acts, some derived from Christianity (such as the nailing of the cross, *koma*, meaning "hit the nail," whence Croix Koma), others derived from Kongo traditional religion, emerged from the Munkukusa. Croix Koma preserved a corporate kinship purification in a Christian idiom.

In contrast to the foregoing, the corporate purification of a non-kin group is exemplified in the rituals of the Church of the Holy Spirit (a generic term for a variety of decentralized independent churches of Lower Zaire). A corporate membership, frequently residing in monasticlike villages, maintains a highly disciplined routine of work and worship. In a rite called "the blessing" the entire attending audience receives a laying on of hands from the prophets (normally, all male members). In the "weighing of the spirit," each worshipper, as dancer, is evaluated in terms of the "weight" or force of his spirit. This is accompanied by confessions. In the "healing," a fancifully choreographed, dancing exorcism of evil spirits takes place, followed by spiritual healing and laying on of hands and prayers. The motif of purification is dominant throughout these rites, pervaded by symbolic white denoting purity, the beyond, sanctity, and spirit.

Purification and initiation therapy—whether pagan or neo-Christian, whether expressed individually or corporately, by purifying with water, anointing with oil or plant incense, laying on of hands, prayer, blessing, identifying with a sacred figure, ritual seclusion or permanent initiation to a cultic order—provides a composite and unique approach to healing within the total medical system (see Figure 16).

Western Medicine

Western medicine brought spectacular relief for such endemic diseases as sleeping sickness, yaws, and leprosy. The Lower Zaire was especially privileged to receive systematic immunization, pediatric, obstetric, and gynecologic care, as well as widespread nursing, surgical, and physiotherapeutic care from mission societies, the colonial government's medical services, and health organizations after independence. No other region of Zaire received the benefits of Western medicine to this extent.[13]

13. Willy de Craemer and Renée C. Fox, *The Emerging Physician* (Stanford, 1968), p. 18.

This systematic pervasion of Western medicinal techniques permitted the public to develop a rather clear concept of its major focus and its limitations. Western medicine thus became a separate therapy system in public consciousness, considered competent to deal with serious physical diseases as well as chronic but less debilitating illnesses or those that recurred. Western medicine was not regarded competent, however, to deal with social and personal contexts of these afflictions, nor to offer the sufferer and his managers an inclusive etiology. Therefore dimensions of illness such as anxiety, anger, social conflict, witchcraft, and magic were seen as outside Western medicine's range. Western medicine's capability lay in handling natural, "of God," afflictions, in a category roughly shared with herbalists (*banganga mbuki*).

In their zeal to replace native medicine, Western medical practitioners refused to deal with broad etiologies and denied the validity of their clientele's expectations in this regard, thereby unwittingly reinforcing the popular image of Western medicine's limited competence. In the popular thinking of BaKongo, denial of the reality of witchcraft was not an acceptable substitute for kinship therapy; confession of sin was not a particularly good way of dealing with "anger illnesses"; unexplained foreign medicines did not substitute for symbolically powerful sacred medicines.

While most practitioners of Western medicine had misjudged the impact they had made, the effectiveness of Western medicine for treating physical pathologies was apparent. The norms of dealing with its personnel could be learned. One simply did not bring up the request of wider social etiologies in their presence. Kinship reunions continued to be held in village or town compound. Rather than ask the mission staff for permission to withdraw the sufferer from the ward to attend the reunion, it was less troublesome for him to leave at night. The perceived niche of Western medicine was readily translated into a system of referrals. Relief for a symptom was sought at the dispensary or hospital, while a follow-up purification and imputation of etiology was sought from an *nganga* or *ngunza*. Or, *banganga* such as Nzoamambu were called to see patients in the dispensary. (European hospital staff members were unaware of those referrals and practices to which African staff members gave their consent.) Conversely, most *banganga* and *bangunza* regularly referred their clientele to the dispensary or hospital for cases without serious social or psychological overtones, or more complicated cases after they had finished their therapy. By failing to recognize etiological questions and by denying the validity of alternative therapies, Western medicine's practitioners communicated to their clients the closed, limited nature of Western medicine.

Nevertheless, from its incursion into Africa, Western medicine enjoyed official support. Its practitioners wielded considerable power in African society. This was true not only of the European medical doctors and nurses, it extended to African personnel in their employment, who, in their turn, enjoyed power in local circles. In one community we studied, people were afraid to enter any dispute with an assistant nurse or his clan, lest he use the power of Western medicine at his disposal to harm them. Magical qualities were ascribed to Western medicine, and some took advantage of this. One nurse's aide and pathology assistant in a mission hospital, for example, sold small pieces of cadaver as a powerful fetish, reinforcing the fear that in performing autopsies (i.e., tampering with the dead), the missionaries "ate" parts of the body to strengthen themselves.

The technology of Western medicine contributed to the awe in which its practitioners were held. Injections, intravenous feeding, artificial limbs, laboratory equipment, and above all, surgery, were the elements that inspired this attitude. Some were seen as parallels of traditional techniques, evoking a stoical respect on the part of a patient awaiting surgery, a painful injection, or a dental visit. Surgical interventions in a Western hospital were sometimes compared to an *nsamba* incision (also "African injection") which, when used to remove a cancer, tumor, or hernia, took on the purificatory character of the cupping horn extraction of an offending substance. Surgery was also sometimes compared to a witchcraft ordeal. Historically, survival of the poison ordeal was evidence of innocence and was followed by a feast. Similar feasts celebrated the successful outcome of surgery as proof of witchcraft innocence.

As long as foreigners in colonial, mission, or aid organization staffed key medical roles, a distant and awesome regard was held of the Western medical professional. But as Africans began receiving advanced training in nursing, pharmacy, laboratory technology, and medicine, a professional African "Western medical" group of healers emerged. African nurses, medical assistants, and doctors, as members of the new salaried bourgeoisie, tended to live like their foreign counterparts had, enjoying large houses, servants, and greater mobility. They practiced medicine largely as they had been taught in classroom and clinic by their European teachers. Only when they became ill did they tend to act like their kinsmen (see the case of Nsimba).

But these new professionals were full members of their own society, not an expatriate class of technocrats. Their role gradually shifted as they became more numerous, filled with other expectations and new tensions. The African medical assistants who were rapidly trained after independence in 1960 to become the country's first indigenous doctors, experienced these changes personally. First of all, their motivations to enter medicine were a unique set of perspectives and values, differing considerably from their European counterparts. They had been greatly impressed in their youth by the technology and gadgetry of Western medicine and the status of the Western practitioner. In addition, they wished to serve fellow men and country, a goal they had absorbed in the Catholic schools most of them had attended. The traditional role of the *nganga* in Bantu culture, respected and sacrosanct, appealed to them, and they could transfer it to the modern healing profession. A number of these medical assistants had, like *banganga* and *bangunza*, experienced visionary callings to medicine when challenged with having a serious illness.[14]

Despite these unique goals and values, the difficult circumstances into which these medical assistants (Zaire's first doctors, many of whom were BaKongo) returned after 1963 exacerbated personal conflicts and compromised high aims. As aspirants to a middle-class way of life, they found they could not live

14. *Ibid.*, pp. 11–20.

on the salary assigned to them, and they opened private practices, contrary to their belief in the universality and nonpecuniary character of the healing arts.[15] Others were obliged to enter politics or become administrators, contrary to their conviction that medicine is apolitical. Many found they could not survive in the isolated bush hospitals to which they had been assigned. Others learned that their own ethnic identity made it impossible for them to work in certain parts of the country. A number of such factors conspired to rank the Zairian Western medical professional lower in his own society than had been the case with his expatriate counterpart, particularly the European doctor. Thus, Western medicine in Zaire had become politicized like many other institutions.

The years 1965–1975 have seen the maturation of Zairian Western medical professionals. In tune with the national government and the party, the Mouvement Populaire de la Révolution, they have sought to shape a medical policy consistent with national priorities. By 1971 medical institutions, like other institutions devoted to public service, had begun to be nationalized and centralized. A single medical school, serving the entire country, was located at Kinshasa, and administered by the state instead of the Catholic university. Hospitals across the country having been operated by missions, large companies, and other agencies were taken under control by Zairian officials. Strong political overtones accompanied these transitions, and in some instances health care declined in quality. Yet, the problem of adequate salaries for Zairian health workers persisted, with expatriate doctors and nurses drawing far greater salaries than they. The lure of the urban centers and private practice thus increased. To counteract this, the government imposed a medical draft to staff needy, often rural, hospitals. By 1975, half of the doctors in the Lower Zaire were African.

The doctrinaire and exclusive quality of Western medicine perpetuated by expatriate professionals had begun to mellow. Western medicine began to include some psychiatry and social

15. *Ibid.*, pp. 29–42.

medicine. The emergence of the governmental policy of "cultural authenticity" stirred a greater awareness of traditional healing arts. Zairian doctors were involved in a research project on the real nature of *banganga, bangunza*, and other aspects of traditional healing.

The Therapy Course Reconsidered

The total universe of Lower Zairian medicine has been presented as four therapeutic systems. The criterion of a therapeutic system used throughout this book has been the correlation of therapists' roles and therapeutic techniques with problems or symptoms. Analysis of the diagnostic ideas and the therapeutic choices of these systems has shown that several types of specialists and therapies are commonly needed to satisfactorily terminate a case. This association of several therapy systems over time creates the framework of a "diachronic structure" of referral (see Figure 17).

Even though Lower Zaire has seen the building up of Western medical institutions and possesses its own indigenous class of Western medical professionals—doctors, nurses, pharmacists, administrators—the referral structure in most cases at the popular level continues to be much like it was before. To our knowledge, this referral structure has been described only once in anthropological and medical literature, by the Belgian ethnographer Jan Van Wing in 1910 before Western medicine entered the picture. Van Wing's description is that of a normative, hypothetical case, but since it is the case of a chief and freeman, all options are stated. Initially, such a person's illness is treated with home medications and simple, self-applied, protective magic. If, after several days, the illness persists or worsens, a diviner is consulted. He diagnoses the nature of the illness and its possible causes: an *nkisi* that has attacked? a "water" or "land" force? a Simbi or Nkita spirit? displeasure of the ancestors caused by the violation of clan rules? After all these measures have been exhausted and there is still no successful outcome, the entire clan of the sufferer is convocated. Gifts are exchanged, and the sufferer swears under oath that he is not practicing witchcraft. His

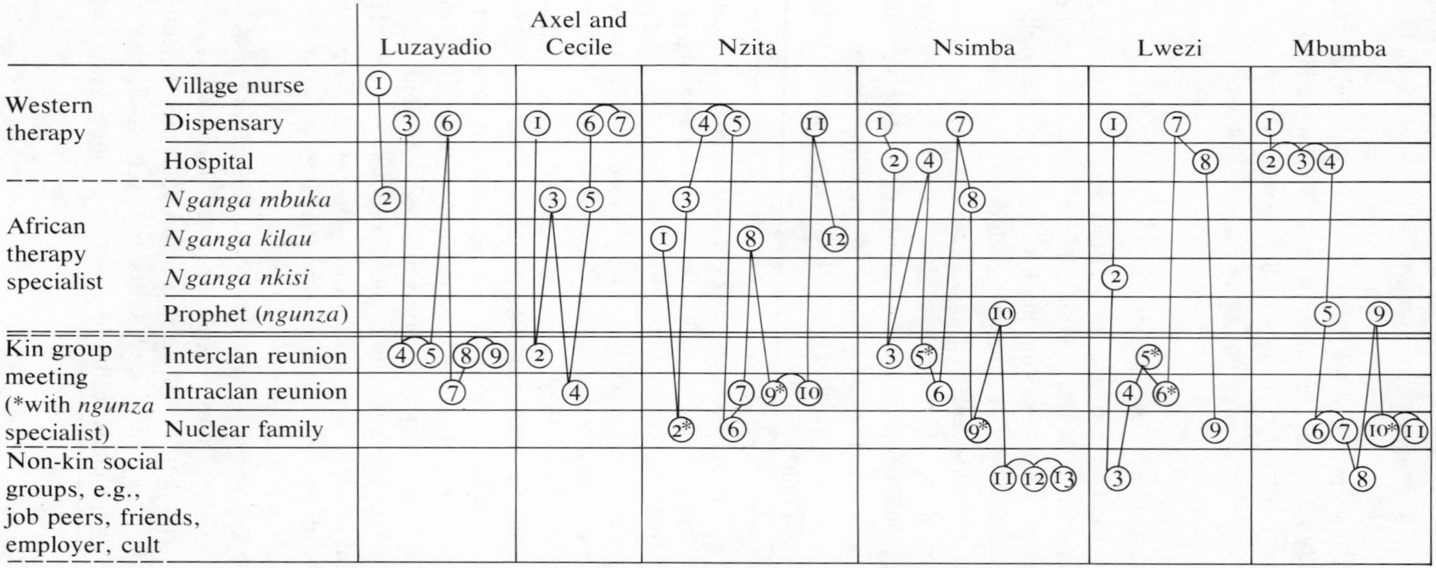

FIGURE 17. The course of therapy: case by case, episode by episode

kinsmen, each in turn, swear the same or confess bad thoughts and grudges to him.[16] Van Wing intimates that symptomatic therapy may persist throughout these alternative therapies.

The addition of Western medicine, the attenuation of certain traditional treatments, and the greater mobility of the populace have not changed the logic of the hierarchy of resort appreciably from Van Wing's hypothetical example. It is similar to that which we have seen in the cases in this book. A set of propositions may be used to establish the normative structure of therapeutic recourse in contemporary Lower Zaire society.

All cases begin, by preference, either with Western medicine or with an *nganga*. If, in due course, healing results, or the expected death of someone like an old person occurs, a tacit evaluation is made that the illness was natural, "of God." Many illnesses and etiological evaluations end here. But if the affliction does not respond to symptomatic treatment, then it is suspected to be "human caused," or "supernaturally caused," resulting from the sufferer's self-abuse, outside or mystical aggression (*nkisi*), or structural and social causes (*kindoki*). These areas are researched, evaluated, and dealt with by the therapy managing group on its own or with the help of a ritual counsellor (as aspects of kinship therapy). Because such deliberations are usually put off until the case is serious, they result in further therapeutic action in kinship therapy, by an *nganga* skilled in treating "anger" illnesses, or a variety of blessing, exchanges, and confessions.

The therapeutic course may continue indefinitely, but few groups or persons have the resources or the will for unending rounds of therapy. Pressure is put upon the sufferer or his kin to seek "closing" therapy and to resolve the impasses. If the sufferer recovers by moving, joining a cult or peer group, then individualized purification and initiation has closed the case. If, contrariwise, permanent impasses, chronicity, or untimely death, occur, the social field around the sufferer(s) becomes the scene of collective purificatory action, such as sacrifices, witchcraft eradi-

16. Jan Van Wing, *Etudes BaKongo* (Bruxelles, 1959), pp. 231–40.

cation, or enrollment in a purificatory rite so that corporate well-being may be reestablished.

Separate but complementary therapeutic systems in Kongo society each possess an internal rationale, linking therapeutic technique to symptom or problem, and these to the role of the practitioner. A broad set of diagnostic ideas and the widespread pattern of lay therapy management prevents separate therapy systems from becoming irreconcilably disparate. In the past, the diviner apparently played a pivotal role as chief diagnostician. In contemporary medicine, this diagnosing and choosing role has been taken over by lay therapy managers. Western medicine has been absorbed into this overall medical system, its unique competence as much a part of the popular consciousness as any other therapy. A complementary medical pluralism reigns at the popular level. Evidence points to increasing sanction of this state of affairs by medical professionals and governmental policies.

Lower Zaire's medical system is not like that in many Western countries where many therapies coexist within one complex bureaucratic network, and unofficially many more may be found, some semilegal, others popularly endorsed. Nor is it to be compared with a situation such as in India where several parallel traditions, both "high" and "low," professional and popular, enjoy official status. In Lower Zaire one finds a complementary medical pluralism in which sufferers or their advocates may routinely and legitimately consult all systems in connection with a single affliction.

CHAPTER TWELVE

Toward an Integrated Medicine

The task of this work has been to accurately describe and analyze the total medical scene of one region of Lower Zaire. This conclusion reviews our theoretical assumptions and priorities. They may offer guidance for further comparative study of medical systems and for the improvement of medical care.

One concern has been the accounting of Western medicine's penetration into Lower Zairian life and consciousness. During the decades that practitioners of African and Western medicine were involved in mutual misunderstandings of the sort exemplified by the exchange between the Mbundu rainmaker and Dr. Livingstone, untold numbers of lay therapy managing groups were creating a unified popular medical system that included a new synthesis of therapeutic alternatives. Western medicine's unique competence was accepted and appreciated, but not at the expense of tradition-derived therapies.

A related concern has emerged in this work's focus on the pluralistic medical system. Medical systems, pluralistic and homogeneous alike, have been defined here as concepts and values relating to techniques practiced by individuals in corresponding role relationships. In Lower Zaire, four contemporary tendencies have been identified as the art of the *nganga*, kinship therapy, purification and initiation, and Western medicine. Each of these therapy systems is couched in a *social consensus*—a shared set of rules regarding relationships—and a *cognitive consensus*—an agreement in ideas.[1] This consensus implies that medical ideas, values, techniques, and role relationships are rooted in more inclusive social, ideational, and ritual orders. We will review first the several modes of social consensus in Kongo medicine.

The hierarchic dyad of practitioner and sufferer has its own unique type of social consensus best exemplified by Western medicine and certain instances of purification and initiation. Contemporary Western medicine elevates the notion of privacy and confidence between an authoritative physician and a compliant patient to an ethical ideal and a conceptual model of practice. The sufferer must convince the physician of the reality of his symptoms, and the physician must persuade the patient, on authority of his status, knowledge, and fee, to accept the treatment he recommends. In Zaire, Western medicine is trusted, but only over a limited range of physical symptoms and signs. Because practitioners tend to assume their authority is total, there is a high degree of noncompliance. Misunderstanding, disbelief, and disagreement on the part of the sufferer is common, even though Western medicine's potential is very highly regarded. Some of this difficulty could be alleviated by improving mutual comprehension between practitioner and patient. But much of the difficulty of noncompliance is due to the same cause as in Europe and North America, namely, inadequate patient comprehension of the professional's rationale for acting.[2] The impersonal, bureaucratized mode of Western medical authority, also, is not

1. We are indebted to Don Bates of the Department of History of Medicine, McGill University, for these labels of this important distinction, and for his application to Western medical settings, in our seminar at McGill, 1971.
2. See, for example, the article by Barbara Korsh and Vida F. Negrete, in *Scientific American* 227 (August 1972), reviewed in *Medical Anthropology Newsletter* 4 (May 1973): 3, in which a survey of 800 doctor-patient interactions is reported. The results revealed that nearly half of the clients in a pediatric clinic in Los Angeles left the hospital unaware of what had been found wrong with their children. A high correlation was found between such unawareness of the doctor's rationale and noncompliance in carrying out the prescription.

consonant with most Zairian notions of therapeutic legitimation. Only in a sufferer's intense relationship to a prophet or cult leader is a comparable degree of loyalty exacted, but it is personal. In tradition-derived therapies, the notion of privacy between practitioner and patient is not found. Rather, séances are public. Traditional healers, not enjoying the support of the state, nor of modern science as an ideology, do not assert their expertise in the authoritative manner of Western practitioners. *Banganga* spend considerable efforts lauding their own skills, and they appeal to mystical authority. But their most common appeal for authority is to the sufferer's therapy managing group, which is asked to exert appropriate pressures toward compliance on the sufferer. The mode of consensus here involves the practitioner and sufferer, as well as a third party.

When the third party, in the form of a kin group, is prevalent in therapy management, yet another form of consensual context is apparent. An effort is usually made by a kin group to determine collectively which ill feeling or conflict caused the illness, thereby permitting therapeutic action to proceed. While social consensus is obviously needed for this step, it can only be taken through prior cognitive consensus. Where cognitive dissension appears, a third party must enter to take the impasse off "dead center," making action possible because of agreement, the basis of legitimacy. The contrast with the hierarchic dyad of practitioner and patient is noteworthy. A kinship group cannot impose agreement or action upon itself unless it achieves a considerable measure of both social and cognitive consensus.

The concern with consensus in a pluralistic medical framework has thus been a third major focus in this work. Consensus between practitioner and patient, between them and the lay therapy managing group, or between members of a kin diagnostic group, does not by itself deliver adequate therapy. In one instance it condemned a helpless person by witchcraft accusation and led to a lengthy treatment with wrong medications. But consensus, combined with correct diagnostic judgment, is an absolute prerequisite for effective delivery of medical care. It is a point that has often been ignored by modern practitioners; but if a physician cannot get his message across to the patient in a consensual man-

226 / The Quest for Therapy in Lower Zaire

ner, his knowledge and competence is often of little avail.[3] This work has argued, as well, that the legitimacy bestowed by a closely knit social group upon a therapeutic course is just as strong as the patient's individual belief in the rightness of the physician who treats him. The implications of this discovery for public hygiene campaigns are noteworthy.

The shift in focus from an exclusive analysis of practitioners' techniques and concepts to an analysis of these *and* popular expectations and images of practitioners, has afforded a much greater insight into the phenomenon of illness and therapy management in Lower Zaire. The therapy managing group is of crucial importance in understanding how coordinated diagnostic ideas can lead to the pluralistic use of techniques and roles. Most therapy managing groups were desirous of continuing specific physical treatment, preferably in a Western medical institution, until the patient had recovered. But their conviction that less tangible social and mystical causes had intervened obliged them to intersperse visits to dispensary or hospital with visits to *banganga*, who could deal with anger, to convene kinship councils to settle conflicts, or to see prophets for council in life crisis decisions.

The theoretical importance of using diagnostic ideas held by decision-makers seems to be central in comparative studies of medical systems. Once such a set of diagnostic ideas, or "theories of disease,"[4] has been identified, we can begin to exercise critical judgment on the consequences of their use.

The major issue that emerges from this investigation of the total medical picture of Lower Zaire, and that facing diagnosticians in every case of illness as well as medical institution builders and policy makers, is the following. How can the practical responses to physical disease in Western medicine be combined with the deeper social, emotional, and mystical responses of African

---

3. *Ibid.*
4. Horatio Fabrega has recently proposed an evaluation of the efficacy of a theory of disease. One must "judge whether the theory leads to behaviors that prevent the onset, limit the spread, diminish the intensity, promote the eradication, and/or control the manifestations of disease." In *Disease and Social Behavior* (Cambridge and London, 1974), p. 280.

medicine, without exacerbating the afflictions of individual sufferers?

One solution already documented in this work, is for practitioners to refer cases to the appropriate "other" if they are unable to complete treatment. Inspirational diviners such as Mama Marie have begun to refer to the hospital cases which, like the child coughing and spitting phlegm, required immediate medical attention. Said Mama Marie to the mother, "No! The child's condition has not been 'caused by somebody in the family.' It is an illness the dispensary can best treat, so get the child there at once!" An *nganga*, realizing that he could not complete a case, referred accompanying kin to a prophet, whom he asked by letter to conduct an investigation on incest and, if necessary, to see to it that the clan sacrifice be made to "sever the blood" permitting the child to become well. All African practitioners we witnessed referred to all other types and to Western medical institutions. African practitioners of Western medicine called in *banganga* or allowed the clan to be present in the hospital. Only European practitioners of Western medicine limited their referrals to their own kind. A well-informed referral network is a key feature of total therapy in a pluralistic medical system such as exists in Lower Zaire.

Another aspect of synchronized plural therapy lies in the efficacy of traditional experts. They will continue to be a part of Kongo medicine, in any case, and the diagnostic ideas that they work out with the clients permit, as Nzoamambu's discussions have shown, the simultaneous physical treatment of disease alongside social investigation and ritual therapy. It is in the logistics of multiple therapy courses that difficulties arise. Frequently life-saving medication is overlooked while excruciating social conflicts are resolved.

A few innovative medical administrators have sought to combine Western medical care with African problem-solving by transporting the sufferer as well as Western medical personnel nearer to the traditional therapist. This is the strategy used in the well-published experiment of Dr. T. A. Lambo of Nigeria. Lambo, a British-trained Nigerian psychiatrist, saw the need for a psychiatry informed by African culture. When he joined the Ibadan University faculty, he created a liaison center in a nearby village to house his patients. Diviners from the area were paid a stipend to receive patients and help them, all the while they were under Lambo's supervision and nursing staff care.[5] In the Kongo setting this would mean that the mother who brought a coughing child to Mama Marie would have immediate care for it rather than have to trudge ten miles on foot to a dispensary, risking the loss of her child because of a wrong diagnosis.

The expertise of good inspirational diviners in resolving conflict and alleviating anxiety is remarkable. Many people seek their counsel. These practitioners have an uncanny gift for second-guessing their clients' problems and a disarming manner of laughing sympathetically at fears not founded in fact. But they react in moral indignation to foolish folks' abuse of one another or themselves, and scold them like a loving parent might. They have the temerity of spirit to probe deeply into dreams, to lay bare hidden motives in tacky situations. The best ones do not stir up conflict in the analysis of conflict. They know when to ease the séance away from direct interpersonal encounter to projected social symbols such as an ancestor or a genealogically remote set of twins. In short, they are significant agents of social integration. Medical planners could integrate the Zairian therapy system considerably by offering auxiliary medical services alongside the work of these diviners.

Another solution to the problem of synchronizing services would bring the ritual therapist and social analyst into the Western hospital. The "Chikore experiment" incorporated a pastor with the gift of divining and counselling into the staff of the large Chikore Hospital in Rhodesia. He was provided with a grass-roofed palaver house in the hospital compound near the wards. Patients' families freely consulted him about kinship problems, witchcraft suspicions, guilt feelings, and other typical issues ac-

5. T. A. Lambo, "A Plan for the Treatment of the Mentally Ill in Nigeria: The Village System at Aro," in *Frontiers in General Hospital Psychiatry,* ed. Louis Linn (New York, 1971), pp. 215–31; "Patterns of Psychiatric Care in Developing African Countries," in *Magic, Faith and Healing,* ed. Ari Kiev (New York and London), 1964, pp. 443–53.

companying disease, while the sufferer simultaneously received Western medical care nearby.[6] A final type of solution to the problem of synchronizing services combines functions of Western medicine with those of traditional therapy. We would regard our intervention into one therapy managing group as accidental; nevertheless, it is one possible combination of therapies that would greatly assist the integration of services. The therapy managing system is not closed, and Western practitioners could, like traditional practitioners, enlist the sanctioning strength of kinsmen and friends to reinforce their therapy. In the *Psychopalavre*, begun by Dr. Bazinga at the Neuropsychiatric Institute of Kinshasa, the sufferer participated alone initally while learning to role play and gain detachment from the setting that had caused his distress. When he was strong enough to meet his familial or job situation again, kinsmen were invited to participate in the *psychopalavre*. The therapy management group of kinsmen was thus utilized by Western medicine to sanction improvements experienced by the sufferer during group therapy,[7] a technique not unlike that used by certain healing cults and prophets.

The interrelated types of medicine in Lower Zaire are rapidly evolving. Health officials and physicians are now more often than not Zairian. Therapy management, the fundamental institution of Kongo medicine, is still performed by kinsmen, although increasingly friends, job peers, coreligionists, and neighbors of the sufferer substitute for them. Whatever form health care takes in Zaire in coming years, may both the rising expectations of full physical health and the profound metaphysical balance of *kisi-nsi* be contained in it. There is surely great wisdom in the words of *nganga* Masamba to Dr. Arkinstall: "*Nge i nganga ku nseke, kansi mono i nganga ku masa.*" ("You are a doctor of the land, but I am a doctor of the water.") Freely translated in the mood of the moment uttered, this means, "You and your medicine are great, but they are temporal; ours is the eternal medicine of the ancestors."

6. Franklin Donaldson, "Sister Buck Memorial Hospital Project in Spiritual Healing" (Chikore, Rhodesia, 1966/67).
7. Dénis Bazinga, *Psychopalavre* (Kinshasa, 1968/69).

APPENDIX A

Episodes of Case Studies Reported in Chapters 3-8

The following charts represent reconstructions of case episodes, many of which we witnessed directly. The left column of each episode indicates symptoms, problems, and diagnoses identified by sufferer, therapy managing group, or specialist. These are frequently multiple, separated by asterisks, reflecting different levels of conceptualization and labelling as well as alternative sources of information from factions or segments in the therapy managing group. Direct quotations of labels have been used wherever possible. The right column of each episode indicates therapeutic action undertaken. Elsewhere in the book, these episodes are cited by chapter and episode number, for example, 3.1, "swelling of limbs" and "weakness" treated by "penicillin injection."

CHAPTER 3: Luzayadio's case.

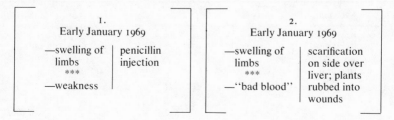

1. Early January 1969	
—swelling of limbs *** —weakness	penicillin injection

2. Early January 1969	
—swelling of limbs *** —"bad blood"	scarification on side over liver; plants rubbed into wounds

CHAPTER 3 (*Continued*)

3. January 13, 1969	
—swelling of face —enlarged heart —cough *** —swelling of limbs —swelling of liver —malaria & amoeba	cure of emetine & chloraquin; hospitalization 3 days

4. Mid-January 1969	
—swelling —cough	restricted meeting of father, mother, brother; decision to hold larger reunion

5. Mid-January 1969	
—swelling —cough *** —imputation of incestuous union of sufferer to suitor —unfinished marriage	examination of paternal and maternal kinship; mutual confessions, kin to sufferer & vice versa

6. January 26, 1969	
—peripheral dependent edema —cardiomegaly —loud systolic murmur down LSB & apex—soft short distalic murmur, increased jugular venous pressure—R cardiac failure, 2° tricoipid insufficiency *** —suspected rheumatic fever	digitalis & diuretics; hospitali- zation

7. February 2–13, 1969 Death, Funeral (I)	
"death by man" *** "death by God"	reunion of maternal clan and examination of maternal kinship

8. February 13, 1969 Conflict over death payment, Funeral (II)	
—accusation by maternal kin toward paternal kin	payment offered by paternal kin refused

CHAPTER 3 (*Continued*)

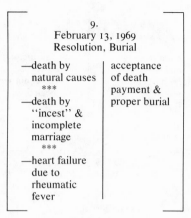

```
                    9.
           February 13, 1969
           Resolution, Burial

   —death by            acceptance
    natural causes      of death
        ***             payment &
   —death by            proper burial
    "incest" &
    incomplete
    marriage
        ***
   —heart failure
    due to
    rheumatic
    fever
```

Chapter 4: Axel and Cécile's child's case, March 1966.

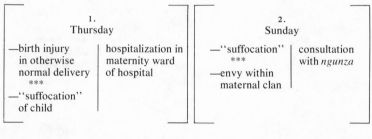

```
         1.                              2.
      Thursday                         Sunday

—birth injury    hospitalization in   —"suffocation"   consultation
 in otherwise    maternity ward           ***          with ngunza
 normal delivery of hospital          —envy within
     ***                               maternal clan
—"suffocation"
 of child
```

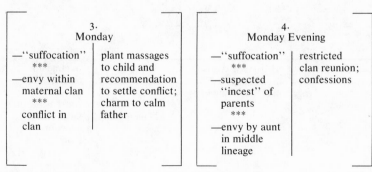

```
         3.                              4.
       Monday                       Monday Evening

—"suffocation"   plant massages      —"suffocation"   restricted
    ***          to child and            ***          clan reunion;
—envy within     recommendation      —suspected       confessions
 maternal clan   to settle conflict;  "incest" of
    ***          charm to calm        parents
 conflict in     father                   ***
 clan                                 —envy by aunt
                                       in middle
                                       lineage
```

CHAPTER 4 (*Continued*)

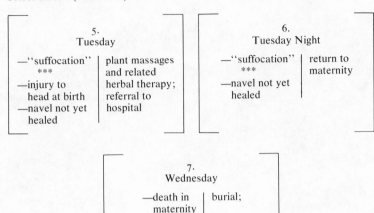

5.
Tuesday

—"suffocation"   plant massages
    ***   and related
—injury to   herbal therapy;
   head at birth   referral to
—navel not yet   hospital
   healed

6.
Tuesday Night

—"suffocation"   return to
    ***   maternity
—navel not yet
   healed

7.
Wednesday

—death in   burial;
   maternity

Chapter 5: Nzita's case.

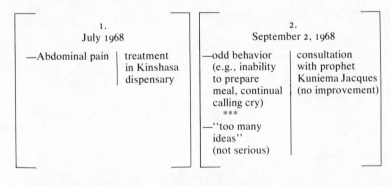

1.
July 1968

—Abdominal pain   treatment
               in Kinshasa
               dispensary

2.
September 2, 1968

—odd behavior   consultation
   (e.g., inability   with prophet
   to prepare   Kuniema Jacques
   meal, continual   (no improvement)
   calling cry)
     ***
—"too many
   ideas"
(not serious)

3.
September 5, 1968

—odd behavior   herbal treatment
    ***   from *nganga*
—"too many   (no improvement)
   ideas"
—(not serious)

4.
September 14–30, 1968

—odd behavior,   treatment at
   (e.g., burning   medical dis-
   clothes)   pensary in
     ***   Kinshasa with
—Thinking too   intravenous
   much   injection
—insomnia   (improved)
—anorexia

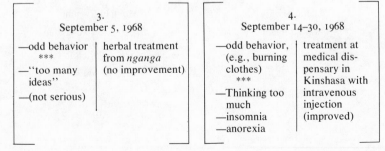

CHAPTER 5 (*Continued*)

5.
December 30, 1968

—odd behavior *** —anorexia (refusal to eat for 4 days) *** —insomnolent nights	treatment at medical dispensary in Kinshasa, intravenous infusion (improved)

6.
Late January 1969

—odd behavior (e.g., refusal to make bed)	return to village with husband

7.
Late January–February 7, 1969

—odd behavior *** —concern for maternal aunt's health	maternal clan meeting

8.
February 9, 1969

—odd behavior —sporadic recognition of close kin *** —young man in family "playing with a fetish"	prophetess Mama Marie consulted; clan reunion recommended

9.
February 10, 1969

—odd behavior *** —young man "playing with fetish"	reunion of clan; confession of kin to patient; letter written to Kinshasa kin (decision to consult "*féticheur*") *** Pastor in family dissents— recommends hospitalization

10.
February 10, 1969

—odd behavior *** —madness (*lauka*)	Bilumbu consulted; medication until the 20th

CHAPTER 5 (*Continued*)

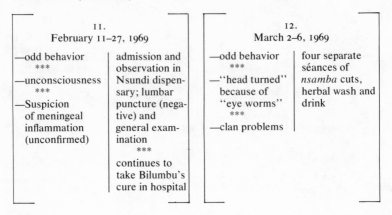

11. February 11–27, 1969	
—odd behavior *** —unconsciousness *** —Suspicion of meningeal inflammation (unconfirmed)	admission and observation in Nsundi dispen- sary; lumbar puncture (nega- tive) and general exam- ination *** continues to take Bilumbu's cure in hospital

12. March 2–6, 1969	
—odd behavior *** —"head turned" because of "eye worms" *** —clan problems	four separate séances of *nsamba* cuts, herbal wash and drink

Chapter 6: Nsimba's case.

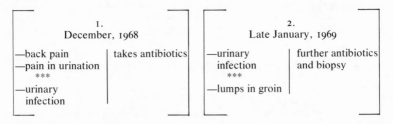

1. December, 1968	
—back pain —pain in urination *** —urinary infection	takes antibiotics

2. Late January, 1969	
—urinary infection *** —lumps in groin	further antibiotics and biopsy

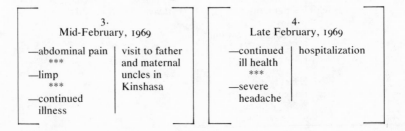

3. Mid-February, 1969	
—abdominal pain *** —limp *** —continued illness	visit to father and maternal uncles in Kinshasa

4. Late February, 1969	
—continued ill health *** —severe headache	hospitalization

CHAPTER 6 (*Continued*)

5. Late February, 1969	
—headache not curable in hospital ***	clan analysis by prophet
—"evil actions" ***	
—snake familiar	

6. Early March, 1969	
—"hands on patient and kin" ***	confession by paternal kinsmen; paternal blessing
—unmet demands for cash	

7. Early March, 1969	
—headache	symptomatic therapy in dispensary
—dizziness	
—delirium	
—fears of death ***	
—no physical findings	

8. Mid-March, 1969	
—headache	treatment for *mumpompila* (head pack of water & grassland plants)
—"splithead (*mumpompila*) ***	
—desire to move	

9. Late March, 1969	
—*nkatanga* "rheumatism of head" "loss of intelligence" ***	entire family spends week at prophet's center baths, prayer, oil, etc.
—"somewhat better but not well" ***	
—whole family sick	

10. Late March, 1969	
—fetish found in house ***	consults with prophet on identifying perpetrator of fetish
—conflict with job-related non-kin	

CHAPTER 6 (*Continued*)

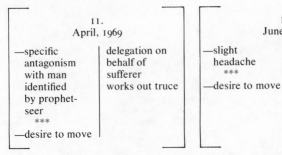

11.
April, 1969

—specific
antagonism
with man
identified
by prophet-
seer
***
—desire to move

delegation on
behalf of
sufferer
works out truce

12.
June, 1969

—slight
headache
***
—desire to move

meeting &
extended retreat
for professional
peers of sufferer;
move okayed

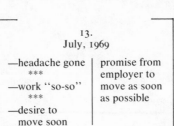

13.
July, 1969

—headache gone
***
—work "so-so"
***
—desire to
move soon

promise from
employer to
move as soon
as possible

Chapter 7: Lwezi's case.

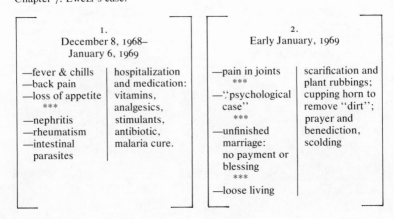

1.
December 8, 1968–
January 6, 1969

—fever & chills
—back pain
—loss of appetite
***
—nephritis
—rheumatism
—intestinal
parasites

hospitalization
and medication:
vitamins,
analgesics,
stimulants,
antibiotic,
malaria cure.

2.
Early January, 1969

—pain in joints
***
—"psychological
case"
***
—unfinished
marriage:
no payment or
blessing
***
—loose living

scarification and
plant rubbings;
cupping horn to
remove "dirt";
prayer and
benediction,
scolding

CHAPTER 7 (*Continued*)

3. February 10, 1969	
—unsolicited diagnosis by Arkinstall: chronic urinary infection; —musculo-skeletal pain & weakness)	(remains in maternal village; clan apprised of medical findings)

4. Mid-February, 1969	
—"psychological problem" *** —problems throughout matrilineage *** —talisman —fetish —unpaid bride price	examination within matrilineage; decision to seek outside help

5. February 19, 1969	
—"psychological problem" *** —problems in clan *** —fetish —talisman *** —unfinished marriage —no paternal blessing —interclan conflict	mutual reconcil-iation of parents; confessions of ill will: sufferer to parents and vice versa; payment of bride price & paternal blessing urged by presiding prophet

6. Early April, 1969	
—pains set in anew	ritual bath, prayer and anointment with oil; purification and liturgies

CHAPTER 7 (*Continued*)

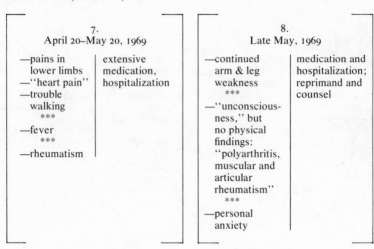

7. April 20–May 20, 1969	
—pains in lower limbs —"heart pain" —trouble walking *** —fever *** —rheumatism	extensive medication, hospitalization

8. Late May, 1969	
—continued arm & leg weakness *** —"unconscious- ness," but no physical findings: "polyarthritis, muscular and articular rheumatism" *** —personal anxiety	medication and hospitalization; reprimand and counsel

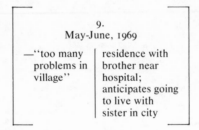

9. May-June, 1969	
—"too many problems in village"	residence with brother near hospital; anticipates going to live with sister in city

Chapter 8: Mbumba's case.

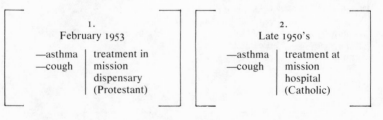

1. February 1953	
—asthma —cough	treatment in mission dispensary (Protestant)

2. Late 1950's	
—asthma —cough	treatment at mission hospital (Catholic)

CHAPTER 8 (*Continued*)

3. Early 1960's	
—asthma —cough	treatment at large hospital (Protestant)

4. July 1965	
—asthma —cough	treatment at state hospital after X-ray (negative)

5. July, 1965	
—asthma —cough *** —resistance to "call" to serve church	drink holy water upon each cough; prayer; dream analysis: to become deacon

6. October 26, 1965	
—public acknowledgment of resistance to "call" and wish to become deacon	announcement before village assembly of need to be deacon

7. November 1, 1965	
—wish to be deacon	acceptance by village/ clan church; recommend sufferer to regional church; clan blessing

8. December 1965	
—wish to be deacon *** —deaconship created	consecration as deacon before regional church conference

CHAPTER 8 (*Continued*)

9. Early 1966	
—local post of deacon empty *** —asthma attacks whenever at home in own village	takes up residence with prophet as deacon and helper for the prophet

10. 1967	
—"afflictions" of several clan brothers (including sufferer)	clan reunion with two prophets; helping; confessions of clansmen to all sufferers and vice versa

11. 1968	
—"afflictions" of same several clan brothers (including sufferer)	clan reunion without any ritual expert; confession of clansmen to each other

Herbarium of Medicinal Plants

This herbarium, assembled by Dr. Arkinstall in conjunction with our field study in 1969, includes a few plants that appear in the case studies as well as many more collected from *banganga* whose practices we observed and with whom we conversed at length. Some duplicates will be noted. These were collected to cross-check naming consistency and plant uses from region to region and herbalist to herbalist, as well as to identify plant types in indigenous gender classifications. Some variations in the KiKongo spelling will be noted, reflecting the range of local dialects and prefix uses, singular and plural expressions. Thus, *ndidi = mundidi*; *nlulu = minlulu*; *lemba-lemba = kilemba-lemba*; *mvete = luvete = luhete,* and so on. The Botany Department of the National University (Kinshasa campus) received a duplicate set of this herbarium, and we are grateful to Professor Evrard and his staff there for identifying these plants following standard botanical nomenclature.

1. *Kuta-kuta*	Biophytum sensitivum (L.) DC.=Oxalid.
2. *Lukasa*	Psendarthria hookeri Wright et Arn. =Papilionaceae.
3. *Mitoko-toko*	Nymphaea lotus L.=Nymphaeac.
4. *Mudidi*	Tetrorchidium didymostemon (Baill.) Pax et K. Hoffm.=Euphorbiaceae.
5. *Munzeke-nzeke*	Abrus precatorius L.=Papil.
6. *Lubala-mukanga*	Manotes griffoniana Baill.=Connar.
7. *Kangaya* (male)	Setaria megaphylla (Steud.) Th. Dur. et Schinz.=Gramineae.

8. *Kangaya* (female)	Setaria megaphylla (Steud.) Th. Dur. et Schinz=Gram.
9. *Tumvumfu*	Sida acuta Burm. f.=Malvaceae.
10. *Kienga*	Nauclea latifolia Sm.=Rubiaceae.
11. *Nlulu*	Annona arenaria Thonn.=Annonaceae.
12. *Kinsangula*	Maprounea africana Mull. Arg.=Euphorb.
13. *Mumpala-mbaki*	Crossopteryx febrifuga (Afz. ex. G. Don) Benth.
14. *Nsangania*	Hymenocardia ulmoides Oliv.=Euphorb.
15. *Nkunga-mbwa*	Pteridium aquilinum (L.) Kuhn.=Pterd.
16. *Mvuka*	Millettia sp.=Papil.
17. *Nsingu-nkabi*	Tetracera cfr. potatoria Afz. ex G. Don. =Dilleniaceae.
18. *Nsumbi-nsumbi*	Combretum=Combretaceae.
19. *Mansiu-nsiu*	Ocimum gratissmum L.=Labiat.
20. *Yuka-yuka*	Bryophyllum pinnatum (Lam.) Oken=Crassulaceae.
21. *Fula*	Cassia occidentalis L.=Caesalpiniaceae.
22. *Lemba-ntoko*	Solenostemon monostachyus (P. Beauv.) Brio=Labiateae.
23. *Nkamba*	Chlorophora excelsa (Welw.) Benth. =Moraceae.
24. *Mupuluka*	Jatropha curcois L.=Euphorb.
25. *Fumu-dia-nseke*	Erigeron floribundus (H. B. et K.) Sch. BiP.
26. *Kideka*	Trichopteryx fruticulosa Chiov.=Gramineae.
27. *Mundanda-njila*	Schwenckia americana Linn.=Solanaceae.
28. *Luhete*	Hymenocardia acida Tul.=Euphorbiaceae.
29. *Nsingu-nkabi*	Tetracera cfr. potatoria Afz. ex G. Don. =Dilleniaceae.
30. *Tumvumvu*	Sida acuta Burm. f.=Malvaceae.
31. *Mundumbu*	Emilia coccinea (Sims) G. Don.=Compositae.
32. *Ba-dia-nseke*	Curculigo pilosa (Schum.) Engl.=Amaryllidaceae.
33. *Mumpoko*	?
34. *Munsanga-vulu*	Costus cfr. Lucanusianus J. Br. et K. Schum.=Zingberaceae.
35. *Mfilu*	Vitex cfr. madiensis Oliv.=Verbenaceae.
36. *Lubota*	Millettia versicolor Welw. ex Bak. =Papilionacceae.
37. *Kinkuba-mbu*	Asparagus sp.=Liliaceae.

38. *Mbunzi*	Alchornea cordifolia (Schumach) Müll. Arg.=Euphorbiaceae.
39. *Mpoko*	?
40. *Mufuma*	Ceiba pentandra (L.) Gaertn.=Bombacaceae.
41. *Munkula-mvumbi*	Steganotaenia araliacea Hochst.=Ombelliferae.
42. *Kilemba-nzau*	Gardenia sp.=Rubiaceae.
43. *Patakani*	Cfr. Lactuca sp.=Compositeae.
44. *Mbala-mukuyu*	?
45. *Muzeke-zeke*	Tristemma sp.=Melastomataceae.
46. *Mufilu*	Vitex Cfr. madiensis Oliv.=Verbenaceae.
47. *Lubata-bata*	Costus spectabilis (Fenzl.) K. Schum. =Zingberaceae.
48. *Saka-dia-mukanka*	? =Rubiaceae.
49. *Munungu-musitu*	Rauvolfia mannii Stapf.=Apocynaceae.
50. *Yombo*	Quassia africana (Baill.) Baill.=Simarubaceae.
51. *Mpamba-munti*	Culcasia cfr. sascatilis A. Chev.=Araceae.
52. *Munsele-bende*	?
53. *Lunama*	Desmodium velutinum (Willd) DC. =Papilionaceae.
54. *Mulondo*	Schwenckia americana Linn.=Solanaceae.
55. *Meso-nkama*	?
56. *Lemba-lemba*	Brillantaisia patula. T. Anders.=Acanthaceae.
57. *Mwakasa*	Cassia cfr. cannii Oliv.=Caesalphiniaceae.
58. *Kuluba*	Ochna cfr. afzelii R. Br. ex Oliv. =Ochnaceae.
59. *Mansiu-nsiu* (male)	Ocimum cfr. basilicum L.=Labiateae.
60. *Mansiu-nsiu* (female)	Ocimum gratissimum L.=Labiateae.
61. *Koyi-bangala*	?
62. *Mulala-mansangi*	Cfr. Canthium sp.=Rubiaceae.
63. *Mpuku-mwifi* (female)	Palisota sp.=Commelinaceae.
64. *Muntense-mankelele*	Maesopsis Eminii Engl.=Rhamnaceae.
65. *Mpuku-mwifi* (male)	Palisota sp.=Commelinaceae.
66. *Meso-nkama*	?
67. *Fuma-dia-nseke*	Erigeron floribundus (H.B. et K.) Sch. Bip.=Compositeae.
68. *Mbanga-ntela*	Caloncoba welwitschii (Oliv.) Gilg. =Flacourtiaceae.

69. *Bubu*	Ficus sp.=Moraceae.
70. *Mumvuka*	Phyllanthus sp.=Euphorbiaceae.
71. *Manguansi*	Ocimum cfr. basilicum L.=Labiateae.
72. *Mansiu-nsiu* (female)	Ocimum cfr. basilicum L.=Labiateae.
73. *Mansiu-nsiu* (male)	Ocimum gratissimum L.=Labiateae.
74. *Kilembe-lembe kia nseke*	Virectaria Multiflora (Sm.) Bremek. =Rubiaceae.
75. *Lemba-ntoko*	Piper Umbellatum L.=Piperaceae.
76. *Kilonga-longa*	Nymphaea lotus L.=Nymphaeaceae.
77. *Lunsongi*	Leonotis nepetifolia (L.) Ait.=Labiateae.
78. *Diamba-koko*	Chenopodium ambrosoides L. =Chenopodiaceae.
79. *Kimbanzia*	Eleusine indica L.=Gramineae.
80. *Kidoka-doka*	Centella asiatica (L.) Urb.=Ombelliferae.
81. *Mwindu*	Bridelia ferruginea Benth.=Euphorbiaceae.
82. *Nseke-nseke*	Abrus cfr. precatorius L.=Papilionaceae.
83. *Mfilu*	?
84. *Tumvumvu*	?
85. *Nkila-mbwa*	Pennisetum polystachyon (L.) Schultes. =Gramineae.
86. *Yeye*	Piptadeniastrum africanum (Hook. f.) Brenan.=Mimosaceae.
87. *Munkula-ndozi*	Steganotaenia araliacea Hochst.=Ombelliferae.
88. *Kinsangani*	Gardiospermum Grandiflorum Swartz. Sapindaceae.
89. *Lunama-nama*	?
90. *Nsanda*	Ficus sp.=Moraceae.
91. *Dinsongi*	Leonotis nepetifolia (L.) Ait.=Labiateae.
92. *Mpuluka*	Jatropha curcois L.=Euphorbiaceae.
93. *Kazuwa*	Anacardium occidentale L.=Anacardiaceae.
94. *Nlulukulu*	Vernonia colorata (Willd.) Drake.=Compositeae.
95. *Nsanda*	Ficus sp.=Moraceae.
96. *Tumvumvu*	Sida acuta Burm. f.=Malvaceae.
97. *Nungu*	Capsicum frutescens L.=Solanaceae.
98. *Kazuwa*	Anacardium occidentale L.=Anacardiaceae.
99. *Mfuluta*	Psidium guajava L.=Myrt.
100. *Nkomo* (lunzila-nzila)	?
101. *Mpese-mpese*	?
102. *Mfundu*	Boerhavia diffusa L.=Nyctaginaceae.

103. *Luyuki*	Bryophyllum pinnatum (Lam.) Oken. =Begoniaceae.
104. *Tula*	Laggera alata (D.Don) Sch. Bip. ex Oliv.=Compositeae.
105. *Nsudi*	Gossypium barbadense L.=Malvaceae.
106. *Wayeya*	? Acanthaceae.
107. *Nkama-nsongo*	Cfr. Hyptis suavacolens Poit.=Labiateae.
108. *Kimvumina*	Euphorbia hirta L.=Euphorbiaceae.
109. *Masisia-sisia*	Aframomum sp.=Zingiberaceae.
110. *Makangaya*	Setaria megaphylla (Steud.) Th. Dur. et Schinz.=Gramineae.
111. *Mumbala-mbala*	Cissus rubignosa (Welw.) ex Benth. Planch.=Vitaceae.
112. *Dinkondo dia kimbiti*	Anchomanes difformis (BL.) Engl. =Aracaea.
113. *Dinkondo dia kimbiti*	Anchomanes difformis (BL.) Engl. =Aracaea.
114. *Munkwinsia*	Costus sp.=Zingiberaceae.
115. *Mumpala-mbaki*	Crossopteryx febrifuga (Afz. ex G. Don) Benth.=Rubiaceae.
116. *Mungye-ngye*	Spondias mombin L.=Anacardiaceae.
117. *Luvete*	Hymenocardia acida Tul.=Euphorbiaceae.
118. *Votolo*	Psorospermum febrifugum Spach.=Guttiferaceae.
119. *Lolo ntumbi*	Nauclea cfr. gilletii (De Wild.) Merr. =Rubiaceae.
120. *Ma nwa nsongi*	?
121. *Nkadi-nkadi*	Vitex sp.=Verbenaceae.
122. *Kilemba*	Solanum sp.=Solanaceae.
123. *Dia ba mvudi*	Eupatorium africanum Oliv. et Hiern. =Compositeae.
124. *Diza-kia-nlembo*	Euphorbia tirucalli L.=Euphorbiaceae.
125. *Sa kongo*	(a) Hibiscus acetosella Welw. ex Hiern. =Malvaceae. (b) Hibiscus sp.=Malvaceae.
126. *Mfilu*	Vitex sp.=Verbenaceae.
127. *Nlolo*	Annona arenaria Thonn.=Annonaceae.
128. *Diza dia kinene*	Euphorbia sp.=Euphorbiaceae.
129. *Luvuka*	Milletia sp.=Papilionaceae.
130. *Nkuki*	Cfr. Symphonia globulifera L. f.=Guttif.
131. *Vamu*	? Euphorbiaceae.
132. *Nsolo-nsonso*	Rottboellia exaltata L. f.=Gramineae.
133. *Mpunga*	Triumfetta cordifolia A. Rich.=Tiliaceae.

134. *Bumi* (female)	Cassia alata L.=Caesalpiniaceae.
135. *Bumi* (male)	Tephrosia Vogelii Hook. f.=Papilionaceae.
136. *Luyangu-yangu*	Cymbopogon densiflorus (Steud.) Stapf. =Gramineae.
137. *Luyangu-yangu*	?
138. *Luvangu*	Dichrostachys cinerea (L.) Wright et Arn.=Mimosaceae.
139. *Dingwanzia*	Ocimum cfr. basilicum L.=Labiateae.
140. *Lemba-ntoko*	Piper Umbellatum L.=Piperaceae.
141. *Kanga-ngoyo*	Cissampelos owariensis P. Beauv. ex DC.=Menispermaceae.
142. *Nkazu*	?
143. *Mbuba*	Myrianthus arboreus P. Beauv.=Moraceae.
144. *Ntutu-tufi*	? Ranouculaceae?
145. *Makinda-ngolo*	? Verbenaceae.
146. *Mansiu-nsiu* (male)	Ocimum gratissimum L.=Labiateae.
147. *Mansiu-nsiu* (female)	?
148. *Zanga bia nzi*	Vigna unguiculata (L.) Walp.=Papilionaceae.
149. *Nsolokoto*	Bidens pilosa L.=Compositeae.
150. *Nsaka-nsaka*	Luffa cylindrica (L.) M.J. Roem.=Cucurbitaceae.
151. *Mumpala-mbaki*	?
152. *Nkizu*	Syzygium guineense (Willd.) DC.=Myrtaceae. .
153. *Votila*	?
154. *Luvete*	Hymenocardia acida Tul.=Euphorbiaceae.
155. *Bole*	Dalbergia gentilii De Wild.=Papilionaceae.
156. *Nkanga-ngoyo*	Cissampelos owariensis P. Beauv. ex DC.=Menispermaceae.
157. *Mvête*	Hymenocardia acida Tul.=Euphorbiaceae.
158. *Nsaku-nsaku*	Cyperus articulatus L.=Cyperaceae.
159. *Nkizu*	Syzygium guineense (Willd.) DC.=Myrtaceae.
160. *Mumpoko*	Asystasia gangetica (L.) T. Anders.=Acanthaceae.
161. *Ngie-ngie*	Abrus precatorius L.=Papilionaceae.
162. *Munzeke-nzeke*	Tristemma sp.=Melastomataceae.
163. *Munzeke-nzeke*	Tristemma sp.=Melastomataceae.
164. *Fumu dia nseke*	?

165. *Lunama*	Desmodium veltinum (Willd.) DC.=Papilionaceae.
166. *Votila*	Crossopteryx Febrifuga (Afz. ex G. Don) Benth.=Rubiaceae.
167. *Luhete*	Hymenocardia acida Tul.=Euphorbiaceae.
168. *Luvuka*	Milletia sp.=Papilionaceae.
169. *Nsingu-nkabi*	Tetracera sp.=Dilleniaceae.
170. *Kienga*	Nauclea latifolia Smith.=Rubiaceae.
171. *Mulolo*	Cfr. Vitex sp.=Verbenaceae.
172. *Tumvumvu*	Sida acuta Burm. f.=Malvaceae.
173. *Kinsangula*	Maprounea africana Müll. Arg.=Euphorbiaceae.
174. *Luangu-luangu*	Cymbopogon densiflorus (Steud.) Stapf.=Gramineae.
175. *Kifusa*	Albizia adianthifolia (Schum.) W. F. Wight. =Mimosaceae.
176. *Kilembe-lembe kia mpembe*	Erigeron floribundus (H. B. et K.) Sch. Bip. =Compositeae.
177. *Kilembe-lembe kia mbwaki*	Virectaria Multiflora (Smith.) Brem. =Rubiaceae.
178. *Mansiu-nsiu* (male)	Ocimum gratissimum L.=Labiateae.
179. *Muzeke-zeke*	Abrus precatorius L.=Papilionaceae.
180. *Mangwansia*	Ocimum cfr. basilicum L.=Labiateae.
181. *Mbangu-mbangu*	Vernonia sp.=Compositeae.
182. *Ngenga*	Canna bidentata Bert.=Cannaceae.
183. *Nsaku-nsaku*	Cyperus articulatus L.=Cyperaceae.

Bibliography of Works Cited

Babutidi. Notebooks 7–8. Lidingö: Svenska Missionsforbundet Archives, Laman Collection.

Bain, S. T., and Spaulding, W. B. "The Importance of Coding Presenting Symptoms." *Canadian Medical Association Journal* 96 (October 14, 1967).

Balint, M. *The Doctor, His Patient, and the Illness*. New York: International Universities Press, 1957.

Bates, Don. Personal communications. November 24, 1971.

Baumann, H., and Westermann, D. *Les peuples et les civilisations de l'Afrique*. Paris: Payot, 1967.

Bazinga, Dénis. *Psychopalavre*. Kinshasa: Institut Neuropsychiatrie (typescript of séances), 1968/9.

Beck, A. *Changing Lifestyles and Sleeping Sickness: A History of the British Medical Administration of East Africa, 1900–1950*. Cambridge: Harvard University Press, 1970.

Bloom, Samuel W. *The Doctor and His Patient*. New York: Russel Sage Foundation, 1963.

Boswell, D. M. "Personal Crises and the Mobilization of the Social Network." In *Social Networks in Urban Situations: Analyses of Personal Relationships in Central African Towns*. Edited by J. Clyde Mitchell. Manchester: Manchester University Press, 1969, pp. 245–96.

Brodsky, C. M. "Decision-Making and Role Shifts as They Affect the Consultation Interface." *Archives of General Psychiatry* 23 (1970), 6: 559–65.

Buakasa, Gérard. *L'impensé du discours: "kindoki" et "nkisi" en pays kongo du Zaire*. Kinshasa: Presses Universitaires du Zaire, 1973.

———. "A Classification of Disease." *Journal of the College of General Practitioners and Research* 6 (1963): 204–16.

Conklin, Harold. "Hanunuoo Color Categories." *Southwestern Journal of Anthropology* 11 (1955): 339–44.

de Craemer, Willy, and Fox, Renée C. *The Emerging Physician: A Sociological Approach to the Development of a Congolese Medical Profession*. Stanford: Hoover Institution Studies No. 19, 1968.

Crowder, Michael. "Indirect Rule, French and British Style." *Africa* 34 (1964), 3: 197–205.

———. "Doctor-Patient Communication." *Medical Anthropology Newsletter* 4 (1973): 3.

Donaldson, Franklin. "Sister Buck Memorial Hospital Project in Spiritual Healing." Chikore, Rhodesia: Mimeograph, 1966/67.

Douglas, Mary. *Purity and Danger*. London: Routledge and Kegan Paul, Ltd., 1966.

———. *Natural Symbols*. New York: Praeger, 1970.

Duff, R. S., and Hollingshead, A. B. *Sickness and Society*. New York: Harper and Row, 1968.

Dupont, Edouard. *Lettres sur le Congo*. Paris: C. Reinwald, 1889.

Evans-Pritchard, E. E. *Witchcraft, Oracles, and Magic Among the Azande*. Oxford: Oxford University Press, 1937.

Fabrega, Horatio. *Disease and Social Behavior*. Cambridge and London: Massachusetts Institute of Technology Press, 1974.

Fannon, Franz. *Les damnées de la terre*. Paris: Maspero, 1961.

Fernandez, James. "Performances and Persuasions: Of the Beast in Every Body . . . and the Metaphors of Everyman." In *Culture, Myth and Symbol*. Edited by Clifford Geertz. Daedalus (winter 1972.)

Frake, Charles. "The Diagnosis of Disease Among the Subanun of Mindanao." *American Anthropologist* 63 (1961), 1: 113–32.

———. "A Structural Description of Subanun 'Religious Behavior.' " in *Cognitive Anthropology*. Edited by Stephen A. Tyler. New York: Holt, Rinehart and Winston, 1969, pp. 470–86.

Freidson, Eliot. *Profession of Medicine*. New York: Dodd, Mead and Co., 1970.

Fukiau-kia-Bunseki. *Le mukongo et le monde qui l'entourait/N'kongo ye Nza yakun'zungidila*. Kinshasa: Office National de la Recherche et de Développement, 1969.

———. Personal communications, 1969.

———. *Kindoki, ou la solution attendue*. Kumba: Mimeographed, 1973.

Gelfand, Michael. *The Sick African*. Capetown: Juta, 1955.

——————. *Medicine and Custom in Africa.* Edinburgh: E. and S. Livingstone, 1964.

——————. *Witch Doctor, Traditional Medicine Man of Rhodesia.* New York: Praeger, 1965.

Gluckman, Max. *Politics, Law, and Ritual in Tribal Society.* Chicago: Aldine, 1965.

Göbel, Peter. Personal communications, November 11, 1975.

Griaule, Marcel. *Dieu d' eau: Entretiens avec Ogotemmêli.* Paris: Editions du Chêne, 1948.

Harley, George W. *Native African Medicine.* Cambridge: Harvard University Press, 1944.

de Hemptinne, J. "La politique indigène du gouvernement belge." *Congo* 2 (1928): 1–16.

Henderson, L. J. "The Patient and Physician as a Social System." *New England Journal of Medicine* 212 (1935): 819–23.

Horton, Robin. "African Traditional Thought and Western Science." *Africa* 37 (1967): 50–72, 155–87.

Iyeky, Jean-François. *Essai de psychologie du primitif.* Léopoldville: La Voix du Congolais, 1956.

Jansen, G. *The Doctor-Patient Relationship in an African Tribal Society.* Assen: Van Gorcum, 1973.

Janson, H. W. *History of Art.* Englewood Cliffs, N.J.: and New York: Prentice-Hall, 1964.

Janzen, John M. "Vers une phénoménologie de la guérison en Afrique centrale." *Etudes congolaises* 12 (1969), 2: 97–114.

——————. "Kongo Religious Renewal: Iconoclastic and Iconorthostic." *Canadian Journal of African Studies* 5 (1971): 135–43.

——————. "Signs, Symptoms, and Symbols: A Semiotic Interpretation of Kongo Illness and Therapy." Paper presented at the American Anthropological Association, New Orleans, 1973.

——————, with Wyatt MacGaffey. *An Anthology of Kongo Religion: Primary Texts from Lower Zaire.* Lawrence: University of Kansas Publications in Anthropology No. 5, 1974.

——————. "The Dynamics of Therapy in the Lower Zaire." In *Psychological Anthropology.* Edited by Thomas R. Williams. The Hague: Mouton, 1975, pp. 441–63.

King, Maurice, ed. *Medical Care in Developing Countries: A Symposium.* Nairobi: Oxford University Press, 1969.

Kivunda Communal Records. Tableaux de recensement de population: 1956, 1959, 1962, 1964, 1965.

Kolaja, J. "Two Processes: A New Framework for the Theory of Participation in Decision-Making." *Behavioural Science* 13 (1968): 66–70.

Korsch, Barbara, and Negrete, Vida F. "Doctor-Patient Communication." *Scientific American* 227 (August 1972), 3: 66–74.

Kuhn, Thomas. *The Structure of Scientific Revolutions.* Second edition. Chicago: University of Chicago Press, 1970.

Kupferer, H. J. K. "Couvade: Ritual or Real Illness?" *American Anthropologist* 67 (1965): 99–101.

Kusikila, J. *Lufwa evo Kimongi e?* Kumba: Mimeographed typescript, 1966.

LaFontaine, Jean S. *City Politics: A Study of Léopoldville* 1962–3. Cambridge: Cambridge University Press, African Studies Series No. 1, 1970.

Laman, K. E. *Dictionnaire KiKongo-Français.* Bruxelles: Institute Royale Coloniale Belge, 1936.

——————. *The Kongo II.* Uppsala: Studia Ethnographica Upsaliensia VIII, 1957.

——————. *The Kongo III.* Uppsala: Studia Ethnographica Upsaliensia XIII, 1962.

Lambo, T. A. "Patterns of Psychiatric Care in Developing African Countries." In *Magic Faith and Healing.* Edited by Ari Kiev. New York and London: The Free Press, 1964, pp. 443–53.

——————. "A Plan for the Treatment of the Mentally Ill in Nigeria: The Village System at Aro." In *Frontiers in General Hospital Psychiatry.* Edited by Louis Linn. New York: International Universities Press, 1971, pp. 215–31.

Lévi-Strauss, Claude. *La pensée sauvage.* Paris: Plon, 1956.

Lévy-Bruhl, Lucien. *L'âme primitive.* Paris: F. Alcan, 1927.

Lewin, Kurt. *Field Theory in Social Science.* New York: Harper, 1951.

Luozi Territorial Archives. Ordinance-law No. 41/81 of February 12, 1953, and Ordinance No. 71/81 of February 19, 1958, on "The Art of Healing."

——————. Dossier P-21, "The Art of Healing."

MacIntyre, Alsadair. "A Mistake About Causality in Social Science." In *Philosophy, Politics, and Society.* Edited by Peter Laslett and W. C. Runciman. Oxford: Oxford University Press, 1962.

Maine, Henry. *Ancient Law.* London: Dent, 1960.

Mannoni, O. *Psychologie de la colonisation.* Paris: Seuil, 1950.

"Markov Chains." *International Encyclopedia of the Social Sciences.* New York: Macmillan and The Free Press, 1968. Volume 9: 581–85.

Matunta. Notebook 306. Lidingö: Svenska Missionsforbundet Archives, Laman Collection.

Mechanic, David. "The Concept of Illness Behavior." *Journal of Chronic Disease* 15 (1962): 189–94.

Mertens, J. "La juridiction indigène chez les BaKongo orientaux." *Kongo-Overzee* 10–18 (1944–1952).

Metzger, Duane, and Williams, Gerald. "Tenejapa Medicine I: The Curer." *Southwestern Journal of Anthropology* 19 (1963): 216–34.

Murdock, George P. *Africa, Its Peoples and Their Culture History.* New York: McGraw-Hill, 1959.

Murphy, Jane M., and Leighton, Alexander H., eds. *Approaches to Cross-Cultural Psychiatry.* Ithaca: Cornell University Press, 1965.

Nicolai, Henri. *Luozi: Géographie régionale d'un pays du Bas-Congo.* Bruxelles: Association de la Recherche des Sociétés d'outre-Mer, 1961.

Nsemi, Isaki. Notebook 391. Lidingö: Svenska Missionsforbundet Archives, Laman Collection.

——————. "Sacred Medicines" (*Min'kisi*). In *Anthology of Kongo Religion.* Compiled by J. M. Janzen and Wyatt MacGaffey. Lawrence: University of Kansas Publication in Anthropology 5 (1974): 34–38.

Ombredane, A. *Etude psychotechnique des Baluba, T. I.: Application experimentale du test d'intelligence "Matrix 38" à 485 noirs Baluba.* Bruxelles: ARSC, 1957.

Parin, Paul, Morgenthaler, Fritz, and Parin-Matthèy, Goldy. *Fürchte deinen Nächsten wie dich Selbst: Psychanalyse u. Gesellschaft am Modell der Agni in Westafrika.* Frankfurt am Main: Suhrkamp Verlag, 1971.

Parsons, Talcott. *The Social System.* New York: The Free Press, 1951.

——————. "Definition of Health and Illness in the Light of American Values and Social Structure." In *Patients, Physicians and Illness: Sourcebook in Behavioral Science and Medicine.* Edited by E. G. Jaco. New York: The Free Press of Glencoe, 1958, p. 165 ff.

Pearse, I. H., and Croitar, L. H. *The Perkham Experiment.* London: 1949.

Pechuel-Loesche, E. *Volkskunde von Loango.* Stuttgart: Strecker u. Schroeder, 1907.

Pouillon, Jean. "Malade et médecin: le même et/ou l'autre? Rémarques ethnologiques." *Incidences de la Psychanalyse: Nouvelle Révue de Psychanalyse* 1(1970).

Price-Williams, D. R. "A Case Study of Ideas Concerning Disease Among the Tiv." *Africa* 32 (1962): 123–31.

"Problem-Oriented Medical Records." *The Lancet* (February 5, 1972).

Rapport annuel sur l'exercise 1931. Bruxelles: Fonds Reine Elisabeth pour l'assistance médicale aux indigènes du Congo Belge (FOREAMI), 1932.

Read, Margaret. *Culture, Health, and Disease.* London: Tavistock Publications, 1966.

Romney, Kimball A., and D'Andrade, Roy G., eds. *Transcultural Studies in Cognition.* American Anthropologist Special Publication, *American Anthropologist* 66 (1964), 3, Part 2.

Sapira, J. D. "Reassurance Therapy." *Annals of Internal Medicine* 77 (1972): 603–04.

Sautter, Gilles. *De l'Atlantique au fleuve Congo: Une géographie du sous-peuplement.* The Hague: Mouton, 1966.

Stanley, Henry M. *Through the Dark Continent.* Two volumes. New York: Harper, 1879.

Statistical Yearbook, 1959. New York: Statistical Office of the United Nations, 1959.

Statistical Yearbook, 1971. New York: Publishing Service of the United Nations, 1972.

"Time Series." *International Encyclopedia of the Social Sciences.* New York: Macmillan Co. and The Free Press, 1968. Volume 16: 73.

Trolli, G. *Rapport sur l'hygiène publique pendant l'année 1929.* Bruxelles, (FOREAMI) 1931.

——————, and Dupuy. *Contribution à l'étude de la démographie des BaKongo au Congo belge 1933.* Bruxelles: Est. M. Cock (FOREAMI), 1934.

Turner, Victor W. *Schism and Continuity in an African Society.* Manchester: Manchester University Press, 1957.

——————. *The Forest of Symbols: Aspects of Ndembu Ritual.* Ithaca: Cornell University Press, 1967.

——————. *Drums of Affliction: A Study of Religious Processes Among the Ndembu of Zambia.* Oxford: Clarendon Press, 1968.

Van Wing, Jan. *Etudes BaKongo.* Bruxelles: Desclées de Brouwers, 1959.

Verhaegen, Benoit. *Rébellions au Congo, I.* Bruxelles: Centre de Recherche et d'Information Socio-Politique, 1966.

Verstig, "Tata" Paul. *Makaya ma Nsi masadisa Nitu.* Ninth edition. Matadi: Imprimèrie Notre-Dame Médiatrice 1966.

Vilen, A. *Rapport annuel 1937 de l'oeuvre médical SMF.* Kibunzi: Typescript, 1938.

Vyncke, J. *Psychoses et nevroses en Afrique centrale.* Bruxelles: Académie Royale des Sciences Coloniales, 1957.

Weed, Lawrence L. *Medical Records, Medical Education, and Patient Care.* Cleveland: Case Western Reserve University Press, 1969.

Weiss, Herbert. *Political Protest in the Congo.* Princeton: Princeton University Press, 1967.

White, Kerr L. "Classification of Patient Symptoms, Complaints, and Problems." *World Health Organization Document DHSS/WP/70.5*, 1970.

Wintringer, G. *Considerations sur l'intelligence du noir d'Afrique.* Anvers: Institut Haurais de sociologie, économie, et de psychologie des peuples, 1955.

World Health Organization. *International Classification of Diseases.* Eighth edition. Geneva: 1965.

World Health Statistics Annual 1969. Volume III. Geneva: W.H.O., 1970.

Zola, I. K. "Culture and Symptoms: An Analysis of Patients' Presenting Complaints." *American Sociological Review* 31 (1966): 615–30.

Glossary-Index

Abdomen, in medical cosmology, 158, 169–75, 162; pain in, 9, 114, 187; swollen, in child, 170–71; noisy, 188; see *Vumu*

Agni, tribe, 5–6

Agriculture, of Lower Zaire, 12–15; and nutrition, 31; and disease, 26

Alliance, *see* Marriage

Anatomy, 128, 162–63, 169, 170–71, 175, 187–88; in organization of metaphor and cosmology, 160–69; symmetry in, 171

Anemia: sickle cell, 26, 31; nutritional, 26; "bad blood" as, 187

Anger, illness, 120, 194–95; see *Mfunia*

Anxiety, illness cause, 9–11

Arkinstall, W., xiv, xvii-xxi, 31–32, 34, 68–74, 81–82, 87, 95–96, 158–60, 229, Pl. 6

Asthma, 114–17, 157, 240–41

Authenticity, campaign, xvii, xx, 57–58, 218–19

Authority, 23–25, 50, 115–16, 120–21, 169–70; see *Mfumu. See also* Decision-Making; Chiefship.

Babutidi, T., 48–49, 130, 177

Bain, S.T., 191n

Balint, M., 8n, 141n

Bana bambuta (sing. *mwana mbuta*), children born to males of matrilineage, 22, 116; see *Se. See also* Patrifiliation

Bates, D., xviii, xxi, 145n, 224n

Baumann, H., 12n

Bayindula, *nganga*, xx, 105–06, 111, 117, 142, 146, 195, Pl. 15, 16

Bazinga, D., psychiatrist, xxi, 114, 121, 145n, 229n. *See also* Psychopalavre

Beck, A., 15n

Belgian Congo, *see* Congo; Colonialism; Medical policy

Bilharzia, 25, 31–32

Bilumbu, *nganga*, xx, 85–86

Blessing, paternal, 95, 172; and bride payment, 105–112; and ending of illness, 171, 185; lack of in illness, 105-12; prophet's, 97

Blood, as life principle, 175–76; menstrual, 172; stigma, 78; in medical cosmology, 158, 171, 176; in theory of conception and descent, 171, 202; in urine, 173; *lubanzi* as "drop of bad blood", 177; "bad blood," 186, 231, 188–89; coughing with, 187

Bloom, S. W., 8n, 141n

Boils, 186, 202

Boswell, D. M., 5, 5n, 131n

Brazil, xiii, 29

Brazzaville, xix-xx, 19, 35, 53, 113

Breath, as life principle, 175; see *Mpeve. See also* Asthma; Suffocation; Pneumonia; Respiratory System